Edward Williams Byron Nicholson

Golspie

Contributions to its Folklore

Edward Williams Byron Nicholson

Golspie
Contributions to its Folklore

ISBN/EAN: 9783744777964

Printed in Europe, USA, Canada, Australia, Japan

Cover: Foto ©Thomas Meinert / pixelio.de

More available books at **www.hansebooks.com**

❧ *Golspie* ❧

Contributions to its Folklore

by Annie and Bella Cumming, Jane Stuart,
Willie W. Munro, Andrew Gunn,
Henri J. MacLean, and Minnie Sutherland
(when pupils of Golspie School)

Collected and edited,
with a chapter on ' The Place and its Peopling,'
by Edward W. B. Nicholson, M.A.,
Bodley's Librarian
in the University of Oxford

With illustrations,
chiefly from photographs by A. M. Dixon

London
David Nutt, 270-271 Strand
1897

Oxford
HORACE HART, PRINTER TO THE UNIVERSITY

TO

THE REV. JAMES MAXWELL JOASS, D.D.,

IN MEMORY OF

CONSTANT HELP AND KINDNESS RECEIVED

CONTENTS

Contents

Contents

Contents

Contents xiii

ILLUSTRATIONS

* From photographs by Mr. A. M. Dixon, Golspie.

INTRODUCTION

WE had left the pleasant uplands of Glen Shee
for the sands, the waves, the bracing breezes of
Nairn—and to our dismay Nairn was full already.
We had then turned our eyes to the varied coast-
line opposite, stretching away for league upon
league toward the Orkneys, and had resolved to
try Tain. We had found Tain peaceful and picturesque—but alas! its shores were not for the feet
of the paddler or the spade of the digger, and so
we had sped northward still, to Golspie.

And at Golspie we had found all that we craved.
On the north of the bay, where we first sought it,
there was just sand enough—we had not yet seen
the miles of smooth sand which lie south of the
village. Before us, across the steely sea rose far
and dim the line of Moray hills; while in front of
us the seabirds swam, wheeled, and settled. Behind,
brown kye and snowy geese were dotted over
a broad belt of green pasture. To left stood the
woody heights and gleaming turrets of Dunrobin.
To right swept a low shore backed by a crescent

B

of mountains. And Golspie Burn! with its beautiful fall, babbling rapids, and clear pools of brown water! its rocks and trees and ferns and mosses! and its dusky rabbits scudding away wherever we bent our steps! Yes, certainly we should have found content at Golspie—even if the Sutherland Arms had been less homelike; even if our host, the Duke's whilom gardener, had not joined to it one of the most delightful of simple old-fashioned gardens; even if every noontide a robin (or was he an enchanted prince?) had not come in at the window and by his example gracefully invited us to partake of the newly spread luncheon.

I had gone into the village one morning to buy something, and as I came back the boys and girls were at play in the steep playground which slopes down from the School to the road. I stood looking at them, and especially at a game which some of the girls were playing. They were dancing in a ring, reciting as they danced, and then they would suddenly reverse and dance the other way round, still reciting. Presently some of the younger ones—children of perhaps seven or eight—came down and formed a ring in the road before me. In a minute or two some of the older girls did the same. I thanked them all and spun up a sixpence for them to scramble for: then they had to go back into school and I went on to the Sutherland Arms. There I sat down and wrote the proposal for a prize-competition from which you will find some extracts at p. 328.

GOLSPIE BURN

Not being quite certain how that proposal might be generally received, I took it to the Minister of the Established Kirk at Golspie, Dr. Joass, a geologist and archaeologist of far higher than 'local' rank, and always ready to help those who come to him. Armed with the assurance of his sympathy, I next approached Mr. James H. Loudon, the then master of the school, now a master in Kelvinside Academy, Glasgow. He at once entered heartily into the plan, and it is to him that I owe the possibility of carrying it out.

In February 1892 Mr. Loudon sent me, as the result of my proposal, the essays of the seven girls and boys whose names are on the titlepage. At p. 331 you will see some particulars as to their ages, parentage, and places in the competition at large and in the several branches of it. As six out of the seven afterwards won 'district prizes,' it cannot be said that the competitors were not a good representative team.

The italicized extracts from those essays which form the basis of this book are in the exact words and spelling of the originals [1], and each is followed by its writer's initials: everything else, including notes and headings, is mine. But I have not felt myself bound to follow the writers in their [2] punctuation (in which I include the hyphen and

[1] In a few cases where I suspected a mere slip, I gave the writer the chance of looking at his or her MS. of the passage and making a correction—but never pointed out an error.

[2] I have never altered it where there was any question of a shade of difference in the sense.

apostrophe), their use of capitals, or their division into paragraphs or verses.

It would have been easy to bestow on the editing all my leisure for several years. I have not been able to spare the time for that; and what is wanted at present is not so much to comment as to collect. If the folklore of the entire kingdom were collected and classified, it would to a great extent annotate itself. Nevertheless I have tried by explanation and illustration to make a substantial contribution of my own to the study of British folklore.

The chief books and articles which have been consulted for the purpose of annotating the work of the contributors I quote for brevity by author and page only: they are these:—

Dempster (Miss) The folk-lore of Sutherlandshire[1]. In the Folk-lore journal, vol. 6, 1888.

Napier (James) Folk lore: or, superstitious beliefs in the West of Scotland within this century. 1879.

*Gregor (Rev. Walter) Notes on the folk-lore of the North-East of Scotland. 1881 (Folk-Lore Soc., vol. 7).

*Henderson (W.) Notes on the folk-lore of the Northern counties of England and the Borders. 1879 (Folk-Lore Soc., vol. 2).

*Shropshire folk-lore. Ed. by Charlotte S. Burne from the collection of Georgina F. Jackson. 1883.

[1] May I entreat Miss Dempster and all the other people without number who speak of Sutherland as 'Sutherlandshire' to do so no longer? When a shire is named after a town, it is natural, and generally necessary, to use the word 'shire,' as in 'Lincolnshire': but when it is not so named, but is the title of a more ancient territorial division, the use of 'shire' is both needless and derogatory. We shall talk of 'Essexshire' and 'Suffolkshire' next!

Choice notes from ' Notes and Queries,' Folklore. 1859.

*Chambers (Robert) Popular rhymes of Scotland.

*Northall (G. F.) English folk-rhymes. 1892.

*Halliwell [1] (James Orchard) Nursery rhymes and nursery tales of England—an undated edition containing xv + 352 pp.

Udal (J. S.) Dorsetshire children's games, etc. In the Folk-lore journal, vol. 7, 1889.

*Newell (William Wells) Games and songs of American children. New York, Harper & brothers. 1884.

Bolton (Henry Carrington) The counting-out rhymes of children. 1888.

Allen (Miss) Children's game-rhymes. Copied down from word of mouth by Miss Allen, School house, Hersham, Surrey. In the Folk-lore record, vol. 5. 1882.

*Gomme (Mrs. Alice Bertha) The traditional games of England, Scotland. and Ireland. 2 vols.—being pt. 1. of 'A dictionary of British folk-lore ed. by G. Laurence Gomme.'

The volumes in particular which I have marked * ought to be in every British public library which can afford to buy them.

All the parts of my book which deal with games had been written before I saw the announcement of Mrs. Gomme's very valuable work. The first volume of that was published in 1894, and, although it contained no games from North of the Moray Firth, it afforded me some new illustrations from other parts of the country. I was anxious to get the benefit of her second volume as well, and, since it had not appeared up to the spring of 1896, I took a friend's suggestion and asked her publisher if she would exchange proof-sheets with

---

[1] Afterwards Halliwell-Phillipps.

me. This she has very kindly done, as far as hers were ready (down to 'Sally Waters'), and I hope my young Golspie friends and I may have furnished to her as much aid as she has to me. All my obligations to her are separately acknowledged.

Visiting Golspie a third time in 1893, to complete my book, I came by chance to study the Pictish inscriptions of Scotland, Orkney, and Shetland, which had not hitherto been solved. Their solution will be found in my work on 'The vernacular inscriptions of the ancient kingdom of Alban,' published in 1896, which I cite simply by my own name. Its preparation and printing kept back the present volume for more than two years, but my new study furnished so much additional information which I have been able to use in these pages that the delay proved 'a blessing in disguise.'

Before I came to prepare them I had merely browsed now and then on folklore, as on much else, in a very casual kind of way. There is a Folk-Lore Society, which has many distinguished men among its members, which has published and continues to publish a valuable journal and important works—among them being a Handbook of Folklore[1] which is priceless, and only costs half

[1] By some accident this book, though dated 1890, did not reach the Bodleian till 1893. Had I in 1891 known of its existence, the questions which I put to the boys and girls of Golspie school would have been many more. In a paper in this volume on 'the way to collect folklore' we are told that 'a visit may be paid to the school in the mid-day "recess," and the children may be bribed to play all the games they know for the instruction of the

a crown. If I may offer to that Society some sug-
gestions which occur to me, they are these. Instead
of being a London society without branches, start,
if you can, a branch in every town and considerable village in the kingdom, and set about
collecting. And, when you do so, begin with the
young. They will collect for you not only from
those of their own age but from their elders as
well. And, if a stray tourist can so easily obtain in
one small place in our furthest North the amount of
curious matter which you will find in these pages,
by way of answer to his few hastily prepared
queries, what cannot you collect by organized
effort? Try, gentlemen, try. The public will
surely help you, if you ask it; for we have all been
children once, and many of us would be glad to be
children again.

It is, of course, not only primary schools which
should be encouraged to furnish such collections,
but secondary schools as well. And to those who
are interested in our ' grammar ' and ' high ' schools
I would say—Offer prizes not merely for collections
of the folklore of a district, but for collections of
its old songs; for vocabularies of its dialect; for
accounts of its general history and antiquities, of
the history of its peopling, of the history of its
industries. By so doing you will store up valuable
material which is rapidly being lost, and which, if

visitor' (p. 170), but the idea of offering prizes to the children
for written collections does not seem to have occurred to the
compilers.

it should not attain the dignity of a separate publication, the editor of the nearest newspaper will gladly preserve in print. You will also be leading the boys and girls themselves to take an interest in subjects of importance which are not included in their school-learning. And you will be getting them to teach themselves what South British schools and universities at any rate rarely attempt to teach them—the art of research. Why is the annual literary output of Germany so much more valuable than that of the British isles? Mainly, I believe, because every German university - student has to undertake, and publish the results of, some approved investigation before a degree is granted him. He has learnt to seek for himself and to draw conclusions for himself—and to love doing these things. But, as far as the training he has had from his school and his University goes, the ordinary English B.A., who has not passed through a natural science course, is almost always in the position of Rudyard Kipling's Tomlinson, the weak dependent soul whom Peter drove from the gate of Heaven and whom the Devil scorned to let into Hell—

> 'This I have read in a book,' he said, 'and that was told to me,
> And this I have thought that another man thought of a Prince in Muscovy.'

If the following pages do anything to stimulate in these ways the collection of folklore, they will not have been written in vain. Nor will they if, by giving to any of the young folk of Golspie itself some idea of the wealth of their own neighbourhood in what is ancient and curious, they lead any such boy or girl to study its folklore, its antiquarian remains and history as an inhabited place, or its geology—and to put the results of that study some day on record, for the interest and instruction of their fellow-countrymen, in a volume much more adequate than this.

For my chapter on ' The Place and its Peopling ' has as little pretension to be a history of Golspie as the earlier part of the book has to be a complete collection of its folklore. But some account was needed of the ' folk ' among whom the ' lore ' is current, and of their antecedents. How much that account owes to Dr. Joass I can hardly estimate. It was he who first described to me, and who personally showed me, the weem, the hut-circle, the earth-house, and the broch. And—although I have everywhere read and thought for myself, and am alone answerable for any error of fact or judgement which can be discovered—I have received from him in other parts of that chapter so much correction or assistance, beyond what is there acknowledged, as to leave me greatly his debtor for whatever value I have succeeded in giving to it.

STORIES

STORIES

—·—

THE number of stories contributed has been below my expectations. I cannot suppose that on the N.E. coast it would be easy to make a collection which should rival that of Campbell's celebrated 'Popular tales of the Western Highlands,' but at the same time I can hardly doubt that among the Gaelic-speaking population of Golspie (particularly, perhaps, the fishermen) more of such tales are yet preserved.

In 1837 a Mr. Hugh Macleod presented to the Duchess-Countess of Sutherland a manuscript collection, written by himself, of 'Traditions and Superstitions &c. of the Reay Country'—Reay being on the N. coast of the county. In this little volume, which I have been allowed to see, the writer, who says that he 'cannot look back for many years,' writes as follows (pp. 10, 11):—

'He remembers the time when, during long winter evenings,—the snow "knee deep" upon the ground, the wind howling over the cottage, the hail, every now and then, rattling against the window of the apartment, and the family, with some from the neighbouring families, congregated around a blazing fire,—among other amusements, the aged communicated to the young what happened in days of yore; the young curiously listened and, in their turn, repeated to others what afforded so much entertainment to themselves. He observed, however, as might be expected, considering the mode of communication, many inaccuracies creep in. He observed too, several editions of the same story current,—and not unfrequently he observed it pass through so many changes as to become almost an original. He observed also the same tradition told of very different individuals,—and traditions which related to one district made, with little or no variation, apply to other districts.'

But as regards 'oral tradition in the Reay Country' in times nearer to 1837 the writer says (p. 10) 'Of late years it lost much of its interest amongst the people, — which may, in a great measure, be ascribed to the progress of written knowledge, and the consequent decline of superstition. Old habits too are fast dying out, and with them traditions must fall.'

These remarks of Mr. Macleod's will not only help the reader to understand why the stories he is about to read are so few, but will show him that in certain features to be presently noticed they are not peculiar.

KELTIC STORIES

[THE HORSE-FAIRY]

At a place called Dalnaguillin there is a bothy for the farm-servants. While they were dancing one night to the strains of the bagpipes, a woman dressed in white entered and joined in the dance. While she was dancing, the piper noticed that it was hoofs she had instead of feet; so he thought that the sooner he was out of there the better. He accordingly asked them to excuse him, as he was going to the door for a minute. The woman, however, would not consent unless she held one end of his plaid. Having reached the door he threw off his plaid, and bolted. The woman followed him, but as he was a good runner he soon outdistanced her and so got rid of her for that night. The day, however, as he was returning from work, a colt suddenly appeared on the road and went on in front of him, always keeping the same distance from him. They went on in this way until they came to the mouth of a cave into which the colt disappeared. Immediately afterwards it emerged as the woman of the previous night, and she began to dance wildly about for

*a few minutes; then she disappeared into the
cave again. The piper took some men with
him next day but could find no trace of anything.*   *[A. C.]*

Dalnaguillin is Dal nan Gillean, colloquially
Dalnagillan, 'Meadow of the young men,' that is,
a meadow used for games. It lies about 15 miles
N.W. of Golspie, on the N. side of Strath na Seilga
(' Valley of the chase '): see Ordnance-maps, 6-inch
sheet 76, 1-inch sheet 109.

The idea of a female spirit transforming herself
into a horse will also be found in the next story.

'In Gaelic tales,' says Campbell, 'horses are
frequently mentioned, and more magic properties
are attributed to them than elsewhere in popular
lore.

In No. 1, horses play a very prominent part;
and in some versions of that tale, the heroine is
a lady transformed into a grey mare. . .

. . . In No. 14, there are horses; in one version
there is a magic " powney."

. . . In 51, the hero assumes the form of a horse.
In many other tales which I have in manuscript,
men appear as horses, and reappear as men . . . and
there is a whole series of tales which relate to
water-horses, and which seem, more than all the
rest, to show the horse as a degraded god, and,
as it would seem, a water-god, and a destroyer'
(' Popular tales of the West Highlands,' i. pp.
lxxxv–vi).

[THE WATER-WRAITH OF LOCH LINDIE]

*An interview with the Benvraggie hermit—
from whom I got the following story, or more
particularly tales—as they are many. The old
man thus began: 'In the year 1789 I was page
in Dunrobin Castle: my name was Willie Day
or "Jack of all trades." Getting old and unfit
to work, I was ordered to remove from the
kitchen to the vault below. Here I got the name
of Brunny of the Castle. I saw no one for many
a year save a visit now and then from ghosts,
fairies, witches, kilpies, etc., who delight to frequent dark cells such as my luck was to occupy
at the time. Otherwise I have seen no living
person. I was kept alive by throwing down
crumbs of bread and other scraps which I was
forced by hunger to devour greedily. Even old
shoes would be gladly received. My visitants
took pity on me in my confinement and demanded
my release, which they made good, and settled
my abode in a cave on the top of Benvraggie,
giving me the name of the Hermit of the Hill.
My liberators frequently visited me in my new
abode and introduced a legion of dark spirits
more wicked than themselves: among the number
was Madge the water-wraith of Loch Lindie,
whose power was to transform herself into dif-*

C

ferent shapes—from a woman to a hare, to a cow, to a horse, and sometimes to a raven or to any spirit that would sink terror or frighten the simple or unlearned.' The story of Madge is the one I intend giving you, word for word as the hermit told it to me. ' On a fine summer Sunday evening a number of boys from the down end of the parish, who never heard of Madge, went a strolling to see Loch Lindie. On coming near the loch they all admired both loch and surroundings. Close to the edge of the water was grazing a beautiful piebald pony. One of the boys said to the others ' Come let us have a ride with the pony round the loch.' One went up, and another saw plenty of room for more. They all took their seat on the pony, till twelve took their seat, never taking note as one by one was taking his seat that the pony was inch by inch getting longer. The thirteenth boy (for that was their number), seeing there was no room for him, thrust his finger into the side of the pony, and there it stuck; and, being alarmed, the poor boys tried to free themselves, but impossible. One of the boys on horseback took his pocket-knife and cut off his companion's finger to give the alarm of the sad end of the others. As soon as their parents heard the news, they started for the loch, but to their horror and grief they found nothing and saw nothing but torn caps and the bodies of the boys floating like buoys on the surface of the loch.' ' If this is given to show the power of the water-

*wraith or as a word to the young not to profane
the Sabbath, the hermit only can tell.'* [*J. S.*]

Benvraggie (Ben a' Vraghey, or in strict Gaelic
spelling Beinn a' Bhraghaidh) is the mountain
(1314 ft. high) behind Golspie—the same on which
stands Chantrey's colossal monument to the memory
of the first Duke of Sutherland. Its name, derived
from its shape, means 'Mountain of the neck-and-
shoulders [1].'

There is a cave on Ben a' Vraghey. There was
also a person named Willie Day once in the Sutherland service. And a very few years ago there
died a certain Hugh Sutherland who lived a very
secluded life in a cottage on the mountain. But
there is not, and was not when this story was
written, any 'Benvraggie hermit' at all. He was
simply created for the purpose of supplying a
framework to the Loch Lundie story. His creator
was Mr. William Stuart, railway-surfaceman, the
father of J. S. Mr. Stuart gave the heads of the
narrative to his little daughter and her brother
Duncan, a youth of 16, and they worked it up from
these heads. This is a very good example of the
error into which an incautious collector of folktales
may fall himself, and may lead his readers to fall:
it is an equally good example of the manner in
which a folktale may be embellished in trans-
mission.

[1] *Bhraghaidh* (properly pronounced *Vraghey*) is genitive (aspirated after *a'*) of *braghadh*, which is not to be confounded with the
kindred *bràighe, bràghad.*

C 2

Mr. Stuart says that [1] *Brunny* (pronounced *broony*) is a Gaelic term for an evil spirit which goes about. Willie Day, he says, died hundreds of years ago, and he has heard a story about his being sent on a message from the Earl of Sutherland to the Earl of Caithness. This should have been a two days' journey, and Willie Day should have started in the small hours of the morning, but he overslept himself until about midday: despite this he returned before the end of the following day. Mr. Stuart adds that a hermit used to live on the top of a hill at Rogart, a few miles from Golspie. And, as regards the Loch [2] Lundie story, he says that, when he was a boy, his mother used to frighten him with it.

That, indeed, is one of a class of story, the Kelpie story, common in Gaelic tradition. The following extract from Miss Dempster (p. 246) tells the very same tale of another Sutherland loch, and affords two more instances of the kelpie's connexion with the county.

---

[1] No doubt the 'brownie' of the Lowlands. ' The Brownie is believed in Berwickshire to be the ordained helper of mankind in the drudgery entailed by sin: hence he is forbidden to receive wages' (Henderson, p. 248). The title selected by Mr. Stuart for his imaginary narrator would consequently = 'the drudge of the Castle.'

[2] J. S. wrote Lindie ; she seemed to pronounce something between the ĭ of *linen* and the ŭ of *Whitsun*. See p. 295.

'The Golden Horse of LochnaGillie

A loch on this estate, now small and muddy, but once much larger, at the time when it received its name from the following sad event:—

A dozen lads were playing by its banks, riding and chasing the ponies which grazed among the reeds and rushes. They all quarrelled who should mount a beautiful horse which grazed among the others, but was finer than any they had ever seen ; its skin was smooth, bay-coloured, and shining like gold. Two boys jumped up. " There is room for three," said the next, and got on. " There is room for four," said the fourth lad, and so there was ; for the more boys mounted him the more the golden horse lengthened. At last all the boys sat on him, but two who were brothers. " Come let us up," said the youngest, touching the horse with his forefinger ; but lo! the finger stuck there, it had grown to the golden skin. " Take your knife, Ian, and cut it off," he cried. His brother did so, and the two ran home together, too much frightened to look behind them and to see the fate of the rest. That no one saw, but by an hour after the hair and entrails of the boys were scattered all over the water. The golden horse had plunged in with all his victims, and the loch is called by their name [1] to this day.—(Widow Calder.)

[1] LochnaGillie, as if colloquial for Loch nan Gille, ' the loch of the lads.' And the 1-inch Ordnance-map of 1878 has Loch nan Gillean, which has this meaning. But the 6-inch one published in 1879 has Lochan a' Ghille, ' the little loch of the lad,

[Loch Laggan, also on this property, boasts of a water-horse, and at night a bright light is seen to swim up and down the middle of the lake. Then they say, "The water-horse moves."—(W. M., sheriff's officer.)

A golden horse was once seen, born of the waters of the *Fleet*. It tempted a woman to follow it and try to drive it, but she was warned in time, and so it was foiled of its aim to lure her to a watery grave.

The Grahams of Morphie, in the Mearns, are said to have caught and bridled the water-horse, and made him draw stones for their new castle. This unwilling workman's curse lay on the family for ever, and caused their ruin.

Apropos of manes, a family of Munro, having many generations ago intermarried with the Vaugha of Ben-na-Caulting, were said to have manes and tails till within the last four generations.]'

So Miss Dempster. Her LochnaGillie (Lochan a' Ghille) is nearly 4 miles S.E. of Lairg station, her Loch Laggan (or Loch an Lagain, 'Lake of the hollow') over 4 miles E. of Invershin station.

The Fleet is a river running into the sea some

and the large map of Sutherland executed in 1853, revised in 1868, and based on the trigonometrical survey of 1831–2, has Lochan-a-Ghille. I cannot help thinking that this is the correct title, as the loch is very small, and that the story of the Golden Horse may have been transferred to it from some other loch as a consequence of its proper name having been corrupted or misunderstood. But it is quite possible that the original name was given to it because a lad had been drowned in it, and that this lad's death was attributed to a kelpie.

3 miles S.W. of Golspie, and its broad estuary is called Loch Fleet.

The sticking of the boy's finger to the horse's side is a kind of incident not peculiar to this group of Gaelic stories. For instance, take the following extract from one translated by Campbell (i, p. 36):—

'She asked the lad for a drink of water from a tumbler that was on the board on the further side of the chamber. He went; but out of that he could not come, as he held the vessel of water the length of the night. " Thou lad," said she, " why wilt thou not lie down ? " but out of that he could not drag till the bright morrow's day was. . . . This wooer went and betook himself to his home, but he did not tell the other two how it happened to him. Next came the second chap, and in the same way, when she had gone to rest—" Look," she said, " if the latch is on the door." The latch laid hold of his hands, and out of that he could not come the length of the night, and out of that he did not come till the morrow's day was bright. He went, under shame and disgrace. No matter, he did not tell the other chap how it had happened, and on the third night he came. As it happened to the two others, so it happened to him. One foot stuck to the floor; he could neither come nor go, but so he was the length of the night.'

Was the idea of this kind of magical power derived from the Gael's first acquaintance with the magnet ?

The ' kelpie ' or ' kilpie ' (as J. S. writes) is simply

the personification of *kelp* or *kilp(e)*, i. e. water-weed which, as it streams on the surface, looks like horses' manes : see p. 332.

I am tempted to add a South-Highland variant of the story of the boys. It is connected with a lake not far from Loch Earn, and the book from which it is taken (composed by a Gael with the help of an English dictionary) is one of the most astonishing works ever written in 'English'—I hope before long to bring out a new annotated edition of it :—

'Another elegant lake in Glenogle, adjacent to the top of the hills passage there, famous for fishing . . . Anent certain predication of the ensuing narration of Glenogle, which affirms, that ten children, on certain day, doing something fanciful or in frolic merriments, close to the lake above narrated, they were [1] taken unawares to see a horse from the lake ; his appearance so avariciously, that they were inordinately desirous to mount him. One of them got up on his back ; the rest acted with the same levity, till the ten furnished with room there. No sooner than they were admitted to that dismally seat, than the horse entered the lake concomitantly with the crew ; only the hind-most fell over, who brought home the tiding of the fatal event ' (Angus McDiarmid, ' Striking and picturesque delineations of the grand, beautiful, wonderful, and interesting scenery around Loch-Earn,' 1815, p. 14).

[1] I. e. surprised.

[A SATANIC STORY]

I had the pleasure of a conversation with my old friend the <u>hermit</u> on Tuesday last. No sooner our meeting took place than I caught courage to speak plainly with my old friend, and asked him if he would give me the history of a ghost-story of any kind, which occured in our locality during the age of his long life-time. ' Yes,' was his answer. ' The one I am to give you is a ghost-tale given to me by tradition, from age to age, as <u>dates</u> or writings were not known in those days, so, my good girl, you must take it for good or bad, to the best of my remembrance as brought down to me from my forefathers.' Thus the hermit begins : ' Golspie village was situated on a high hill—say, about a full mile above the <u>present Golspie.</u> The former village was built of turf of rude form, overlaid with sticks, turf, and fir-branches for roofing. Near the miserable village stood a very high tower or castle, built by the old or ancient Picts, from which the village got its name, and retains it to this day, as <u>Golspie Tower.</u> Peterioli de Roma, a good Roman Catholic (for this was the religion in those days) to whom charge was given to look over the castle or tower and keep it clean, during the absence of the owners, who started on a visit to Italy. The ship on which they sailed was either wrecked or lost ; for no trace of the family ever came to

*Peterioli's ears : so the good man had sole check
over the old castle, and ever since the Tower
became the haunts of ghosts. A great many
pilgrims lost their lives sheltering within its
roof, to the great grief of decent Peterioli de Roma.
At this season of the year, the Christmas-time,
it was a common custome of the monks of the
different monasteries to visit each other. So the
father-monk of the diocese of Forttrose was invited by his brother monk of the diocese of
Thurso and the Orkney Isles to come and see
him. He accepted the invitation and prepared
for the journey. Early on the Christmas week,
going round the longest route to shun rivers, as
bridges were far and few on the journey, at last
he arrived at Golspie, where our story begins.
As he was winding his way up the steep foot-
path, he saw a glimmering light, feebly, through
the snow-drift of this dismal night. At ten
o'clock the monk stood at Peterioli's door knocking
for admittance. No sooner than De Roma heard
the knock at the door than he opened it, and to
his surprise saw a man clad in white, for so he
was, owing to the heavy shower of snow that fell
at the moment. ' Oh, what storm ! ' exclaimed
de Roma. ' Come in, sir, come in ; take of the
best hospitality my humble cottage can afford to
strangers ' (believing the monk to be a man of
distinction, owing to his garments). ' Sit down
by the fire, sir ; make yourself as comfortable as
you can, friend.' Turning to Lydia, who was*

*only to bed, saying 'Rise, dear, rise; prepare
food for the stranger, for he is both hungry and
tired, while I go and put his horse into safe
keeping and give the poor animal food for the
night.' By this time good Lydia was also ready
with the supper, so that the stranger was made
as comfortable as possible with such means as
they had. Supper over, Peterioli said 'I am very
sorry, sir, that our house is ¹on one bed; but,
if you accept of ours, Lydia and I will sit by the
fire till you take a rest².' 'No, no—I am thank-
ful of the shelter of your roof on such a stormy
night.' 'Well, my dear sir, are you a timid man
or a man of fortitude and courage? I should
like to know if you are a brave man with a bold
heart³, not given to superstition. I could give
you the best bed in the castle for a night's rest.'
'Thank you, friend, and it's me that will accept
of it, taking chance of all your spirits that you
say haunt the castle.' 'Well, sir, let us proceed,
as the night is far spent and you in need of rest
after so long a journey.' Both men started to
the castle through an old narrow foot-path
overhanging with honey-suckle, black thorn, and
⁴rodin-trees, on the boughs of which sat perching*

---

¹ A Gaelic idiom = 'with one bed,' 'one-bedded.'
² Scottish for 'till you have taken' (Dr. Joass).
³ This and the next sentence are unfortunately not consistent with
the statement that 'a great many pilgrims lost their lives sheltering
within its roof, to the great grief of decent Peterioli de Roma.'
⁴ Another name for the rowan-tree or mountain-ash. The
bunches of red berries are 'rodins,' the trees 'rodin-trees.'

the screech-owl, the whoop-owl, and such like
creatures of the dark as may roam in the night-
time, lifting their nocturnal scream and howl to
the terror of the monk. As soon as they came
to the door, it was instantly opened with an old
rusty key. Peterioli said to the stranger 'Please
come in, sir, until I secure the door behind so
that no human being can disturb you during the
night's rest.' The large hall, the kitchen, and
closets being properly examined, they proceeded
to the upper flat. All the rooms being found
quite safe, the brave monk felt quite at home for
the night. 'Now, dear sir, if Lydia and me are
well in the morning, I will call on you at nine
o'clock for breakfast. And now come down with
me until you see the outer door securely locked.'
While doing so, Peterioli said in a low whisper
'Good night.' The monk, retracing his steps to
his bed-room, felt the first symptoms of fear when
he perceived his lonely position. He placed a
lighted candle on each end of the table, took his
sword and laid it between them, secured the door
of his room, sat in his chair, bible before him,
putting up prayers to the Almighty for his protection, awaiting the awful hour of twelve when
ghosts begin their carnival. Five minutes past
the hour of midnight a rumbling sound like
distant thunder fell on the monk's ear; his heart
failing him, he rose, barricaded the door of his
room as well as he could for safety. In a few
minutes more, the outer door of the castle was

*flung open, and in came a legion of evil spirits
and ghosts, howling like demons, making a great
noise with pots, pans, and dishes, as if preparing
for a great feast.   In a few minutes there was
a hush, and the poor monk thought all was over ;
but, to his horror, he heard foot-steps ascending
the stairs, and afterwards a knock at his door.
The monk calls ' Who is there ?'   ' 'Tis I ; ' said
a rough voice, ' the master wants you down to
supper.'   ' Thank you, sir : I have taken my
supper.'   The bearer descended with the answer
to his master, but again returned (his steps being
much heavier than before, causing the tower to
shake from top to bottom) with the same invitation, ' The master wants you down to supper.'
The third time the same was done, and the
monk, seeing that no refusal would do, took the
candle in his hand, opened the door, where stood
before him the skeleton of an old grey-haired
man who gave him a sign to follow him down
the stairs and through a long dark passage to
the hall-door, where sat a great many round
a well furnished table.   ' Come in, sir, come in ;
we have been waiting on you for so long ; come up
to the head of the table, your place.'   The monk
humbly obeyed from fear, and sat down.   The
good monk put his hand to his brow, shut his
eyes, and prayed thus—' Oh, father, thou hast
always supported me with thy providence until
now ; at this time permit me not to feast with
devils.'   On the good man opening his eyes there*

was nothing to be seen but his candle. The ghosts made their exit. The good man returned to his room, went to bed, partook of a sound sleep, till Peterioli awakened him, saying ' Rise, sir; Lydia is ready with breakfast; just nine o'clock.' [J. S.]

This story, like the last, owes its present form to the narrative talent of J. S.'s father, and was worked up in the same manner: it had to be done twice, Mr. Stuart told me, because the first time it did not altogether agree with the heads which he dictated. There was no such person as Peterioli de Roma (though Petrioli is a real Italian surname), and no such legend about Golspie Tower. *But a similar story was told in Golspie*, and this is it :—

A young minister in British North America was riding on a bad snowy night to a place where there were a number of Highlanders. He saw a light, and found it came from a cottage; so, ' clapping ' at the door with his stick, he asked for lodging for himself and his horse. The cottager and his wife said that there was no difficulty about putting up his horse, but that they had no room for him, as they had only their own bed. There was, indeed, accommodation in an empty old castle hard by (which they were keeping for some nobleman or other great person); but no one who slept there ever came out alive. The minister, after supping with the man and his wife, said he would

run the risk. He took his sword and Bible, and
they led him to a splendid room at the top of the
castle, where they made him a good fire. They
had locked every door after them, so that no one
else might enter; and, when they left the minister,
he let them out and locked every door after him
as he went back. He sat up, with two candles
and his Bible and sword, and heard no sound till
midnight. Then a fearful and unearthly noise
shook the castle under him, a heavy foot came
on to the stair and to the door: there was a tap
at the door, and a voice cried 'The master wants
you down to supper.' The minister replied that
he had already supped. Again the same thing
happened, the noise this time being still greater,
and the unseen visitor's step heavier. A third
time the noise was heard, and this time more
terrible than ever: a third time the step came,
and this time so heavy that at every footfall the
castle seemed about to come down. The door
opened, and an evil spirit in the shape of a skeleton
stood in it and repeated the summons. The minister
took his sword and Bible, and followed his sum-
moner to the basement of the castle, where he
found a table laid, and round it a number of devils
grinning at him. He was invited to sup with
them, and said he would. He then shut his eyes,
and said 'O Lord, wilt thou permit me to eat with
devils?'—opened his eyes again, and found all
gone. He went upstairs again, thanked God, went
to bed, and slept all night. In the morning the

cottager and his wife came, thinking to find him dead, but found him 'jolly and laughing.' They gave him further entertainment, and indeed there was nothing they were not anxious to do for him.

That is the original story, put in my own words except where quotation-marks are used, but faithful in all details to the notes which I made while Mr. Stuart told it to me. And, taking it as it was told, I venture to suggest that the minister's fears, assisted perhaps by an indigestible supper, gave him a very bad dream. As he was a 'minister,' we are of course sure that none of the incidents were due to his own invention!

British North America, however, is not the most likely part of the world in which to meet old castles, and, even if for 'old castle' we substitute 'haunted house,' the kernel of the story seems decidedly mediaeval: I fully expect to find some day that it is at least four centuries old.

The statement about the site of the original Golspie is very curious. There are two hamlets of Golspie Tower. The very scanty remnants of the tower itself (see p. 285) are in the lower of these two, but A. C., B. C., J. S., and M. S. (the only young people I asked) had never seen them and did not know where the tower was; while A. C. told me that Golspie Tower is 'just the name of a village,' and pointed, not to the lower hamlet (close to which she was standing), but to the upper hamlet nearly half a mile away. It is clearly this upper hamlet which is referred to as the original Golspie.

The ground on which it stands was certainly raised above the sea while the site of the present Golspie was still under the waves, but we have no reason to suppose that the district was inhabited until after that site had become dry land. Still, settlements made during the times of Saxon and Norse piracy might very well be placed high up, for safety.

Golspie Tower was a mediaeval castellated house. It *may* have been built where an old 'Pictish tower' once stood, but there are no records or evidences to this effect.

STORIES OF HAUNTINGS

There is a place in the middle of a wood[1] *here where they used to hang people long ago. No one would go to this wood after dark, as strange sounds were heard and the spirits of the people that were hung haunted the place.* [H. J. M.]

There is another place which is called the Devil's Gate[2], *where it was said a lady robed in*

---

[1] In the grounds of Dunrobin.

[2] On the Dunrobin estate, over the burn. It led to the old nursery, and the railway now runs over its site.

*white was seen to wander every night to the fear
of the country-people.   [H. J. M.]*

STORIES OF GHOSTS THAT WERE
NO GHOSTS

From several of these stories it seems as if ghost-
shamming has been a favourite practice in and
about Golspie. I myself, when a boy, have wrapped
up in a sheet on a bright moonlight night, floured
my face, and come suddenly round the corner when
a friend was about to turn it from the other side.
I did not do that twice—I was too much frightened
at my friend's fright. Sudden alarms of this kind
have sometimes caused people to lose their reason,
and probably any one suffering from certain forms
of heart-disease might quite easily be killed on the
spot. So, young folk of Golspie, forbear, and, if
you will not take my caution, take that of Burns—

'For monie a ane has gotten a fright—
    An' liv'd an di'd deleeret—
            On sic a night.'

*In a neat little cottage about three miles from
the village of Golspie there lives a man who once
had recourse to act the part of a ghost for
reasons which will afterwards be told. Every
night his wife dressed herself, and, leaving him
in charge of the bairns, started for the village.*

Thinking that she was getting tired of him, and that her purpose for going so often to the village was to meet some other man, he determined to give her a fright. After putting the bairns to bed, he covered himself with a white sheet, and, taking a candle in his hand, he stationed himself near a house in which a man died a week before who resembled this man very much. About ten o'clock (she always came home a little after ten) he took off his boots and lighted the candle. He walked round and round this house waiting for her arrival. Needless to say that his plan met with success after repeating it several times; for it not only cured her but many others. She would never go to the village afterwards without her husband being with her. He found out a short time after that he was supposed to be the ghost of the man who had died.   [A. C.]

A boy who lived in one of the country-places which surround Golspie, and who spent all his money in strong drink and smoking-materials, was made to abandon his evil habits in the following way. The boys of the village, sorry to see such a young boy indulging in such evil habits, made an agreement that two of them would put a white sheet and chains on themselves and frighten the boy on his way home. As they heard the footsteps of the boy, they crept out of their hiding-place and stood on the road, at the same time rattling their chains so as to attract the attention of the boy. When the boy saw the lads dressed in white he thought they were ghosts. He prayed to God for protection, and then begged the ghosts not to touch him—in return for which he promised to abandon his evil habits. The 'ghosts' went away, promising to come again if he would not fulfil his promise. Then they went to their companions and told them all about their interview with the boy. They were pleased to see how their plan succeeded, for the boy never indulged in his evil habits again. [B. C.]

Before I begin to relate my stories, let me tell you that I do not believe in ghosts, and none of the stories of which I am going to tell you proves contrary to my statement. You may then say (if you believe in ghosts, as some people do) that they are not ghost-stories, but all the same I shall tell them to you. [W. W. M.]

A friend of mine (in fact, a relation) was returning home, from being on some business, at a very late, or I should say a very early hour, as it was about one o'clock in the morning. On his way home he had to pass over a bridge which was said to be haunted by ghosts, and when crossing this at full gallop (for he was on horse-back) he thought he saw something very like a shadow passing him. He rode on past the bridge, but, like myself, not believing in ghosts, returned to find out what it was. After riding back several miles, he overtook a man who went about selling tea, and who was riding on a Shetland pony which had no shoes on. My friend had not heard the pony passing him, the night being very windy, and he did not recognise the man, the night being very dark. [W. W. M.]

A man was one night passing our churchyard at a very late hour. He saw some object moving among the tombstones, and, being very superstitious, he thought this was a ghost. He ran away, but, meeting some neighbours, he told them what he had seen, and returned with them to discover what it was. It turned out to be the horse of the village carter, which he had put into the churchyard to feed on the luxuriant grass, thinking that nobody would notice it, and which, being white, the man had mistaken for a ghost.

[W. W. M.]

The fishers being of a very superstitious nature, a young man who was very fond of a lark determined to take advantage of this superstition. He dressed himself up in the usual dress which a ghost is supposed to wear, and, having procured some chains from a cart, he personified the ghost for several nights with great success. But the fishers at length found out that it was a trick which was being played on them, and so they set a watch for the ghost one night. When the ghost came to his usual place of operation, which was an ash-pit near the gas-works, from which he threw up clouds of ashes, the fishers gave chase. Of course the ghost ran away, and they followed. The ghost jumped over a [1] *dike at the alms-cottages, and the fishers, not being very sure but that it was a ghost after all, thought that the ground had swallowed it, and so gave up the chase.*   [W. W. M.]

Once there was an old woman who was afraid of nothing. She was asked one day if she would go to the old ruins of a [2] *church at twelve o'clock at night. Inside the church were old skulls and bones, and she had to take out two skulls. And if she did this she was going to be rewarded with a sum of money. One man went to the church before twelve o'clock and dressed himself in a large white sheet. When the old woman came, she went in, and she saw the white object standing in the centre of the church. The old woman never said one word, but began looking for two skulls. She liftet one skull and she looked at it. The white object said in a trembulos and shaking voice 'That's my skull.' The old woman never stirred, but began looking for another skull. She found a skull. The white object repeated the same words over again. And when the old woman was going out she said 'Be quiet with you, ye haven't two skulls.'*   [A. G.]

[1] In Scotland 'dike' = bank, or wall.
[2] A. G. says it was in Caithness.

Once an old man used to watch his bees all night beside the church-yard, because the boys used to come and steal them. The boys one night made up their minds to give the old man a fright. So two of the boys dressed themselves one in a white sheet and the other in a black sheet. They were hiding behind a grave-stone, and, when they thought everything was quiet and still, the white deil began running through the church-yard and the black deil chasing him. They were running about like this for a while, and the man called out ' The black deil can chase the white deil, but I'll watch my bees.' [A. G.]

Once a man was coming home a very dark road one night. And as he was walking on he saw a white thing on the road a little bit in front of him. He stopped and heard the white thing making a noise. He was not going to stop for this, and so he went on, and as he came near he found that it was a goat caught in a fence by the horns. [A. G.]

It was generally believed in the Highlands that there were ghosts, and indeed some people believe in them still. To pass a churchyard alone at night was thought to be the height of courage. Indeed our school was at one time supposed to be haunted by ghosts, and I have been told that for a time the scholars would not go near it in the morning till the teacher would come. The ghosts in this instance were given to rattling chains and pulling the desks about with a great noise. [1] *Morrvich House, in the vicinity, was also supposed to be haunted, and the tenant, a retired soldier, sat up for nights in one of the rooms with loaded guns watching for the ghosts —which, however, it is said, never came. There are several places in the district where, it is said, ghosts were seen, but most frequently on the road between the* [2] *Porter Lodge and Dun- robin* [3] *Mains.* [M. S.]

Mr. Andrew Lang, to whom I mentioned the story about Morvich, has written me a letter which I venture to quote. ' Morvich,' he says, ' is our *stammschloss,* in a way. None of us, I think, in 3 generations, ever heard of a ghost there, certainly *I* never did, but I could make inquiries. I have stayed in it at divers times, and never saw a spook, through 40 years, nor heard of one. . . . A shoot- ing party in the strath was lately evicted by a ghost, but not from Morvich.' Morvich House was built at some time after 1784 and before 1819. If the ghost-story belongs to it at all, it may have been nothing but a hoax on the old soldier.

---

[1] Morvich is close to the line, about 5 miles W. of Golspie.

[2] Southrons would have expected Porter's, but there is no mistake.

[3] Mains are farm-lands, farm-buildings, &c., attached to a mansion.

HISTORICAL AND GEOGRAPHICAL TRADITIONS

There is a tradition that hundreds of years ago a vessel landed at a place called the Little Ferry, three miles from Golspie.   It is said that the captain landed and was attacked by a pack of wild cats, and succeeded in killing them all, after being dangerously wounded.   It is said that the Earls of Sutherland get their coat of arms from this.   *[H. J. M.]*

The Little Ferry, otherwise Unes, is to the S.E. of Golspie.   [1] Wild cats still exist in the neighbourhood of Golspie.   The tradition is given as follows by Sir Robert Gordon on pp. 14, 15 of his 'Genealogical history of the earldom of Sutherland,' written in 1639 and published in 1813 :—

'In the raigne of Corbred the second, surnamed Gald, that famous King of Scotland (whom Tacitus calleth Galgacus), sone to Corbred the first, the yeir of Christ fourscore and elevin, Domitian being emperour of Rome, ther aryved in the river of Tay a great company of Germanes, named Catti and Vsipii, a valiant people, of mightie bodies, who were banished out of their owne native land for killing of a Roman generall, with his legione, Domitian having befor triumphed over their nation . . .

---

[1] Mostly, perhaps, half-breeds ; but the true breed is occasionally seen.

At their first arryvale in the river of Vnes (a commodious and saffe haven in that cuntrey), ther captane went to the shore for to recreatt himself, and to spy the land; wher he wes suddentlie invaded by a company of monstrous big wild catts, that much indomaged and molested the countrey. The feght betucen them was cruell, and continued long, yet in end (being grivouslie wounded in severall places of his bodie) he killed them all, with great danger of his lyff. From hence the thaines and erles of Cattey or Sutherland evin vnto this day, doe carie in their crest or bage, abowe ther armes, a cat sitting with one of his feett vpward, readie to catch his prey; some doe think that from this dangerous adventure this countrey wes first called Cattey: for Catt, in old Scottish (or Irish language) signifieth a catt.'

You will see that this account really combines two different explanations of the ancient name of the country—one that it is called from German immigrants named Catti, the other that it is called from its wild cats.

The wild cat derivation would be more likely if we knew that wild cats were uncommon in other parts of the country: but I have no reason to suppose that they were.

As to the Catti, the story about them is without historical foundation and to the last degree improbable. There was a tribe of Catti who lived near the Severn in Caesar's time, and there might have been other tribes of the same name in our isle. These Catti were of course Kelts, as were the inhabitants of Sutherland.

There is, however, no doubt that the Earls (now Dukes) of Sutherland have a cat for their crest; that the Gaelic name of their clan is Clann Cattach (= Clan 'Cattish'); that the original 'Sutherland' (the E. coast region—see p. 280) is still called Catuᵛ ('Cats'), and was formerly also called Cat ('Cat'). Some of these facts have been explained by others before me. The clan were called Cats; the country was called Cats after the clan, according to a practice prevalent in Old Gaelic; and the Sutherland crest is also adopted from the name of the clan. But why was the country called not only 'Cats' but also 'Cat'? And how did the 'Cats' themselves get their name? These are questions to which I hope to give a satisfactory answer.

The proper names of ancient Keltic chiefs were often derived from the names of animals. Generally the animal was the dog. The ancient Kelt's idea of a dog was—not a Skye terrier, but—a staghound, boar-hound, or wolf-hound, an animal swift, strong, and brave, so that in Old Irish Gaelic *cu* 'dog' was used metaphorically to signify a champion or warrior. Hence among the Britons King Cunobelinus's name meant 'bright-coloured dog,' King ¹Cuneglasus's 'tawny dog'; while that of

¹ His contemporary Gildas says that Cuneglase means *canis fulve*, which has been corrupted in the MSS. into *lanio fulve*

St. Kentigern (Conthigirnus)—the son of a princess—meant 'dog-chief' or 'king of dogs.' Similarly the great Irish hero Cuchulainn had a name into which the word *cu* 'dog' enters; indeed he is sometimes called simply Cu. And among the Picts we find from inscriptions that in Conningsburgh in Shetland there was a man (apparently a chief) named Cu Morr ('Big Dog')[1], and that at Kilmadock in Perthshire there was a man named U Culiæn ('Descendant of Whelp')[2].

But sometimes it was another animal. Sometimes, for instance, the bear, *art*, *arth*, as in Artur, Arthur[3], 'Bear-man' or 'Bear-male.' Sometimes the cat, *catt* or *cat*, as in the name of St. Catán ('Little Cat'). In those days the idea conveyed by such a name was quite different from what it would be now. The domestic cat, which is not a native of these isles, was almost totally unknown in them: if it existed here at all, it was only as a curious animal brought over from the continent by some Roman family, some military officer who wanted to keep the mice from his stores, or in later times some priest or other pilgrim who had been to Rome or Gaul. But the wild cat—which [4] 'attains a length of 3 feet including the tail'—'was

through confusion of the ancient Ɛ *c*) and L: see my letter in *The Academy* of Oct. 12, 1895.

  [1] Nicholson, pp. 4, 9. App. 21, 35-6.

  [2] See a letter by me in *The Academy* of May 23, 1896.

  [3] See my letter of Oct. 12, 1895, above-mentioned.

  [4] This and the following quotations are from the article 'Cat' in the Encyclopædia Britannica.

formerly abundant throughout the wooded districts of Britain.' ' The fierceness of its disposition, its strength, and its agility are well known; and although it does not seek to attack man, yet when disturbed in its lair, or when hemmed in, it will spring with tiger-like ferocity on its opponent, every hair on its body bristling with rage. " I never saw an animal fight so desperately," says Mr. Charles St John (*Wild Sports of the Highlands*), " or one which was so difficult to kill." '

Consequently Cat(t) was a good name to give a young chief in a fighting age, and the Irish translation (made not later than the 12th century) of the Welsh chronicler Nennius tells us (Irish p. 50, Eng. trans. p. 51) that ' Cruithne . . . seized the northern part of the island of Britain, and his seven sons divided his territory into seven divisions, and each of them gave his name to his own portion. The seven sons of Cruithne are Fib, Fidach, Fotlaid, Fortrean, Cat, Ce, Cirig. As Columbkille said,

> Seven of the children of Cruithne
> Divided Alban into seven portions;
> Cait, Ce, Cireach of the hundred children,
> Fib, Fidach, Fotla, Foirtreann.

And Aenbeagan, son of Cat, son of Cruithne, took the sovereignty of the seven divisions [1].'

Now Cruithne is the Old Irish name for ' Pict,'

---

[1] For references to and instances of the name and its derivatives I am indebted to an article by Stokes ' On the linguistic value of the Irish annals ' in Bezzenberger's *Beiträge zur Kunde der indogermanischen Sprachen*, xviii. p. 92.

and this story of Cruithne and his seven sons is just the sort of story which is imagined all over the world by uncivilized or half-civilized people in order to account for their own names and those of the countries they inhabit. But, putting it aside altogether, there is no reason why there should not have been a Pictish chief named Cat(t). And, if so, it was natural that the territory he ruled should be called Cat(t) after him. For in the Pictish inscriptions homesteads commonly bear the name of the past or present occupiers—and that not in the genitive case, as we might speak of Mr. Cameron's farm as 'Cameron's' but in the locative case, as if we spoke of it as 'Cameron¹.' Thus at St. Vigean's near Arbroath the homestead of Forcus was called Ett F'orcus (Àit-Fhorcus), at St. Ninian's isle in Orkney the ground belonging to the priest Mo-bhaist was itself called Movvest; while another property at St. Vigean's, two at Greenloaning in Perthshire, probably two more near Doune in the same county, two (at Aboyne and Carden Moor) in Aberdeenshire, one at Burrian in North Ronaldshay (Orkney), two others (at Conningsburgh and Lunasting) in Shetland, were all named after the families who then or formerly occupied them. And, when we get so large a number of instances as these out of only some 22 Pictish inscriptions yet discovered, we see that it was natural that Cat(t)'s territory should itself be called Cat. This is the

¹ Nicholson, pp. 3 &c.

name the country bears in another passage of the same Irish chronicle (p. 148).

Another very strong reason for believing that the clan get their name from a man is that all Highland clan-names are taken from persons who existed or were supposed to have existed. If ever a clan seems to be named from a territory, such as Clan Ross, and Clan Sutherland itself, it is only because the name of the territory had previously become the name of a person : thus Clan Sutherland means the Clan of the Earl of Sutherland. For the ordinary meaning of *clann* in Gaelic is ' progeny, children.'

Not only is there a Clann Cattach or 'cattish,' but a Clann Catanach or 'kittenish,' and the latter name is certainly of personal origin. I have mentioned the Irish saint named Catán, 'Little Cat.' It was common to give children names expressing dedication to some saint. For instance Malcolum meant ' Bald one [monk] of St. Columba,' Gillicolaim 'Lad of St. Columba'—names afterwards shortened into Calum. In the same way Gillacatain meant 'Lad of St. Catan' and from a certain Gillacatan was named Clann Gillacatan [1], otherwise Clann Chattan or Clann Catanach.

Granting, then, a chief named Cat(t), his ' clann '

---

[1] My instances and forms are from Macbain's Etymological dictionary of the Gaelic language, pp. 358, &c. If it be said that Malcol*u*m and Gillacat*a*n are not correct genitives, the reply is that in ancient Highland Gaelic the vowel of the nominative is not always modified in writing : thus we have *vor* for modern *mhoir* (Nicholson, p. 76).

or 'children' (whether really such or only those who were in his service or put themselves under his protection) would each call themselves Cat(t), and the clan would be called Cait(t), 'Cats,' or Clann Cattach, 'Cattish,' just as every follower of a De Comines or Gunni is a Cuimein (Cumming) or Guinne (Gunn) and the clan is called Clann Cuimeanach or Gunnach[1]. And, as in Old Gaelic it was common to call a country from its inhabitants, so Sutherland and Caithness (*Old Norse* Katanes) would be called in Pictish in the locative case Catev or Catov ('Cats'). In mediaeval Irish they are called Cataib ('Cats,' pronounced Catev or Cataiv); in Sutherland Gaelic of to-day the name is Catu[v], a mere variety of the same case. The original chief, or his successor, might be known as the Cat(t) Mor, the Big or Great Cat, just as the Duke of Argyll is Mac Cailein Mor (*or* Mhoir) and the head of the McKenzies of Kintail is Mac Coinnich Mor (*or* Mhoir) Chinntaile[2]. Probably this *mor*

[1] See note, p. 47.

[2] The latter instance I owe (through the Rev. D. MacInnes of Oban) to the Rev. James MacDougall of Duror by Ballichulish. He says that in both cases *mor* has been corrupted into *mhoir*. *Mor* (nominative) would give the epithet to the present chief, *Mhoir* (genitive) to his ancestor. There is a Cailean Mor in the Argyll pedigree, and Dr. Joass believes that in this case Mhoir is right. On the authority of the late Dr. John MacIntyre, a tutor in the family of Glengarry, he compares Glengarry's title, Mac 'ic Alasdair Mhoir, borne by him as descendant of Alasdair Mor. Mr. MacInnes, on the other hand, says that Glengarry's title is Mac 'Ic Alastair. Scott, who writes Mac Callum More, might excusably mistake Cailein (sometimes pronounced Callen) for Callum: but 'More' shows that he heard Mor, and not Voir or

was once a mere epithet of size, denoting the 'big' father of a family as contrasted with his children, the 'big' brother as contrasted with the little brothers[1]. I do not know whether the head of Clann Cattach has ever been called Cat(t) Mor, but he is called Morf hear Chatt, 'Great man of Cats.' For on Golspie bridge is an obelisk bearing the following inscription, ' MORFHEAR CHATT *do Cheann na Droichaite big* GAIRM *Chlann* CHATTICH *nam Buadh*,' i.e. ' GREAT MAN OF CATS *to Head of the* [2] *little Bridge* (in ?) CALLING *of Clann*

Woir. His 'Rob Roy,' in which the style occurs, was published in 1818.

In Capt. Simon Fraser's collection of Highland music (first published in 1816) I find the Lord Lovat of 1745 called *Mac Shimi mor* in the title of no. 59, and MacDonald of the Isles called *Mac Dhonaill Mòr nan Eillan* in that of no. 217. He also gives Glengarry's title as *Mac mhic Alastair* (no. 29), not *Mac mhic Alastair Mhoir.*

[1] Nicholson, p. 55.

[2] The 'little Bridge' was close to the mouth of the burn, on the site of the present wooden bridge (substantially rebuilt in 1895). It was to the head of this bridge that the chief of the Sutherlands called the clan, by messengers who carried a wooden cross with its tips burnt and dipped in blood, and who may have recited this form ; and the war-cry of the clan was 'To the head of the little bridge.' The 'head' was probably on the Dunrobin side, where there is a long and wide pasture ('the Dairy Park') through which ran the old Caithness road, still easily traceable. The road was diverted to its present course in 1811, when the stone bridge was probably erected. But the obelisk is somewhat older, and was moved from an earlier site—doubtless at the 'head of the little bridge.' The 'little' bridge may have been so called in contradistinction to the high stone bridge at Brora. There was a bridge at Brora at least as early as 1610 (*Origines parochiales Scotiæ*, ii. pt. ii, p. 723'.

E

Cattach of the Victories.'   Above this is an earl's coronet, surmounted by a cat's head.

[A CAVE AT BACKIES]

Another is that, when an old woman was herding cattle near a cave at Backies, one of the animals suddenly disappeared into the cave, and she was just in time to lay hold of it by the tail, and held on till she came out at a place five miles distant.   *[H. J. M.]*

The cave is known as Uamh (Uaigh) Thorcuil or ' Torquil's cave.'   Torquil is the Gaelic representative of the Norse Thorkill, so that the name may be taken either from a Highlander or from a Norseman.   It lies about 900 ft. above the sea, a good bit higher than the Pictish tower, and is simply part of a rift on the mountain-side which can be traced some distance.   I have been in it, but consideration for my light-coloured clothes prevented me from squeezing myself through a very dripping aperture where the cave takes a sudden turn.   I have, however, been assured by Dr. Joass, and by the late Mr. Thomas MacDonald (one of the oldest members of the Dunrobin estate staff), that the tradition is an impossible one.

The supposed exit was ' 4 Scotch miles ' away, S. of the River Fleet (Keith, writing in 1799 in the *Statistical account of Scotland*, xxi, p. 225).   And Dr. Joass tells me that numberless caves in various parts of the kingdom are supposed to have distant outlets.

SUPERSTITIONS

E 2

SUPERSTITIONS

—••—

If this book is read by any large number of
people, it will almost certainly be read by a number
of superstitious people. Superstition is not confined to Golspie, or to Sutherland, or to Scotland,
nor is it confined to fishermen and crofters—many
a well educated person in London or Oxford,
who would laugh at the idea of its being unlucky
to see the first lamb of the season with its tail
turned towards him, would think it unlucky to sit
down to dinner 13 in number[1], and would bring
a child in to make 14, lest one of the party should
die within the following twelvemonth! Let me,
then, explain what I mean by superstition.

So far as we know, everything has a cause.
When anything happens and a person *does not*
attribute it to any cause in the universe known to
our sensations, or to any action *which can ration-
ally be accounted for* on the part of invisible beings

[1] This superstition I have heard, read, or imagined to arise
from its being the number of those who sat down to the Last
Supper.

—but *does* attribute it to apparently irrational and motiveless action on their part, or else to something which he calls 'luck' or 'ill-luck' (which is not a being of any kind, nor a part of the known universe)—then I call that person's belief on the subject a superstition.

Perhaps he will say that he has known the superstition 'come true.' He has known 13 sit down to dinner and one of them die in the next twelvemonth. Perhaps he has. But has he ever counted the number of times when 13 sat down to dinner and one did *not* die in the next twelvemonth? Or has he ever counted the number of times that 12 or 14 sat down to dinner, and one died in the next twelvemonth? And has he ever considered that a man *must* die within a year of eating *some* dinner, however few or however many people sit down with him from day to day?

It may be suggested on behalf of the superstitious that perhaps they do not regard 'omens' as causes of good or ill fortune, but only as signs from invisible beings that good or ill fortune is being prepared for them. Any such suggestion is entirely inconsistent with the nature of a large class of omens, of which various examples will be found in the following pages—I refer to those omens which become omens or not as we ourselves choose. If, for instance, I meet any one on the stairs and pass him, it is unlucky. If, knowing that fact, I turn back, I avoid the ill-luck!

I have no doubt that many more superstitions

might be collected in this neighbourhood. In my notes I have alluded to several which have come to my ears.

SUPERSTITIONS ABOUT FISHING

Dread of the hare.

If a fisherman, when going to sea, sees a hare cross his path, he takes that as a sign of misfortune.   *[J. S.]*

Also, if they find a hare's foot on the bottom of their boat, they will not go to sea that day.
     [H. J. M.]

So on the other side of the Moray Firth ' To say to a fisherwoman that there was a hare's foot in her creel, or to say to a fisherman that there was a hare in his boat, aroused great ire, and called forth strong words. The word " hare " was not pronounced at sea.

To have thrown a hare, or any part of a hare, into a boat would have stopped many a fisherman in by-gone days from going to sea ; and if any misfortune had happened, however long afterwards, it was traced up to the hare ' (Gregor, p. 128). Mr. Gregor adds ' A hare crossing the path portended mishap on the journey.'

See also pp. 76, 334, '**Witches as hares.**'

Consulting a witch.

Another instance of belief in witchcraft is, that certain of the fishers consult a supposed witch in the parish of Clyne before they go to the herring-fishing, to find out whether or not they will be lucky that season.   *[M. S.]*

Clyne is the next parish northward along the coast.

The praying over the boats.

Before starting for the herring-fishing they get some good old man to pray over their boats: this is thought to bring them a good fishing.

[H. J. M.]

Note that it is *not* 'the minister' (the reason will be found presently). That is why I class the belief among superstitions.

Boats not to be counted.

If you count boats when they are going out for fish, one of them is sure to be lost.   *[A. C.]*

'On no account must the boats be counted when at sea, neither must any gathering of men or women or children be numbered. Nothing aroused the indignation of a company of fishwomen trudging along the road to sell their fish more than to point towards them with the finger, and begin to number them aloud :—

· " Ane, twa, three,
   Faht a fishers I see
   Gyain our the brigg o' Dee,
   Deel pick their muckle greethy ee." [1]
(Gregor, p. 200).

Compare the story of the numbering of the people in ii Sam. 24 and i Chr. 21. Has this frightened the fisherfolk? or are men in an early stage of civilization afraid of calling the attention of some unseen being, and exciting either his anger at their pride or his malice at their good fortune? Dr. A. Neubauer, the eminent Hebraist, tells me that even now there is a Jewish uperstition against counting persons &c. except by letters of the Hebrew alphabet or other indirect means: if they were counted by numbers, it is supposed that there would be mortality!

Unluckiness of 'the minister,' &c.

If a minister come on board, it is a sign of bad luck. [*H. J. M.*]

So on the other side of the Moray Firth ' When at sea, the words " minister," " kirk," " swine," " salmon," " trout," " dog," and certain family names, were never pronounced by the inhabitants of some of the villages, each village having an aversion to one or more of the words [1].

[1] Dr. Buchan, the distinguished meteorologist, tells me that in Shetland the minister is in such a case called the 'upstander,' and the kirk and kirkyard the ‘bany-hoose,’ i. e. the bony-house. To these substitutes he thinks no objection exists.

When the word "kirk" had to be used, from several of the churches being used as landmarks, the word "bell-hoose" or "bell-'oose" was substituted. The minister was called "the man wi' the black quyte." A minister in a boat at sea was looked upon with much misgiving[1]. He might be another Jonah ' (Gregor, p. 199).

Mr. A. Polson, Dunbeath, in a paper on ' Some Highland fishermen's fancies ' printed in the Transactions of the Gaelic Society of Inverness, vol. xviii, pp. 42–7, says ' One of their most peculiar fancies is, that it is unlucky to meet a minister on their way to sea ; and if they see one, they take some trouble to get out of his way. They also have the strongest aversion to take ministers aboard or to give them a passage from one port to the other. On inquiry, it has been found that some Caithness sailors of long ago, took a number of ministers to Leith to attend a General Assembly, and that the passage was exceedingly stormy. But when Leith was reached, and as soon as the ministers were landed, the wind ceased. The sailors, from this circumstance, formed the belief that the prince of the power of the air thought that while they were on the waters he might, by exercising his power, get these men, who were the enemies of his kingdom, out of the way. Similarly, a fisherman who gets a minister's blessing on going to sea will have the prince of the power of the air

---

[1] *Choice Notes*, p. 60.

as his enemy, and it is therefore questionable if ever he may come ashore again.'

The following very different explanation had occurred to me, and I am not at all sure that it is wrong. At Preston Pans on the Firth of Forth Sunday is (or quite lately was) the lucky day on which to start for the fishing[1]. Until the Reformation, there would have been no objection to this on the part of the clergy; but the Puritan doctrine that the Christian First Day was under the religious law of the Jewish Seventh Day was of course hostile to the practice. Hence, if a boat was starting, or had started, on Sunday, any reminder of the clerical prohibition would have seemed to put the boat under a ban.

Why was Sunday the lucky day on which to start? Perhaps because of its special sanctity. But perhaps for some purely pagan reason, as being the day of the sun. It was not only lucky to start on a voyage on Sunday, but also to sail the way of the sun. In the West of Scotland ' One very ancient and persistent superstition had regard to the direction of movement either of persons or things. This direction should always be with the course of the sun[2]. To move against

[1] ' It is a favourite custom to set sail on the Sunday for the fishing grounds. A clergyman of the town is said to pray against their sabbath-breaking ; and to prevent any injury accruing from his prayers, the fishermen make a small image of rags, and burn it on the top of their chimneys' (*Choice Notes*, p. 271—signed U.).

[2] The Ogam inscription on the Carden Moor stone (at Logie Elphinstone in Aberdeenshire) is written on a circular line, so

the sun was improper and productive of evil con-
sequences, and the name given to this direction of
movement was *withershins*' (Napier, p. 133).

So on the other side of the Moray Firth, when
a boat was pushed into the water, ' The prow was
always turned seaward in the direction of the sun's
course' (Gregor, p. 199).

And Miss Joass tells me that in Golspie many
things are done the way of the sun, and that sometimes a funeral will go some distance round in order
to travel with the sun.   Dr. Joass adds that when
you go out first in the morning it is ' lucky' to
turn first to the right—which is the way of the sun
—and ' unlucky' to turn to the left.

Not taking a dead body into the boat.

If they [the fishermen of this place] *find a dead
body at sea, they will not take it into the boat, but
tow it; for if they put it in their boat they are
afraid that it will bring bad luck to them.*

[H. J. M.]

Probably this superstition arises from the idea
that good luck and bad luck attend particular
persons and things, and that the same bad luck
which killed the man will cling to his body and
affect the place in which it lies.

that it presents an imitation of the sun. The stone is a boundary-
stone of a homestead; the inscription gives its name, which was
the name of the family living in it (Ovobhv = Omhaibh); and the
mode of writing it was evidently meant to bring luck or ward
off ill-luck. It is probably as old as the 7th century. See
Nicholson, pp. 3, 19, App. 37–40, 78–9.

Burt in his 'Letters from a gentleman in the North of Scotland' (1754 ed., ii, p. 215) says he has heard that English seamen 'don't care for a Voyage with a Corps on Board, as tho' it would be the Occasion of tempestuous Weather.'

SUPERSTITIONS RELATING TO ANIMALS

Black snails as money-bringers.

If you catch a black snail by the horns and throw it over your head, you will find some money shortly after.   [*A. C.*]

The following parallel to this cruel superstition is from Lancashire :—' If black snails are seized by the horn and tossed over the *left* shoulder, the process will insure *good luck* to the person who performs it ' (T. T. Wilkinson, Burnley, in *Choice Notes*, p. 187).

Cockcrowing at night.

A cock crowing at night was a bad sign.
                                        [*B. C.*]

If you hear a cock crow at an unusual hour of the night, it is a sign of someone's death.
                                        [*J. S.*]

So in the Border counties of Scotland and England ' Another death-omen is the crowing of a cock at dead of night ' (Henderson, p. 49).

Cuckoo's cry before a door a death-omen.

If the coocoo comes and calls before any door, it is believed that there will be a death in the house. [*J. S.*]

Compare a belief of the Borders, 'The flying or hovering of birds around a house, and their resting on the window-sill, or tapping against the pane, portends death' (*ib.*).

Much folklore attaches to the cuckoo, and particularly to the first hearing of it. In Golspie to hear it when you are fasting is unlucky: see **First sight of beasts,** p. 64.

Peacock's feather unlucky.

A peacock's feather, it is said, means 'Ill-luck.' [*M. S.*]

I am told that if such feathers are put over the pictures in any house it is believed that the husband and wife will quarrel.

A superstitious fear of peacocks' feathers is believed to exist in 'some parts of Ireland' and is 'common in the eastern counties of England' (F. C. H. in *Notes and Queries,* 3rd S. ix, pp. 305–6), has been heard in Cheshire (J. L. Warren, *ib.*, 5th S. vii, p. 508), and is 'general in Derbyshire and the surrounding counties' (Llewellyn Jewitt, *ib.*, 3rd S. ix, p. 187). On the other hand, 'A group of these feathers, stuck behind a picture-frame or a looking-glass, is a very common cottage or farmhouse ornament in the north of England' (P. P., *ib.*, p. 109). And when I called on a married farmer, with a good Gaelic name, in Golspie parish, I saw peacock-feathers on his mantelpiece: his ideally cheerful countenance would be enough of itself to discredit the local superstition.

As to the origin of the dread, Mr. James Tod asks ' May not the *Evil Eye* have something to do with it ? ' (*ib.*, 3rd S. viii, p. 529). I have no doubt that he is right, that it is the eyes in the feathers which first made them feared.

Hares.

See p. 55, '**Dread of the hare,**' and pp. 76-9, 334-9, ' **Witches as hares.**'

First sight of beasts.

If the head of a beast is turned toward you the first time you see it, you will be lucky; if it is the tail, you will be unlucky.   *[A. C.]*

That, the first time in a year you saw a young beast, if the face was turned to you you would be fortunate; if the back was turned to you, you would be unfortunate.   *[B. C.]*

So on the other side of the Moray Firth ' Omens of good or bad luck were drawn from the lamb or foal first seen during the season. If the animal's head was towards the observer, the year would bring prosperity, but, if the animal was standing in the opposite position, misfortune would crown the year ' (Gregor, p. 130).

So too on the Borders ' When you see the first

lamb in the spring, note whether its head or tail
is turned towards you. If the former, you will
have plenty of meat to eat during the year ; if the
latter, look for nothing beyond milk and vegetables.
As far south as Lancashire it is thought lucky to
see the first lamb's head, and unlucky to see its tail '
(Henderson, p. 120).

And Miss Dempster has noted that in Sutherland
it is an unlucky omen ' To see the first lamb of the
year with its tail towards you ' (p. 233).

Dr. Joass writes (May 18, 1896) ' There is still
real distress here over hearing the 1ˢᵗ Cuckoo
fasting or before breakfast, as well as at seeing the
first lamb, or a calf of your own for the first time,
' tail on,' & you should make a noise to attract
its attention and bring its head round before you
enter the [1] byre.' And he refers me to the following
passage in Nicolson's ' Gaelic Proverbs ' (p. 144):—

' Chuala mi 'chubhag gun bhiadh 'am bhroinn,
Chunnaic mi 'n scarrach 's a chùlaobh rium,

. . . .

'S dh'aithnich mi nach rachadh a' bhliadhn'
ud leam.'

which is literally :—

I heard the cuckoo without food in my belly,
I saw the foal and its rump to me,

. . . .

And I knew that that year would not go
with me.

[1] Cow-house.

Horse-shoes.

If the first shoe that was ever on an entire horse be hung on the byre door, no harm will happen to the cow while in your possession.

[A. C.]

In the case of two neighbours quarrelling, if a horse-shoe is placed between their houses, no harm can happen one by the other's wish.

[A. C.]

That a horse-shoe could keep away witchcraft.

[B. C.]

If a horse-shoe is hung above a door, it is believed that it will keep away both the witches and evil spirits.

[J. S.]

A horse-shoe, it is said, means 'Luck.'

[M. S.]

The belief in the luckiness of horse-shoes is so wide-spread through Great Britain that it is not worth while to give more than one or two quotations. Miss Dempster has noted that in Sutherland it is lucky 'To find and pick up a horseshoe' (p. 233). And the Rev. Walter Gregor says that at Achterneed in Ross 'It is almost the universal custom to keep one or more old horse-shoes in the house, or affixed to some part outside' (*Folk-lore Journal*, vi, p. 264). The belief is no doubt connected with the idea that horses and fairies are associated with each other—see p. 16.

SUPERSTITIONS ABOUT PARTICULAR TIMES

Cutting nails on Sunday[1].

He who on Sunday pares his horn
Twere better for him he had ne'er been born.

[A. G.]

So on the Scottish and English Borders :
' Better a child had ne'er been born
Than cut his nails on a Sunday morn !

Another variation of the verse runs thus—
Friday hair, Sunday horn,
Better that child had ne'er been born !'

(Henderson, p. 17.)

And again (*ib.*, p. 18) :
' Cut them on Monday, cut them for health,
Cut them on Tuesday, cut them for wealth ;
Cut them on Wednesday, cut them for news,
Cut them on Thursday, a pair of new shoes ;
Cut them on Friday, cut them for sorrow,
Cut them on Saturday, a present to-morrow ;
But he that on Sunday cuts his horn,
Better that he had never been born !

In Sussex they simply say " Cut your nails on Sunday morning, and you'll come to grief before Saturday night." '

---

[1] 'In Lancashire & Cheshire, it is a superstition that he who cuts his nails on Sunday will all thro' the week be ruled by the devil' (The Rev. John Cort, Sale, through Dr. Joass). And see Northall, p. 172.

Monday unlucky.

Anything begun on Monday would have an unsuccessful end. [B. C.]

Miss Dempster has noted that in Sutherland 'Friday and Monday are unlucky days,' and that 'A servant-maid will not go to a new situation on Monday' (p. 234).

And so on the other side of the Moray Firth 'Monday was accounted an unlucky day on which to begin a piece of work. There were parents who would not enter their children at school on this day' (Gregor, p. 149).

A belief in the unluckiness of Friday is of course very common, I suppose from the Crucifixion having taken place on that day. As for Monday, with the Highlander, as with the 'Saxon,' that is Moon-day, *Di-luain* or *Di-luan*. Now from *luan* 'moon' is formed an adjective *luaineach* 'changeable, inconstant, fleeting, fickle, uncertain,' so that the idea seems to be that anything begun on the day connected with the moon would not be steadfastly carried out, and that a servant going to a new place on that day would soon have to 'change.'

New moon.

If you had anything in your hand that signified comfort when the new moon appeared, you would be happy until the next moon appeared.

[B. C.]

So on the other side of the Moray Firth 'To
have something in the hand on the first sight of
the new moon was lucky, and indicated a present
before the moon had waned' (Gregor, p. 151).

Hallowe'en's night.

*If on Hallowe'ens night you go round a hay-
stack backwards nine times, you will either see
your lover catching you in his arms or a ghost.*

[J. S.]

You may make yourself so giddy that you can
see anything!

SUPERSTITIONS ABOUT 'THE EVIL EYE'

*It was also believed that certain individuals
had what was called an evil eye, which they
fastened on any person who had offended them,
and the person thus looked upon was supposed
to suffer some injury to person or property.*

[H. J. M.]

*It is believed that if a witch looks on you with
an evil eye it means misfortune.*   *[J. S.]*

Miss Dempster says (p. 245): 'The evil eye is
very common. Children, cattle (milch cows), and
poultry, suffer most from it. But the evil wishes,
it is remarked, often fall back on the utterer,
because to the "mischief" it is a matter of indif-
ference on which of the two the spell or the wish
falls.

[A Turkish nurse objects just as a Sutherland woman does to your looking at the baby. A pasha's daughter explained to a friend of mine that this was because of the evil eye.]'

And so on the other side of the Moray Firth ' The power of the "evil eye" was possessed by some. It was supposed to be inherent in some families, and was handed down from generation to generation to one or more members of the families. The power was called into use at the will of the possessors, and was exercised against those who had incurred their displeasure, or on behalf of those who wished to be avenged on their enemies, and paid for its exercise * ' (Gregor, p. 34).

There is a special book on this superstition—' The evil eye,' by Frederick Thomas Elworthy, 1895.

Feared in churning.

Many people while churning would not allow any other people see them, because they might [have] *an evil eye and it would keep the butter from coming.* *[A. G.]*

Counteracted by a red thread.

People often tie a red thread round their arms to keep off evil eyes, because there is a charm in red. *[A. G.]*

Mr. Napier says (p. 36): ' The Romans used to hang red coral round the necks of their children to save them from falling-sickness, sorcery, charms,

' * Cf. Henderson, pp. 187, 188.'

and poison. In this country coral beads were hung round the necks of babies, and are still used in country districts to protect them from an evil eye. Coral bells are used at present.'

And on page 80, ' Mr. Train describes the action of a careful farmer's wife or dairymaid thus :—

" Lest witches should obtain the power
Of Hawkie's milk in evil hour,
She winds a red thread round her horn,
And milks thro' row'n tree night and morn;
Against the blink of evil eye
She knows each antidote to ply." '

In these verses Hawkie is a cow, and the virtue of rowan-tree is that its berries are red.

And by a live coal.

Some people throw a coal of fire after people who go out of their house, in case they might cast an evil eye on anything.　　　*[A. G.]*

Doubtless because the coal is red.

And by water, &c., in which a silver coin has been put.

Another belief was that the effect of the evil eye could be cured by placing a piece of silver in the water which was to be drunk by the person or animal affected.　　　*[H. J. M.]*

I have been told by a person who witnessed it that a crooked sixpence was put into a pig's

*trough to cure what was thought to be the effects
of the evil eye.* *[H. J. M.]*

Compare the following: ' In the north-west of
Scotland, according to Dr. Mitchell, the " gold and
silver water " is the accredited cure for a child
suffering from an evil eye. A shilling and a sove-
reign are put into water, which is then sprinkled
over the patient in the name of the Trinity ' (Henderson, p. 188).

So at Achterneed in Ross the following ' Cure
for the Evil Eye ' is used :—

' The father of the patient takes the marriage
ring, a penny, a six-pence a shilling, and a florin,
puts them into a wooden ladle—the one in use in
the household—and goes with the mother and the
patient to the nearest stream, fills the ladle with
water, and with that water sprinkles the sufferer.
This goes by the name of " silver water " ' (The
Rev. Walter Gregor in *The Folk-lore Journal*, vi,
p. 264).

And the following antidote to 'the Ill Ee ' is or
was in use on the other side of the Moray Firth :—

' Go to a ford, where the dead and the living
cross, draw water from it, pour it into a "cog"
with three " girds " over a " crosst shilling," and
then sprinkle the water over the victim of the
" ill ee " in the name of the Father, the Son, and
the Holy Ghost † ' (Gregor, p. 42).

The stipulation that the ford must be one over
which funerals pass is paralleled by a fact men-

' † Cf. Henderson, p. 188.'

tioned in ' The Inverness Courier ' of March 20, 1892. In a certain superstitious process used somewhere in Sutherland for discovering the seat of a disease, three stones (representing the head, the heart, and the rest of the body) ' are selected from the burn beneath a bridge, where Life and Death have passed.'

SUPERSTITIONS ABOUT BIRTH, MARRIAGE, AND DEATH, &c.

Child's first airing at Christening.

That a child should not be taken out until it was christened.   *[B. C.]*

' In the southern counties of Scotland children are considered before baptism at the mercy of the fairies, who may carry them off at pleasure or inflict injury on them.   Hence, of course, it is unlucky to take unbaptized children on a journey— a belief which prevails throughout Northumberland, and indeed in many other parts of the country ' (Henderson, p. 14).

See also p. 75, ' **Woman's first airing.**'

Child-curing with gold-and-silver water.

If a child who is not christened is out and is taken ill, a witch is blamed.   The child is bathed in water taken from a stream where very few go for water.   The water must be fetched by a woman who does not belong to the child.   Gold

*and silver must also be put into the water before
the spell is broken.* [A. C.]

*That, if a child was taken suddenly ill, a witch
had cast an evil eye upon it, and that it could
be cured in the following way. Some one, not
belonging to the child, went for water to a burn
not near a public road. They put some gold or
silver ornaments into the water and washed the
sick child in it, thinking that in this way the
power of the witch would be destroyed.* [B. C.]

*When some people's children are ill, they put
into a bath of water gold and silver ornaments;
and they believe that putting gold and silver
ornaments into a bath of water cures the children.* [J. S.]

Miss Dempster (p. 235) says that in Sutherland
'A new-born infant must be washed with a piece
of silver in the water: the larger the sum the better
the luck. The midwife's fee of five shillings is
generally put in the bath; but to make matters
safe, in poor houses, where there is no fee, the
midwife wears a silver ring.

[In Russia children are generally baptized in a
silver font. A rich Greek merchant will make
a point of this for luck, and even a Presbyterian
minister will use a silver basin at a christening.]'

Marriage-contract by whom written.

*Before marriage a contract is always written
out: this must be done by a person who has*

heard nothing of the intended marriage, and he must be taken out of bed after midnight.

[H. J. M.]

Perhaps it is desired to avoid choosing any person who may have wished ill to the marriage. The fetching out of bed after midnight is probably a precaution against the possibility of the writer having incurred ill-luck for the day. Had he gone out of doors when people were about, the first person he met might have been a red-haired woman! Had he only gone downstairs when the house was astir, he might have passed someone on the stairs! Had he only dressed himself by daylight, he might have seen through the window the first lamb of the year with its tail turned towards him!

Brass candlesticks to be used at marriage and death.

Another superstition is that nothing but long brass candlesticks should be used at a death or marriage.   *[H. J. M.]*

Losing the wedding-ring omen of husband's death.

If you would lose your wedding-ring, your husband would die.   *[B. C.]*

On the Borders of Scotland and England ' the wife who loses her wedding ring incurs the loss of her husband's affection. The breaking of the ring forebodes death ' (Henderson, p. 42).

Woman's first airing after childbirth to be at churching.

The first place a woman should go after giving birth to a child was to church.   *[B. C.]*

So on the other side of the Moray Firth 'Strict watch was kept over both mother and child till the mother was churched and the child was baptised, and in the doing of both all convenient speed was used. For, besides exposure to the danger of being carried off by the fairies, the mother was under great restrictions till churched. She was not allowed to do any kind of work, at least any kind of work more than the most simple and necessary. Neither was she permitted to enter a neighbour's house, and, had she attempted to do so, some would have gone the length of offering a stout resistance, and for the reason that, if there chanced to be in the house a woman great with child, travail would prove difficult with her ' (Gregor, p. 5).

And so on the borders of Scotland and England: 'As to the mother's churching, it is very " uncannie " for her to enter any other house before she goes to church; to do so would be to carry ill-luck with her. It is believed also that if she appears out-of-doors under these circumstances, and receives any insults or blows from her neighbours, she has no remedy at law. I am informed that old custom enjoins Irish women to stay at home till after their churching as rigidly as their English sisters. They have, however, their own way of evading it. They will pull a little thatch from their roof, or take a

splinter of slate or tile off it, fasten this at the top
of the bonnet, and go where they please, stoutly
averring afterwards to the priest, or anyone else,
that they have not gone from under their own
roof' (Henderson, p. 16).

SUPERSTITIONS ABOUT WITCHES, &c.

Witches as hares [1].

*Not very long ago in this part of the High-
lands witchcraft was believed in by a good many
people, and it was thought that those professing
to have the power of witchcraft had the power of
transforming themselves into various animals,
especially the hare. A few years ago, within
a few miles of this village, a man while returning from his walk had to pass through a field
where there was ploughing going on. The
ploughman had startled a hare: he instantly
threw a stone at it, and, as he thought, killed it.
The man who witnessed the affair asked for
the hare, remarking at the same time that, as the
ploughman was a single man, he could not get
it properly cooked. His request was readily
granted; so he put the hare under his coat to
conceal it. When he got near the village, he
considered it would be safer to put it in his*

---

[1] See also p. 334.

*pocket-handkerchief. He accordingly laid it on
the ground, and spreading his handkerchief
turned round to lift the hare; when, to his con-
sternation, he saw it making for the village at
full speed. After heaving a deep sigh over his
loss, he came to the conclusion that it was a well
known old woman who enjoyed the reputation of
being a witch.*   *[H. J. M.]*

*A witch when on the way to do evil is never
seen except as a hare.*   *[A. C.]*

*That a witch exercised her powers not in her
natural form but in the form of a hare.* *[B. C.]*

So on the other side of the Moray Firth 'Great
aversion was shown towards the hare both by the
fishing population and by the agricultural, except
in one instance. It was into a hare the witch
turned herself when she was going forth to perform
any of her evil deeds, such as to steal the milk
from a neighbour's cow' (Gregor, p. 128).

Miss Dempster (p. 234) notes that in Sutherland
it is unlucky 'To meet a hare or an old woman.'

Which are to be shot only with silver.

*When a witch is in the form of a hare, the
hare cannot be shot with* ¹*grain, but with silver
coins.*   *[A. C.]*

¹ I. e. grain-shot.

*That a witch, while in the form of a hare,
could not be shot by grain, but by a silver coin.*

[B. C.]

So on the other side of the Moray Firth
'Against such a hare, when running about a farm-
steading, or making her way from the cow-house
after accomplishing her deed of taking the cow's
milk to herself, a leaden bullet from a gun had
no effect. She could be hit by nothing but by a
crooked sixpence. If such a hare crossed a sportsman's path, all his skill was baffled in pursuit of
her, and the swiftest of his dogs were soon left far
behind *.

The hare was aware of her power, and would
do what she could to annoy the sportsman. She
would disappear for a time, and again suddenly
start up beside him, and then off like the wind in
a moment out of his reach. For hours would she
play in this way with man and dogs. She has
been known, however, to have been hit by the
crooked sixpence in an unwary moment. Then she
made to her dwelling with all the speed she could,
and well for her if she reached it before the dogs
came upon her. When the sportsman entered
the hut he saw the hare enter, instead of finding the
hare that had cost him so many hours' toil, he found
an old woman lying panting and bleeding on the bed,
and it was with difficulty he could prevent the dogs
from tearing her to pieces ' (Gregor, p. 128).

' * Cf. Henderson, pp. 202-204, and *Choice Notes*, p. 27.'

So too in Yorkshire: 'Through the Dales of Yorkshire we find hares still in the same mysterious relationship with witches. The Rev. J. C. Atkinson informs me, that, a new plantation having been made near Eskdale, great havoc was committed among the freshly-planted trees by hares. Many of these depredators were shot, but one hare seemed to bid defiance to shot and snare alike, and returned to the charge night after night. By the advice of a Wise-man (I believe of the Wise-man of Stokesley, of whom more will be said bye-and-bye), recourse was had to silver shot, which was obtained by cutting up some small silver coin. The hare came again as usual, and was shot with the silver charge. At that moment an old lady who lived at some distance, but had always been considered somewhat uncannie, was busy tamming, i. e. roughly carding wool for her spinning. She suddenly flung up both hands, gave a wild shriek, and crying out, " They have shot my familiar spirit," fell down and died' (Henderson, p. 202).

And in Shropshire 'It was thought that a witch could only be wounded by a silver bullet' (Jackson and Burne, p. 165).

Dr. Joass has a sixpence (obtained from Mr. Munro, gamekeeper at Innis-an-damh at the S. end of Loch Assynt) which he suspects to have been shot at a hare. It was found on the moor, and is indented by pellets.

Cow-witching, and charms against it.

A woman who lived in [1] *B—— near Golspie was always telling her neighbours that a woman whom they all believed to be a witch had cast an evil eye upon the cow and herself. 'Her milk and butter were spoiled,' she said; and she also told them that in a dream she saw the witch in the shape of a hare come into her milkhouse and drink the milk. One day, when she was in the wood for sticks, her neighbours went into her byre, and, seeing a petticoat on a nail, cut a number of crosses on it and put it in the cow's stall. Then they tied nine rusty nails to a cord with nine knots on it. This cord they tied to the chain on the cow's neck, and then they went away. Shortly after the woman came home she went into the byre, and, seeing the petticoat, nails, etc., ran out to her neighbours screaming, and calling to them to go and see what the witch had done on her. To make them sure that it was the witch's work she showed them the unequal number of nails & knots. Then she took every thing that she thought the witch had handled, and made a fire of them, saying that she could no longer harm any person, because her power was destroyed with the fire.* [B. C.]

If a cow was not giving milk and a witch suspected of being the cause of it, a man's drawers would be placed over the cow's head, and the cow led out of the byre. The cow would wander about and at last stand at the witche's door. [A. C.]

[1] Backies?

In the parish of Golspie a farmer who had a number of cows imagined that the witches were taking the milk from them. One morning before sunrise he put off his drawers and put them on one of the cows' horns (as this was the method of finding out the witches), and then he let out the cow. The cow ran for three miles, followed by the man, until it came to a certain house, and there it stood at the byre-door and began to low. The occupant of the house was an old woman, and she was believed to be the witch, and was demanded by the man to come and give the cows back the milk. [J. S.]

There is [1]presently living in the district a farmer who believes that the wife of a neighbouring farmer is a witch, and that she has the power of taking the milk from his cows. So, after consulting another supposed witch, he was advised to [2]stick silver coins in the tails of his cows, and then the other witch would have no more power over them, and they would give their milk as usual. This he did, but the boy employed by him in attending to the cows, noticing the coins, took them out as often as they were put in, when the farmer was not at hand, and thus for a long time kept himself in tobacco. [M. S.]

---

[1] This is the old sense of 'presently': the *Imperial Dictionary* quotes from Sidney 'The towns and forts you presently have.'

[2] The same kind of charm is used to prevent fairies from milking cows: see p. 87.

G

'According to Mr. Kelly, the proper antidote for witchcraft in the dairy is a twig of rowan-tree, bound with scarlet thread, or a stalk of clover with four leaves, laid in the byre. To discover the witch the gudeman's breeks must be put upon the horns of the cow, one leg upon each horn, when she, being let loose, will for certain run straight to the door of the guilty person[1]. He also mentions a Scottish witch having been seen milking the cows in the shape of a hare' (Henderson, p. 201).

Image-killing.

As an instance of the power which a witch was supposed to possess, a person who wished to be revenged upon another applied to the witch, who made a figure of clay in which she stuck pins, generally about the heart—which was supposed to cause him great suffering—and then laid the figure in a running stream, and, as the water wore away the clay figure, the person on whom he wished to be revenged was thought to be decaying. I have been told that such a figure was found in a burn not many miles from this locality about five or six years ago. [H. J. M.]

A few years ago there was a quarrel between the families of the fishing-population of the village, and, as one of the families was unlucky at the herring-fishing, they ascribed their ill-luck to the evil wishes of the other family. The unlucky family called upon an old woman in the

[1] See also p. 339, 'How to discover a cow-witch.'

village, who was supposed to be well up to all the ways of witches, and, after telling their story to her and as a matter of course paying her a sum of money in silver, she advised them to meet in front of their house at midnight to 'burn the witch,' and she would be with them to see it done. When that night came round, a fire was lit before the house, and all the members of the unlucky family and their relations stood in a circle about it, with their hands joined together. Meantime the old woman, who had prepared a rag model of an old hag with a great number of pins stuck in it, advanced to the fire, and, after muttering a few unintelligible words, threw the model into it, and while it burned away they all danced round, shouting and screaming at the pitch of their voices till it was completely consumed. Then the old woman told the unlucky family that their enemy would have no more power over them, and they believed it. [M. S.]

The practice of image-killing (which is some-times also effected by melting before a fire) is so ancient and has been so widely spread that in-stances of it seem superfluous[1]. I have not the least doubt that it is still frequently carried on in one part or another of the kingdom. The idea at the bottom of it is that a man and his likeness are connected with each other in such a way that any harm done to the latter will affect the former.

[1] For one, see p. 59, note 1.

G 2

Various charms against witchcraft.

It is believed that, if [1] *nine knots of bird-cherry wood* [2] *is sewn into a cow's tail or a man's drawers or a woman's petticoat, or if a four-penny piece be used in the same way, that it shall keep the witches from harming them.* [J. S.]

See also above, p. 72, '**Child-curing.**'

Sham-wizardry.

At a market held not far from this village a wizard was present who wished to buy a cow. Seeing an old woman standing near him who had a cow to sell, he went and asked the price of it. The price being told him, he asked if the cow had any faults. No, she could find no faults with it. The wizard then gave her the money, and asked again, if the cow had any faults, not to hesitate to tell them, as she had the money. The woman said the only faults it had [2] *was that it would eat clothes and money. 'Oh,' said the man, 'I will soon cure her of that: just tie you the money in your handkerchief and give it to me.' The woman gave it to him, and he began whirling it round the cow's head, muttering some words. Then he pocketed the money and went away, after saying to her 'You can keep your cow and her faults with her.'* [A. C.]

---

[1] Compare the nine rusty nails tied to a cord with nine knots on it, p. 80.

[2] See p. 97, note 1, and p. 169, note 1.

MISCELLANEOUS SUPERSTITIONS

Teeth falling out –lucky if not found.

If a tooth fall out of you and you cannot find it, you will be sure to find something of value during the week. **[A. C.]**

Breaking a looking-glass unlucky.

To break a looking-glass, it is said, means ' Ill-luck.' **[M. S.]**

Mr. Henderson (p. 50) mentions among Sussex death-omens ' the breaking of a looking-glass, which they say in Denmark is a sign of utter ruin to the family in which it takes place.'

The reason is obviously the idea that misfortune which has happened to one's image will affect oneself: if a man breaks a looking-glass, his own image is probably upon it at the time, or at any rate has been on it. The ground of the wider belief prevalent in Denmark is perhaps that the looking-glass has received the image of every member of the household.

Crossing on stairs unlucky.

It is not considered lucky to meet and pass anyone on the stairs.   [*A. C.*]

So in Shropshire 'To pass a person on the stairs is very unlucky. Many North Shropshire people will rather turn back than do so; they consider it a sign of a parting' (Jackson and Burne, p. 283).

The idea at the root of the Golspie superstition may be that one's luck, or at any rate the purpose with which one was going downstairs, would be 'crossed.' I am told that, when a fishing-boat is drawn up on the beach, its owners think it most unlucky if anyone steps across the ropes which fasten it, and that if I did so all the ill-luck which attended them in the next week would be put down to me!

Picking up a pin lucky.

If you bend your back to pick up a pin, you'll bend your back to pick up a bigger thing.

[*A. G.*]

[Probably this once ran

If you bend your back to pick up a pin,
You'll bend it to pick up a bigger thing.]

Miss Dempster (p. 233) notes that in Sutherland it is lucky ' To find and pick up a pin.'

In Jackson and Burne, pp. 279-80, we read:
' Pins are held as unlucky as knives in the North

of England [3], and Salopians too say, ' Pick up pins, pick up sorrow.' But side by side with this we have the thrifty maxim—

' See a pin and let it $\begin{cases} \text{stay,} \\ \text{lie,} \end{cases}$

You'll want a pin $\begin{cases} \text{another day,} \\ \text{before you die.} \end{cases}$

See a pin and pick it up,
All the day you'll have gook luck.' '

Perhaps the pin owes its unluckiness in the one case to its power of wounding, and its luckiness in the other to its likeness to silver.

Money in water lucky.

To put money in water, it is said, means 'Luck.' [*M. S.*]

See p. 72, ' **Child-curing.**' Miss Dempster (p. 233) notes that in Sutherland it is lucky ' To wash a baby with a piece of gold in its hand.'

Fairies milking cows.

People often tie a threepenny piece on their cow's tail to keep the fairies from taking the milk away. [*A. G.*]

The same kind of charm is used to prevent witches from taking milk from cows: see p. 81.

' [3] HENDERSON, *Folk-Lore of the Northern Counties*, pp. 117, 230.'

CUSTOMS
ATTACHING TO DAYS

CUSTOMS ATTACHING TO DAYS

—•—

Disappearance of old customs.

I am informed that customs formerly in use have fallen almost, if not completely, into disuse, the customs changing with the times. [M. S.]

HALLOWE'EN: OUTDOOR AMUSEMENTS.

Turnip-lanterns.

The boys go about the village with turnip-lanterns, which they make themselves, doing all kinds of mischief. [B. C.]

On Halloween's night the boys form themselves into companies and go marching about with turnip-lanterns. These lanterns are made of the largest turnips they can find, with the inside cut out, and holes made all round it so as to give forth light. The top part is cut off so as to form a lid, then a piece of candle is placed in it, and thus it is completed. [J. S.]

Blocking up and bombardment of doors.

Blocking up doors with carts. [A. C.]

Attacking the doors of houses with turnips.

[A. C.]

They go to a turnip-field and take away as many turnips as possible. These turnips they use for bombarding and blocking doors. [B. C.]

Blowing smoke through keyholes.

Filling the stalks of cabbage-stocks with tow. Set the tow on fire at one end, and, having applied the lighted end to the keyhole of a door, blow into the other end. The effect of this is that the house will soon be full of smoke. [A. C.]

Getting stalks of cabbage-stocks and making them hollow. They fill the hollow with tow and set fire to the tow. Then they run to the nearest door and put the stalk against the keyhole. The smoke coming from the tow goes through the keyhole, and in a short time fills the house with smoke. [B. C.]

Stopping chimneys.

Stopping the chimneys of low houses with turf, and thus turning back the smoke to the interior of the house. [A. C.]

When they are tired of this work[1] *they get turf, with which they close the* [2]*cans of chimneys,*

---

[1] Bombarding and blocking doors with turnips.

[2] Altered from 'mouths': Dr. Murray in the New English Dictionary quotes '*Act 3 & 4 Will. IV, xlvi. § 10* Chimney cans or pots.'

so that the smoke coming up the chimney is forced down again and in this way fills the house. [B. C.]

Another of their [1] *mischevious tricks is to go about as much disguised as possible and climb up on the tops of houses and stop the chimney with sods.* [J. S.]

Window-tapping.

Take two pieces of string, one long and the other short. Tie one end of the long one to a pin, and tie the short one to the long one, about an inch from where it is tied to the pin. Tie the other end of the short one to a small stone or button. Fix the pin in the wood on the outside of a window, and, with the other end of the string in your hand, take up a position some distance from the window. Pull the string gently toward you and then slacken it. Every time the string is slackened the stone or button strikes the window. Those inside, hearing the beating on the window, come out to find out the cause of it. Then pull the string hard, so that the pin comes out of the window. Repeat the performance whenever they go in, and thus keep on annoying them. [A. C.]

[A most business-like receipt!]

---

[1] J. S, on being asked to read the line, pronounced 'mischievous,' but, when asked whether she did not sometimes pronounce 'mischévious,' said that she did: in English folk-speech 'mischévious' is of course common.

"*The button.*" *A long cord stretching from one side of the road to the other is used. A pin is tied at the end of this cord, and stuck in the wood that surrounds a window. A short cord is tied near the pin, and a button is tied to the end of it. A boy*[1] *has the other end of the cord, and when he slackens it the button strikes the window. If he hears anybody coming, he pulls the cord and the pin comes out of the wood.*

[B. C.]

Sham window-smashing.

Two people go to a window. One of them strikes the window with his hand, immediately after which the other, who carries a bottle, smashes it on the wall. The result is a hurry to the window by those inside who are of the opinion that the window has been smashed.

[A. C.]

Carrying away ploughs, &c.

They[2] *go about doing all the mischief they possibly can, such as carrying all the ploughs, carts, gates, etc., and throw them into the nearest ditch or pond.* *[J. S.]*

Leading horses astray.

Leading horses away from their stables and leaving them in fields a few miles away.

[A. C.]

---

[1] Never a girl?   [2] 'The boys,' of course.

HALLOWE'EN: INDOOR AMUSEMENTS.

[1] Marriage-divination :

by cabbage-stocks;

A girl goes out to the garden blindfolded, and pulls up a cabbage-stock by the root. Then she enters the house, and the bandage is removed from her eyes. If the stalk of the cabbage is crooked, she will get a deformed husband: if it is straight, he will be [2] tall and handsome.

[A. C.]

Compare Burns's ' Halloween,' stanzas 4 and 5.

by nuts;

Put two common nuts in the fire, in the name of a girl and a boy. If both burn together, they love each other : if one separates from the other, they do not love each other. [A. C.]

Putting two nuts in the fire and watching them burn. The nuts stand for a boy and a girl. If they stop beside each other until they burn, the boy and girl will marry. If one nut jumps away, they will quarrel. [B. C.]

Compare Burns's ' Halloween,' stanzas 7–10.

The same form of divination was practised on the other side of the Moray Firth :—

' A live coal was taken, and two peas (nuts were

---

[1] See also p. 68, Hallowe'en's night.

[2] Is there nothing in Golspie between these extremes?

not always to be had) were placed upon it, the one to represent the *lad* and the other the *lass.* If the two rested on the coal and burned together, the young man and young woman (represented by the two peas) would become man and wife; and from the length of time the peas burned and the brightness of the flame the length and happiness of the married life were augured. If one of the peas started off from the other, there would be no marriage, and through the fault of the one whom the pea, that started off, represented' (Gregor, p. 85).

by a ring;

The house is lighted up with turnip-lanterns. A mixture of meal and cream is made, and a ring put in it. The company attack it with spoons, and the one who gets the ring will be married first. [B. C.]

by saucers.

Take three saucers, one with clean water, one with dirty water, and the third leave empty. Let one of the party be blindfolded and led to the other end of the room. From there he or she will have to find their way alone to the table on which the saucers are arranged. She touches a saucer with her hand. If it is the clean-water saucer, she will get a gentleman for a husband. If it is the dirty water, her husband will be poor. And if it is the empty one she will be an 'old maid.'

*If it is a boy who is playing, he will get a lady,
a poor wife, or he will be a bachelor.* [A. C.]

*Three saucers, one with clean water, another
with dirty water, and a third empty,* [1] *is put on
a table. The company is blindfolded and each
selects a dish. If the dish selected is the clean
water, you will get an* [2] *industrious husband or
wife. If it is the dirty water, you will get a* [3] *lazy
husband or wife. If it is empty, you will remain
unmarried.* [B. C.]

Compare Burns's ' Halloween,' stanza 27.

The same form of divination was also practised
on the other side of the Moray Firth :—

' *By Three Caps or Wooden Basins.*—Three
wooden basins were placed in a line on the hearth ;
one was filled with pure, another with dirty, water,
and the third was left empty. The performer was
blindfolded, and a wand or stick was put into her
hand. She was led up to the caps, when she

---

[1] B. C. *may* have been thinking of 'a third' instead of 'three
saucers' when she wrote 'is.' But Dr. Murray in the New
English Dictionary says that in the northern dialect (both of
Middle English and of Modern English) plural nouns take 'is.'
Of modern Scottish and northern English he gives as specimens
'All my hopes is lost' and ' Is your friends coming?', and quotes
instances from the first folio edition of Shakspere (1623), where
the same usage ' is exceedingly frequent.'
An exactly similar doubt arises in a passage by J. S. on p. 84,
but later on that page is a clear instance in a passage by A. C., and
on pp. 123, 169 (where see notes) others by J. S. herself.
[2] Far better than a mere ' gentleman ' or ' lady.'
[3] Far worse than a ' poor' one.

pointed towards one of them. This was done three times, the position of the caps being changed each time. " The best of three " decided her fate ; that is, choosing the same cap twice. The choice of the cap with the pure water indicated an honourable marriage ; the choice of that with the dirty water betokened marriage, but in dishonour. If the choice fell on the empty cap, a single life was to be the lot ' (Gregor, p. 85).

Bob-apple, &c.

A large tub of water in which is placed a number of apples. The amusement of this lies in putting your head beneath the water and trying to take an apple up with your teeth. The same trick is also played with small pieces of money, such as a threepenny piece.   *[J. S.]*

' Throughout Ross and Cromarty Hallowe'en pastimes, such as ducking for apples and pulling kail stalks, were much in vogue ' (Mr. J. M. Mac Kinlay in *The Glasgow Herald*, Aug. 1, 1891).

Get an apple, tie it to a piece of cord, and then fasten the cord to [1] *the top of the house. As the apple swings to and fro, each one tries to get a bite out of it. Anyone is not allowed to touch it with their hands. Some sweet bread will do instead of an apple.*   *[A. C.]*

Another amusement is to cut a number of cakes and to [2] *fill them with treacle, then suspend*

---

[1] I. e. the rafters inside the roof.
[2] At first written *full*.

*them from the ceiling with a string—this trick
being to jump and catch the cake with your teeth
—not only to catch it with your teeth but to take
the whole cake off the string without taking
a piece off with your teeth.* [J. S.]

CHRISTMAS

¹ **Guising.**

*At Christmas the young people of the village
go about 'guising.' The girls dress themselves
in long wide garments, caps belonging to their
grandmothers, and a thick covering of black
muslin, cut in the shape of the face, to hide the
face. The boys dress themselves in long overcoats, large hats pulled over their forehead, and
false whiskers. They also colour their faces with
charcoal, flour, etc. In this dress they go from
door to door singing comic songs and dancing
for a penny.* [A. C.]

*The boy guisers are dressed in long overcoats,
and big hats which they pull over their faces
when they enter houses. Sometimes they wear
false faces and long white beards. The girls
have white gowns thrown over their clothes and
decorated with bright ribbons. In this disguise*

¹ A common term for this amusement in the Northern counties
of England. It means 'putting on a guise' or dress. The verb
' to guise' (cf. ' disguise ') and the substantive ' guiser' (= masker)
are found in literary English.

they visit houses singing and dancing, sometimes for money, sometimes for sport. [*B. C.*]

So on the other side of the Moray Firth ' On Christmas Eve a few of the more sportive of the youth in the villages went along the streets, and besmeared doors and windows with sones. Others disguised themselves, and went in companies of three and four, singing, shouting, and rapping at doors and windows. The houses whose inmates were known to them they entered with dancing, antic gestures, and all kinds of daffing. They were called " gysers." * ' (Gregor, p. 158.)

---

¹ HOG(O)MANAY

The night before New Year's day the boys ramble about the street (waiting for the New Year to come in), doing mischief. Every door, gate, barrow, and cart, or anything that is moveable, is carried away and hid sometimes, but more often put against some door at the other end of the village. Shutters are carried away and tied to the tails of horses. The younger boys of the village content themselves with dis-

'* Cf. Henderson. p. 66.'

¹ ' Hogmanay is the universal popular name in Scotland for the last day of the year,' says Chambers (*Popular rhymes of Scotland*, p. 164). He describes the customs connected with it, which are not in the least like those mentioned as in use at Golspie—where the proceedings are partly a repetition of those in vogue at Hallowe'en. Begging for oaten bread by the poorer children used to be a feature of the day, according to Chambers.

turbing people by drumming on pails or anything
that will make a noise.   Between twelve and one
o'clock the band   marches   through   the   street,
playing 'Auld Lang Syne.'   *[A. C.]*

A. C. gives the name as Hogmanay, B. C. as
Hogomanay: none of the others has written it.
The Southron name is simply New Year's Eve.

I shall discuss the origin of the Scottish name at
the end of this chapter.   It will there be shown
that it comes from a continental original of 4 syllables, not 3; and B. C.'s spelling, and her evidence
given to me personally, are of great interest as
showing the existence of a 4-syllable form in
Scotland also.

The young men spend the last night of the
year in dancing and singing.   The boys do all
the mischief.   They block up doors with carts,
barrows, gates, etc.   They tie the shutters of
shop-windows to horses' tails.   The band goes
through the village between twelve and one o'clock
in the morning to welcome the New Year and
bid farewell to the Old.   Then there is shaking
of hands and drinking to the health of friends.
Then the people go home and wait for the first
visitor, as the luck of the coming year depends
upon him or her.   *[B. C.]*

Miss Dempster (p. 233) mentions that in Sutherland it is lucky 'To see a person of the opposite

sex first on New Year's Day,' and unlucky ' To see a woman the first thing on New Year's Day ' (*ib.* p. 234): but, if the former of these omens be everywhere current, it should have been lucky for a *man* to see a woman first on that day.

So on the Borders 'On New Year's Day much importance is attached to the first foot which crosses the threshold. That of a fair man is luckier than of a dark one, but (alas for the chivalry of the North!) should it be a woman's, some misfortune may certainly be looked for. The servant girls are desirous that their "first foot" should be a lover, and sometimes they insure it by admitting him as soon as the New Year is rung in. They arrange, too, that he should bring something with him into the house, for, as the Lincolnshire rhyme runs :—

> Take out, and then take in,
> Bad luck will begin ;
> Take in, then take out,
> Good luck comes about.

A friend tells me, that in the western part of the county of Durham he has known a man to be specially retained as " first-foot," or " Lucky-bird," as they call him in Yorkshire; his guerdon being a glass of spirits ; but it was not necessary that he should be a bachelor. The man took care to be at the house by 5 o'clock in the morning, which insured his being the earliest visitor. This custom prevails through all our northern counties ' (Henderson, p. 73).

On [1] *New Year's night the boys make a great deal of damage to anything they can lay their hands on, especially on ploughs, gates, and carts, etc. They go in small numbers in all directions, so as not to be so easily caught when doing mischief. They get a cart and fill it with turnips, and block up the first door they come to, and they take ploughs and put them against doors also. They sometimes put ploughs down the chimney. They carry gates away with them and hide them. Window-shutters are changed from one shop to another. Any shopkeeper who is disliked by the boys gets very often things written on with paint or tar on the shutters or door of the shop.* [2] *People who got trouble with things carried away from them have all their carts and things safe from the boys. People who haven't their things in safety get far more trouble than they who have, because they have to seek for their things.*
[J. S.]

On [1] *New Year's Day it is the custom of the boys to take all the portable property which is*

---

[1] The three writers agree that they mean the night on which the New Year begins, W. W. M. adding that it is usually after midnight when the mischief is done.

[2] I. e. People who have had trouble owing to things having been carried away from them keep all their carts and things safe from the boys. This use of 'got' when a Southron would say 'have got' was paralleled by B. C. who, when asked by me what books she had had for a prize which she had lately gained, replied 'I did not get them yet.'

*found lying about any house—such as carts,
barrows, ploughs, window-shutters which are
not lucky enough to have fastenings, and such-
like—and place them at the doors of the houses,
or carry them to a distance and leave them there
to be brought back when found by the owners.
The older people go about with the whisky-bottle
and treat their neighbours. [W. W. M.]*

*At [1] New Year the boys indulged in a great
deal of horse-play, such as blocking up doors and
windows of houses with boxes, carts, ploughs,
and even boats—in fact anything that came handy
—carrying on the sport, as they called it, even
till daylight. But now, with the exception of
the instrumental band taking a turn through the
village at midnight, the rough play has disappeared. [M. S.]*

Many impossible explanations of the name
Hog(o)manay have been given. There is, I believe, no doubt whatever that in England it is
known only in the extreme north, and that in
Scotland the Highlands have adopted it from the
Lowlands, and not *vice versa.* And John Hill
Burton (whether he originated the explanation or
not) was certainly right in regarding it as the
corruption of a French popular cry, which I should
suppose to have been introduced by the French
retinue of Queen Mary.

The oldest known reference to the cry on this

---

[1] See note 1, p. 103.

side of the Channel seems to be in ' Scotch Presbyterian Eloquence,' which, says Burton in ' The Scot
abroad,' 'will not carry us further back than the
middle of the seventeenth century' (i, p. 300):
indeed, unless I am mistaken as to the book meant,
it was not published before 1692. The passage, as
quoted by Burton (without exact reference) runs
thus :—" It is ordinary among some plebeians in the
south of Scotland to go about from door to door,
on New Year's eve, crying ' Hogmana! ' . . ."

Northall (pp. 180-1) gives the following forms
from the N. of England :—*Hogmina* (Cumberland),
Hagmena (Northumberland), and *hag-man ha!*
(Yorkshire). *Hagmanay* is also known, and (Yorkshire) *Hagman Heigh!* (Gent. Mag. lx, p. 352).

The subjoined definition and early instances from
Godefroy's ' Dictionnaire de l'ancienne langue
française ' will establish the common origin of the
Scottish and French custom and cry :—

'AGUILANNEUF, *aguillanneuf, ang., aguillenneuf,*
aguillenneu, aguilloneu, aguillanleuf, aguillenleu,
aguilanleu, eguilanleu, guillanneuf, haguirenleu,
haguilennef, s.m., jour de l'an, étrennes, fête du
jour de l'an, où les étrennes se donnaient et se
demandaient au cri de *aguillanneuf:*

Item le jour de l'*auguilanleu* onze sols de
fresainges . . . (1353, *Aveu de la seigneurie*
d'Épied, ap. Le Clerc de Douy, t. II, f°6ᵛᵒ, Arch.
Loiret.)

Demanda pour son *aguilanleu* une poule. (1409,
Enq., Arch. Sarthe, E 3, f° 26.)

À certains petiz enffans qui demandoient *aguil-lenleu*, le jour de l'an dernier passé. (1470, *D. de Bourg.*, n° 7072, ap. Laborde, *Emaux.*)

Le jeudi vigille de la Circon[ci]sion plusieurs compaignons faisans grant chere pour l'honneur de la feste que l'en appelle communement *aguil-loneu.* (1472, Arch. JJ 197, pièce 302.)

Le suppliant oyt des chalumeaulx ou menes-triers, . . . et trouva des varletz ou jeunes com-paignons . . . qui alloient par illecques querant *aguillenneu* le dernier jour de decembre. (1473, Arch. JJ 195, pièce 977.)'

In the last edition of La Curne de Sainte-Palaye's 'Dictionnaire historique de l'ancien lan-gage françois' one also finds under ' Haguilenne' an instance of *Hagui men lo* in 1408, as well as of three other forms beginning with *h* and dated 1399, 1409, 1474.

Other French forms worth mentioning are :— *Hoquinano* and *Hoguinané* in Normandy (*ib.*), and *Oguinané* in Guernsey (Moisy, ' Dictionnaire de patois normand,' p. 16).

The origin of the French word has not been discovered. The Druids used to cut mistletoe at the beginning of the year (Pliny, Hist. nat., xvi at end). Accordingly the late form *aguillanneuf* has been explained as À gui! L'an neuf! ' To mistletoe! The New Year!' In support of this explanation the line ' Ad viscum Druidæ, Druidæ cantare sole-bant ' (' " To the mistletoe Druids! " the Druids used to chant ') was quoted as Ovid's in 1605 by Paulus

Merula, but is not to be found in Ovid (Ménage, Dict. etym., ed. 1694, p. 12). It was also quoted by De Chiniac (with the omission of the first ' Druidæ ') from Pliny's Natural history, xvi. 44 (see *L'Intermédiaire* xvii, 464), but it is not there either! And it is obvious that if *-lannen(f)*, which gives a simple meaning and is easy to pronounce, had been the original form, it would hardly have been corrupted into *-lanleu*, which gives no sense and is more difficult to pronounce.

Moreover, there are Spanish forms to be taken into account. A correspondent of the French antiquarian journal *L'Intermédiaire* points out that at Madrid the New Year's Day mass is called the Aguinaldo mass, and says that the Marquis of Santillana, a 15th cent. Spanish poet, asks his lady to set him free from his irons ' pour *anguilando*.'

A Spanish dictionary will show that *aguinaldo* is regular Spanish for a New Year's gift[1]. As regards Santillana, I find in the 1852 edition of his works a poem (p. 437) headed ' El aguilando,' ' The *aguilando*,' in the first verse of which, after asking his lady to free him from chains, he says

> Estas sean mis estrenas,
> Esto solo vos demando,
> Este seu mi aguilando ;

i. e. ' These be my New Year's gifts, this alone I ask of you, this be my *aguilando*.'

---

[1] As Señor Don Fernando de Arteaga y Pereira informs me, it also means a Christmas gift.

Now anyone would naturally suppose that *aguilando* was the gerund of a verb *aguilar*. And I suggest that it points to a popular corrupted form of the verb *alquilar* 'to hire or let oneself out for hire,' so that it would have meant in the first instance 'For hiring,' 'Hiring-money,' or 'Handsel.' And, on referring to this last word in the Imperial Dictionary, I find 'Handsel-Monday . . . The first Monday of the new year, when it was formerly usual in Scotland for servants, children, and others to ask or receive presents or handsel.' And Dr. Joass tells me that this practice still survives, and is accompanied by those of waiting for the first foot and whisky-treating. So that Hog(o)-manay was apparently a mere anticipation, under 16th century French influence, of the customs which attached to Handsel-Monday[1].

Let me add that, since the foregoing pages were put into type, Dr. Murray, the editor of the New English Dictionary, himself a Roxburghshire man, tells me that 'Hogmanay' in Scotland properly means the gift and not the day, 'Hogmanay' as applied to the day really standing for 'Hogmanay-day.'

---

[1] Of course I regard the French forms as corrupted from an earlier Spanish one : the earliest French form yet found begins with *au-*, which suggests an original *al-*.

The Spanish verb itself is derived from the substantive *alquilé*, which is borrowed from the Arabic *al queré* 'the hire' according to Eguilaz y Yanguas *Glosario*, p. 250, and Prof. Margoliouth tells me that *al kira* 'the hire' would be pronounced in most dialects *al kiré*.

GOWKING-DAY (APRIL FOOLS' DAY)

On the 1ˢᵗ of April people send those who do not remember that that is the gowking-day agowking. [W. W. M.]

W. W. M. has also given the following rime,

Never laugh, never smile ;
Send the gowk another mile.

'Gowk' ordinarily means 'fool,' and this is pretty certainly the meaning in the minds of the people who use this rime and who speak of sending others agowking on gowking-day.

But 'gowk' also means 'cuckoo.' And Mr. Henderson (p. 92) refers to White's Selborne as evidence that the bird first utters its note between the 7th and 26th of April, and points out that under the Old Style the 1st of April would have been what is now the 12th. And Jamieson in his Dictionary has suggested that the phrase 'hunt the gowk' arose from young people vainly trying to catch sight of the cuckoo, which flew further off whenever they got near it.

If this were so, the application of the term to the person befooled instead of to the bird which befooled him can only have arisen through the meaning of the phrase 'hunt the gowk' having been entirely misunderstood. As the cuckoo is still called gowk in North Britain, this seems very unlikely : it would be in South Britain, where the bird is no longer so called, that one would expect such a misunderstanding to have arisen—but in South Britain April ' gowks ' are unknown, they are April 'fools.' And the phrase in Dr. Murray's part of Scotland was not ' hunt the gowk,' but ' hund the gowk,' i. e. hound him.

As regards the practice on the Borders, Mr. Henderson says (p. 92) ' We learn from the Wilkie MS. that the second of April shares on the Borders the character which the first bears all England over. There are two April-fool days there, or, as they call them, " gowk days." Unsuspecting people are then sent on bootless errands, and ridiculed for their pains.

But " hunting the gowk " is more fully carried out by sending the victim from place to place with a letter, in which the following couplet was written:

> The first and second of Aprile,
> Hound the gowk another mile.'

The double meaning ' cuckoo ' and ' fool ' is found very early for this word in the Germanic languages. It may be asked whether we are not possibly dealing with two distinct words which have acquired a common sound; but in all probability that is not the case. Apparently some popular belief about the bird, perhaps some legend about it, gave it a reputation for folly, and so fools came to be called cuckoos. And perhaps also the time when the cuckoo's note is first heard was seized on as an occasion for deluding the foolish and chaffing them with their likeness to the cuckoo. For the origin of April-fooling does not seem to have been discovered, if this is not it.

MAY-DAY

On the 1ˢᵗ of May the persons who wish to preserve their beauty rise very early in the morning and wash their faces in the dew, which they say will keep them from being sunburnt.

[W. W. M.]

'On May Day morning in Edinburgh, not many years ago, everyone went up to the top of Arthur's Seat before sunrise to "meet the dew." In Perth they climbed Kinnoul Hill for the same purpose, with a lingering belief in the old saying—that those who wash their faces in May dew will be beautiful all the year' (Henderson, p. 85).

The following relates to Shropshire :—

'Washing in May-Dew was (and no doubt still is) supposed in Edgmond to strengthen the joints and muscles as well as to beautify the complexion. I knew a little idiot boy whose mother (fancying it was weakness of the spine which prevented him from walking) took him into the fields "nine mornings running" to rub his back with May-dew. She explained that the dew had in it all the "nature" of the spring herbs and grasses, and that it was only to be expected that it should be wonderfully strengthening' (Jackson and Burne, p. 190).

GAMES WITHOUT RIMES

1

GAMES WITHOUT RIMES

—•—

Nearly all the rimeless games described to me were games already well known in England. Sometimes, however, the names vary more or less from those by which I knew them or by which they are described in *Cassell's Complete Book of Sports and Pastimes*. I will give Cassell's name for each of these (with a reference to the page), and then the Golspie name.

Name in Cassell's book.	*Name in Golspie.*
Postman's knock (p. 782).	American post. [M. S.]
Buck, buck, how many fingers do I hold up? (p. 252).	Ride the donkey. [W. W. M., A. G.]
Bull in the ring (p. 252).	[1] Bull in the barn. [W. W. M., A. G., H. J. M.]
Follow my leader (p. 256).	Follow the leader. [W. W. M.]
Foot and a half, Foot it, or Fly the garter (p. 255).	Foot and one half. [A. G.]
Hare and hounds (p. 258).	Hounds and hares. [W. W. M.]
Hop scotch (p. 259).	[2] Pot. [A. C., B. C.]
[3] Oranges and lemons (p. 780).	Putting out the ashes. [A. C.]

[1] So called in Shropshire (Jackson and Burne, p. 519).

[2] I have heard this name in England (at Liverpool?), and believe it to be common there.

[3] Called by Chambers (p. 127) 'Scots and English.' 'French and English' (Cassell, p. 257) or 'tug of war' (Cassell, p. 273) is virtually only the latter part of the same game, but the game called 'French and English' in Golspie is quite different.

Name in Cassell's book.	*Name in Golspie.*
Puss in the corner (p. 267).	Pussy in the corner. [A. C., B. C.]
Rounders (p. 225).	¹ Housie meetie. [A. C., B. C., J. S. ('housy meetie'), W.W.M.]
² Spanish fly (p. 269).	Leap frog with bonnets. [A. G.]
Walk, moon, walk! (p. 273).	³ Spague. [A. G.]

The following games are played under names known in England:—Cricket, Football, Golf, Hide and seek (M. S.), Quoits (W. W. M.—sometimes played with a flat stone instead of an iron ring), and Shinty (W. W. M.). The last is more commonly called Clubs, the ball is termed a 'shiney,' and the goals and goal-posts 'hiles' and 'hile-posts' (W. W. M.).

W. W. M. merely mentions, and has now forgotten, Bull in the path. We suspect it to be merely another name of ' Bull in the barn,' which Mrs. Gomme (i, p. 50) calls ' Bull in the Park.'

On the manner in which such games are spread some remarks will be found upon p. 127.

The following games played in Golspie I do not find in Cassell.

¹ Pronounced ' Hoozy meety.' But H. J. M. wrote *Housie mettie*.

² ' Leap frog with bonnets' is only a part of ' Spanish fly.' The late Mr. A. W. L. Whitbread told me that it is part of a game known in Oxford as ' Ships a-sailing.'

³ Boys throw their bonnets between the straddling legs of a blindfolded boy, and then '*tell the boy to spague this, meaning to go and look for the bonnets*' [*A. G.*]. In Jamieson's Dictionary I find that ' Spaig is expl. by Mactaggart, "A person with long ill-shaped legs." '

[1] Bonnets.

In Bonnets all the bonnets of the players are placed in a row, and one player tries to put a ball into one of the bonnets. He into whose bonnet it is put tries to strike one of the players with the ball. He who is struck thrice has to stand three hits from the other players with the ball.

[IV. IV. M.]

In Mrs. Gomme's book (i, p. 14) a variety of this is described from Nairn by the Rev. W. Gregor. The title given is ' Ball and Bonnets.' Mrs. Gomme adds ' See " Eggatt " '; but there is no article " Eggatt " in the volume. Her ' Ball in the Decker,' reported from Dublin, has points in common.

The late Mr. A. W. L. Whitbread told me that the game is nearly the same as one known in Oxford as ' Rats in holes.'

Bullie Horn.

This is a variety of the game called ' Warning ' in Cassell's book (p. 274). It was mentioned, but not described, by A. G., from whom I ascertain that it is played as follows.

One boy puts his hands in his ' wallet ' and tries to ' tip ' (= touch) another boy with it, without taking his hands out. The boy thus ' tipped ' is obliged to carry the tipper on his back to the ' stand ' (= bounds). He then puts his own hands inside his wallet, and he and the tipper unite in

---

[1] I. e. Caps. In Scotland still, as once in England, ' bonnet ' is in common use for a man's or boy's cap.

trying to tip other boys, the game going on as at first until every boy has been tipped and has carried his tipper.

Buttons (W. W. M.) or Buttony (A. G.).

Buttons are played by a stick being set up at which each boy throws a button. He whose button lands nearest to the stick lifts all the buttons, and throws them all up in the air, calling head or tail. All the buttons which land the way that he calls out he gets, and the others are passed on to the next boy, who does the same, and so on until the last boy.   [W. W. M.]

Mr. E. Gass informs me that this is nearly the same as ' Pitch and toss.'   It is perhaps the Forfarshire ' buttony,' but not the Perthshire one as described in the English Dialect Dictionary : Prof. Wright tells me there is a Yorkshire ' buttony.'

Cabbage-stock.

Cabbage stock. Lots are cast and, whoever the lot falls on, that person has to kneel down, and another stand above him and covers his eyes. Then he asks him to appoint a place for each to stand at without letting him know their names. When this is done he calls ' Play on, cabbage-stock,' at which they all run from their appointed places and begin beating him, that is kneeling on his back, and he that is last in has to go under the same proceedings.   [J. S.]

This game is also mentioned by A. G.

French and English.

French & English is played by equal sides being made, one of which is called the French and the other the English. The bonnets of each side are then piled up in two seperate heaps, and the side which obtains the most bonnets are the winners. [W. W. M.]

I find that the two sides occupy different 'stands' and that the bonnets are piled at a point between the two. One boy runs to snatch a bonnet before he can be touched, another from the opposite stand tries to touch him first; whichever of the two is successful carries away the top bonnet.

This is only one of the many varieties of 'Touch,' and is quite different from the game called 'French and English' in Cassell (p. 257). Mrs. Gomme describes a similar game under the Golspie title, but says that it 'is known as " Scotch and English " in the north' (i, p. 145).

King and queen.

This game was mentioned but not described by M. S. I ascertain from her that it is played as follows.

Two chairs are placed facing each other, with a certain space between. Across this space, and over the backs of the chairs, a blanket is stretched. The king then sits on one chair and the queen on the other. A third player is then asked to sit on the blanket between them. As he or she does so, the king and queen rise, and the blanket and third player fall to the ground. The procedure is repeated till all the rest have sat on the blanket.

The game is played in the United States under the same name (Newell, p. 120), and Mr. Newell quotes Strutt's ' Sports and pastimes ' (p. 294) to show that early in this century it was played as a trick on new girls in large English boarding-schools; the new girl, after having a very flattering speech addressed to her, was suddenly let fall into a tub of water. Mr. Newell describes a similar Austrian game called ' conferring knighthood.'

[1] Skeby or Tit for tat.

Skeby, or tit for tat. Two stands are needed to play skeby. There is also a number of girls who call ' No skeby.' The girl who calls the last has to go skeby. She has to go between the two stands. There is a number of girls in each stand. The girl who is skebby is watching till she sees any of the other girls coming out of their stands. When she sees them out of their stands, she pounces on them and tries to give them [2] skeby. If she gives them skeby, then they are skeby, and she goes into one of the stands.

[J. S.]

---

[1] This is only a variety of ' Touch ' (Cassell, p. 273), or Tick. The pronunciation of the name is midway between *skibby* and *skeeby*. It is (Dr. Joass tells me) the Gaelic *sgiobag* (pronounced *skeepak*), ' a slap given in play.'

[2] I ask J. S. what skeby *is*, and she tells me ' touch.'

[1]Smuggle the giggie.

The company is divided into two equal sides (first & second). A large ring called the 'stand' is drawn on the ground. The second side gives some article—as a ring, pencil, etc.[2]— to the first side, who, after getting it go to some corner which the second side cannot see. One of the first side takes the ring from the girl who got it from the second side. Then they all call 'Giggie' and run towards the 'stand.' The second side tries to catch them as they run. If the girl who has the ring gets into the 'stand' without any of the second side catching her, she calls 'Giggie is free' and the first side gets the ring again; but, if the second side catches her, they get the ring. [B. C.]

This game is also described by A. C., J. S., W. W. M., and H. J. M., while A. G. mentions it. I think I played it about 1859 at Liverpool College (Middle School). It is described as a Glasgow game in Jamieson's Dictionary, where it is called 'Smuggle the geg.' It is obviously an imitation of smuggling, and, since W. W. M. explains 'giggie' to me as 'keg,' 'geg' and 'giggie' may just pos-

---

[1] So called by A. C.   B. C. calls it 'Giggie,' J. S. 'Giggie or Smuggle the gig,' W. W. M. 'Smuggle the gauge,' A. G. 'Smuggle,' and H. J. M. 'Giggies Free' (=Giggie's free).

[2] J. S. thrice mentions a 'thumble'—never 'thimble.' Dr. Joass tells me that *thummle* is a local pronunciation, and the new edition of Jamieson gives *thumble* and *thummil* as Scottish.

sibly = 'keg' and 'keggie' with *k* assimilated to following *g*. But Dr. Joass tells me that 'giggie' is a name for a spinning-top (diminutive of Shakspere's 'gig' with the same meaning), and originally a top may have been used in the game—perhaps because its material and shape, and the rings round it, resembled those of a cask.

Stand but(t).

This is played (H. J. M.) by boys as well as girls. It is described by A. C., B. C., J. S., and H. J. M. I shall give it as played by girls.

One girl throws up a ball, calling another girl's name. The girl so named tries to catch it, and, if successful, takes the place of thrower-up. Any girl who fails to catch it throws it at the rest, who are running away. A girl thus hit is called 'one of it' (A. C.) or 'one' (J. S.), and has in turn to take the place of thrower-up. A girl who has been hit three times is called 'three of it' (A. C.) or 'three' (J. S.).

Such a girl, A. C., says, ' has to undergo some punishment.' B. C. says that she ' holds her hand against the wall while each girl hits her hand three times with the ball. This curious punishment is called [1] " paps." ' J. S. says that ' she is in for her baps. That is to say she has to hold her hand

---

[1] Jamieson's Dictionary gives *pap* or *pawp* as Aberdeenshire for ' blow,' but a *bap* is a small roll or loaf of bread (New Eng. Dict.).

against a wall and the other girl's [1] gives her so many hits on the hand.' H. J. M. says that a boy who is so punished ' has to put his hand to the wall; then they all try to strike it with the ball.'

The game is called *Stand bit* by A. C. and J. S., *Standbit* by B. C., and *Stan But* by H. J. M. The *u* in *but, butt,* and *i* in *bit* are so frequently interchanged, or replaced by the same almost neutral sound, that I cannot attach much importance to either way of spelling the second syllable. I suspect the right form to be ' Stand butt,' i. e. ' Stand as a target, stand to be shot at [2].'

The game is said by Mr. Newell (p. 181) to be well known in Austria: a somewhat similar game, he says, was played by New England schoolboys and was known as *Call-Ball, Callie-ball,* or *Balliecallie.* He considers that it is alluded to in the 16th century by Herrick, in the lines

'I call, I call; who doe ye call?
  The maids to catch this cowslip ball.'

And Mr. E. Gass informs me of a variety of it known in Oxford as ' Iddy-iddy-all,' which I describe on p. 339.

---

[1] ' Girl's ' should have been ' girls,' but ' gives ' is good old Scots English — see p. 169, note 1.

[2] Dr. Joass says boys say ' out ' as often as ' but ' in this game. ' But ' in Scots English = ' the outer room,' or ' to the outer room,' and I suspect that ' out ' arises from a mistaken interpretation of ' butt.'

RIME-GAMES

RIME-GAMES

—•—

I have divided the rime-games into 3 classes [1]— those played in a line, those played in a ring, and ' Mrs. Brown.' I have taken the completest or otherwise best version received of each rime, and have printed it without any verbal correction or addition. But it often happens that the version of some other contributor is nearer in some points to what must have been the original form of the rime, so that the variations given in the notes should also be read.

It will be seen that in some of the games a number of quite distinct rimes have been strung together : this, or at least the borrowing by one rime of part of another rime, is a common feature in British rime-games.

It will also be seen that a considerable number of the rimes are known in Shropshire, Dorset, and Surrey, and (so far as we can judge by their present forms, and in some cases by the tunes to which they are sung) have been imported from England into Scotland. Wherever a family of children go, it is natural that they should play their own games and teach them to the children of their

---

[1] ' See the robbers passing by ' forms a 4th class by itself. It was merely mentioned by A. C. in her paper, and I did not know it to be a rime-game. It will be found at p. 340, in ' Additional notes to the contributions.'

new neighbourhood, and nowadays the railroad and the steamship can thus extend the knowledge of a game hundreds or thousands of miles in a few hours or days.

There remain a number of rimes which apparently took their origin north of the Tweed or in the Border counties of England, and of which I have seen no other versions. But even in those rimes to which I shall print parallels from elsewhere the Golspie version often yields some interesting variation. Take for instance ' My delight's in tansies,' which exhibits in a much less incorrect form a rime which in the one version (from Yorkshire) which I have yet seen in print had been corrupted into arrant nonsense ; while a comparison of the Golspie and Yorkshire versions enables us to conjecture pretty closely what was the original text of the rime.

The game-rimes are almost all sung, not spoken. None of the tunes were sent in by the contributors ; but tunes will be found at pp. 197-207, together with the necessary explanation and such notes as it occurs to me to make upon them.

1. Games in a line.

Games with rhymes are divided into two sets, namely those which are played in a line and those played in a ring. In the following games the company stands in a line. One of them stands in front of the others. When they begin to sing, the girl goes backward and forward in

*front of them. At a certain part of the rhyme
the girl who is out takes some other girl out by
the hand and stands in herself, after finishing
the rhyme.* [*A. C.*]

. . . [When the singer takes the other girl out]
*they both sing the remaining part of the rhyme.
Then the girl who sang the last rhyme takes her
place in the line, and the other girl sings the
rhyme over again, or sings another rhyme.*

[*B. C.*]

[Father and mother, may I go?]

'[1] *Father and mother, may I go,
May I go, may I go,
Father and mother may I go
Across the banks of* [2]*roses?* '

' *Yes, my darling, you may go,
You may go, you may go,
Yes, my darling, you may go
Across the banks of roses.* '

[1] M. S. writes 'Father, mother,'—here and in l. 3. Mr. Loudon
tells me that he has heard this as follows :—

> Please, mamma, will I get leave,
> Will I get leave, will I get leave,
> Please mamma, will I get leave
> To cross the banks of roses?

> Yes, my dear, you will get leave,
> You will get leave, you will get leave,
> Yes, my dear, you will get leave
> To cross the banks of roses.

[2] Probably *rosa rubella* (pale pink or cream), growing on sandy
coasts, or *rosa arvensis*, a trailing white hedge-bank rose.

As I went down yon bank, oh!

Clap your [1] *tails and away you go,*
Away you go, away you go,
Clap your tails and away you go
Across the banks of roses.

[As I went down yon bank, oh!]

As I went down yon bank, oh!
Yon bank, oh! yon bank, oh!
As I went down yon bank, oh!
Who did I meet but a lad
With a tartan [2] *plaid?*

[My delight's in tansies]

And my delight's in [3] *tansies;*
My delight's in pansies;
My delight's in a red red rose,
The colour of my Maggie, oh!

Heigh oh! my Maggie, oh!
My very bonnie Maggie, oh!
All the world I would not give
For a kiss from Maggie, oh!

In the third verse you should 'clap your tails'
till the end of the verse. Take some one out at
' The colour of my Maggie, oh!' [A. C.]

[1] Skirts.
[2] Note the pronunciation 'plad,' which is rare in Golspie.
[3] A common tall wild plant with bunches of radiate yellow flowers. Its ordinary Golspie name is 'Stinkin' Willie,' and ' tansy' is probably almost unknown to natives.

The two stanzas beginning 'And my delight's in tansies' are specially interesting because they supply a less corrupted form of a Yorkshire rime given by Northall (p. 386). 'A number of girls,' he says, 'range themselves against a wall, whilst one stands out, stepping backwards and forwards to the tune—

> " Sunday night an' Nancy oh!
> My delight an' fancy oh!
> All the world that I should keep,
> If I had a Katey oh ! "

Then she rushes to pick out one, taking her by the hand, and standing face to face with her, the hands of the two being joined, sings—

> " He oh, my Katey oh !
> My bonny, bonny Katey oh !
> All the world that I should keep,
> If I had, etc."

Then the two advance, and take another girl, etc.'

' Keep ' suggests that not ' give ' but ' gi'e ' is the original word. And ' Sunday night ' suggests ' Some delight[1].' The original may have been

> Some delight in a tansy, oh !
> Some delight in a pansy, oh !
> My delight's in a red, red rose,
> The colour of my Nancy, oh !

[1] So Prof. H. H. Turner of Oxford; it is better than ' One delights,' which I had written.

K 2

Heigh, oh! my Nancy, oh!
My bonnie bonnie Nancy, oh!
All the wor(u)ld I wad gi'e
For ae kiss from my Nancy, oh!

The pronunciation of *world* as two syllables is
quite correct: in old English it was *weorold* (-*uld*),
worold (-*uld*). In Barnes's 'Poems in the Dorset
Dialect' it is regularly spelt *worold*. This pronunciation is also heard in N. England and Scotland,
and 'ae' points to the latter as the birth-country of
the rime. In singing the last line (see p. 198) *a* is
accented, and *my* sung before *Maggie*.

[My name is Queen Mary]

¹ *My name is Queen Mary,*
My age is sixteen;
My father's a farmer
² *In yonder green.*
He has plenty of money
³ *To dress me in silk,*
⁴ *But no bonnie laddie*
Will ⁵ *take me awa.*

¹ B. C. gives the first two lines as
'Queen Mary Queen Mary my heart is with thee.'
² This suggests a much more southern origin. B. C. and M. S.
confirm 'In,' but J. S. has 'On,' which is almost certainly right.
³ J. S. has 'To keep me in silks.'
⁴ B. C. has 'Though,' which is worse. J. S. has 'And some,'
which is also less likely.
⁵ B. C. and J. S. have 'tak,' which is better. J. S. has 'away,'
which is worse.
    B. C. continues with the four lines beginning 'May be I'll get
married' followed by the four beginning 'I can chew tobacco.'
For these see later.

One morning I rose
[1] *And I looked in the glass :*
Says I to myself
' What a handsome young lass ! '
[2] *My hands by my side*[3]*,*
And I laughed [4] *a ha ha !*
For some bonnie laddie
Will [5] *take me awa.*

[(I'll) take her by the lily white hand]
[6] *I'll take her by the lily white hand,*
I'll lead her o'er the water[7]*,*
I'll give her kisses [8] *one two three,*
For she's a lady's daughter[9]*.*

[Roses in and roses out]
Roses in and roses out,
[10] *Roses in the garden :*
[11] *I would not give a bunch of flowers*
For twopence halfpenny [12] *farthing.*

Take some one out at ' I 'll take her by the etc.'

[A. C.]

---

[1] J. S. omits ' And.'

[2] Perhaps in the original

With my hands by my side I laughed ' Ha ha ha ! ' (or
' ahaha ! ').   [3] J. S. ' sides.'   [4] J. S. omits ' a.'

[5] J. S. has ' tak' (better), and ' away' (worse .

[6] J. S. ' We'll' in all three lines. Both *I'll* and *We'll* are
probably insertions: see pp. 139–40, 144.   [7] J. S. ' waters.'

[8] A. C. writes ' One two three' as a separate line.

[9] J. S. ' is the ladies daughter.'   [10] J. S. prefixes ' And.'

[11] J. S. substitutes for these two lines the last two of the previous
stanza—' We'll give her kisses one two three for she is the ladies
daughter.'

[12] In the original rime no doubt ' farden,' which was common in
English folk-speech.

J. S. says that there are two varieties of this set
of rimes.   In the first, the stanza beginning ' My
name is Queen Mary' is followed by the 3rd stanza,
'We'll take her by the lily white hand,' and that
by ' Roses in and roses out.'

In the second, after the stanza beginning ' My
name is Queen Mary' comes the following :—

[I've a lad at Golspie]

I've a lad at Golspie;
I've a lad at sea;
I've a lad at Golspie,
And his [1] *number is twenty-three.*

[I can wash a sailor's shirt]

I can wash a sailor's shirt,
[2]And I can wash it clean;
I can wash a sailor's shirt,
And bleach it on the green.

[I can chew tobacco]

I can chew tobacco,
I can smoke a pipe,
I can kiss a bonny lad
At ten o'clock at night.   *[J. S.]*

[1] Perhaps this rime originated in some place consisting of
one long street or row with the houses numbered.   The houses
in Golspie are not numbered.   But Dr. Joass suggests that the
number of a naval reserve man in a training-ship may be meant.

[2] A. C., B. C., and M. S. sing the line without 'And.'

After which comes the stanza 'One morning I rose &c.'

According to B. C. the 'Queen Mary' stanza is followed by

[May be I'll get married]

May be I'll get married;
May be I'll get free;
May be I'll get married
To the ¹ laddie's on the sea.

⌊I can chew tobacco]

I can chew tobacco,
I can smoke a pipe,
I can kiss a bonny lass
At ten o'clock at night.   [B. C.]

In the last stanza B. C.'s 'lass' is correct, against J. S.'s 'lad.' And the 'I can''s seem to have been originally either 'He can' or, more probably still, 'He canna.' For the stanza appears to be a mere fragment of a long piece which will be found at p. 146.

The 'Queen Mary' stanza is closely connected

---

¹ B. C. writes 'laddies,' but 'laddie 's,' i.e. *laddie that is*, must be meant in the original. Compare ' I have a brother is condemned to die' (*Meas. for Meas.* ii. 2. 33) and other instances in Abbott's ' Shakespearian grammar' (1870 ed., p. 164).

with the English children's rime ' Green gravel.'
Life is too short, for me at least, to resolve each of
these rimes into their original elements, but the
following points of similarity will bear out my
contention.

(1) On p. 199 I print the two tunes to which
' Queen Mary ' is sung at Golspie, and show that
one of them is practically the same to which ' Green
gravel ' is sung at Madeley in Shropshire, Sporle
in Norfolk, and in Lancashire.

(2) The following are the first verses of the
Madeley, Sporle, and Lancashire versions (taken
from Mrs. Gomme's book, i, pp. 172-4).

Green gravel, green gravel, the grass is so green,
The flowers are all faded and none to be seen,
O [Dolly], O [Dolly], your sweetheart is dead,
He 's sent you a letter to turn back your head.

      —Madeley, Shropshire (Miss Burne).

Green meadows, green meadows, your grass is so
    green,
The fairest young damsel that ever was seen ;
O Mary, O Mary, your sweetheart is dead ;
We've sent you a letter to turn back your head.

Or, Green gravel, green gravel, the grass is so
    green,

and following on as above.

      —Sporle, Norfolk (Miss Matthews).

Green gravel, green gravel, the grass is so green,
The fairest young lady [damsel] that ever was seen.
O ——, O ——, your true love is dead;
He's sent you a letter to turn round your head.

—Redhill, Surrey (Miss G. Hope);
Lancashire (Mrs. Harley).

It is clear from these and many other English versions given by Mrs. Gomme that the oldest ascertained beginning of the English rime is 'Green gravel.' As there is a sand known as 'greensand,' there may be some gravel which is green; but it is not likely to be so common as to have been introduced into popular poetry, and one of the Sporle versions alters it to ' Green meadows,' while an Isle of Wight version alters it to ' Yellow gravel'!

Now 'Mary' was once pronounced 'Marry'; indeed the exclamation *Marry!* so common in Shakspere, was originally an invocation of the Virgin Mary. And when we compare the *accented* syllables in the first line of 'Green gravel'

Green grável, green grável, the gráss is so gréen

and in the first line of B. C.'s version

Queen Máry, Queen Máry, my heárt is with thée

we see that their vowel-sounds are identical, if we only pronounce Mary as Marry [1].

---

[1] And might not a young child pronounce 'Queen' as 'Green'?
—whence the transition to 'Green' would be very easy.

Again, if we take the ordinary version,

My náme is Queen Máry, my áge is sixtéen

and give the vowels *old* values, sounding the *a* in *name* and *age* as in the adjective *bad*, and *my* as *me*, we get nearly the same result ; and I believe that ' Green gravel, green gravel, the grass is so green,' was gradually corrupted from this through imperfect hearing. When ' We are all young maidens ' gets turned into ' We all shall have the measles ' (see p. 175), and ' We are three dukes a-roving ' into 'Forty ducks are riding' (see p. 151), any such things are possible.

With this may have been mixed up another rime beginning ' O Mary, O Mary, your sweetheart is dead.'

(3) It will be noticed that the 6th and 8th lines, which ought to rime, do not. This is a pretty sure sign that they are borrowed from different songs. With ' To dress me in silk ' or ' To keep me in silks ' compare the following (from Mrs. Gomme's book) in the ' Green gravel ' song :—

We washed her, we dried her, we rolled her in
   silk (Belfast)

I'll wash you in milk,
And I'll clothe you with silk (Berrington, Os-
   westry)

Wash them in milk, and clothe them in silk
   (Derbyshire and Worcestershire ; also Sheffield)

I'll wash you in butter-milk, I'll dress you in silk
(Isle of Man)

Washed in milk and dressed in silk (Forest of
Dean, Gloucestershire)

They wash 'em in milk
And dress 'em in silk (Wakefield)

As regards the rime ' [I'll] take her by the [1] lily
white hand,' it is apparently only the end of
a stanza, and ' o'er the water ' should probably
be ' to the altar ' (*altar* was also written *awter*
in old times). Compare the [2] two following
parallels :—

(1) From Surrey (Allen, p. 84),

' V. LEMON OR PEAR.

Rosy apple, lemon or pear,
Bunch of roses she shall wear.
Gold and silver by his side ;
I know who will be the bride.
Take her by her lily white hand,
Lead her to the altar,
Give her kisses one, two, three,
Mrs. (child's name) daughter.'

---

[1] I print 'lily white ' as it was written, and not 'lily-white,'
because in a child's rime ' lily ' may = 'lilly,' i. e. 'little.'

[2] A wide variant from Hartford in Connecticut has ' o'er the
water ' (Newell, p. 72).

(2) From Dorset (Udal, p. 210),

'(IV.) ROSY APPLE, LEMON, AND PEAR.

The children form a ring, and one of them is chosen to stand in the middle, as in the last game, whilst the rest circle round and sing:

> "Rosy apple, lemon, and pear,
> A bunch of roses she shall wear;
> Gold and silver by her side,
> Choose the one shall be her bride.

> "Take her by her lily-white hand,
> *'Here the one in the centre chooses one from the ring to stand by her.'*
> Lead her to the altar;
> Give her kisses, one, two, three,
> To old mother's runaway daughter."

On these last words being uttered, the one who was first standing in the middle must run away and take a place in the ring as soon as she can. The second one remains in the centre, and the game is repeated over and over again until all have been chosen. (Symondsbury.)'

I had the last 5 pages in type before I received a proof of the article ' Queen Mary ' in Mrs. Gomme's 2nd vol. The following are the versions she has:—

> I. Queen Mary, Queen Mary, my age is sixteen,
> My father's a farmer on yonder green;
> He has plenty of money to dress me in silk—
> Come away, my sweet laddie, and take me
> a walk.

One morning I rose and I looked in the glass,
I thought to myself what a handsome young
    lass ;
My hands by my side, and a gentle ha, ha,
Come away, my sweet lassie, and take me
    a walk.

Father, mother, may I go, may I go, may
    I go ;
Father, mother, may I go, to buy a bunch
    of roses ?
Oh yes, you may go, you may go, you may
    go ;
Oh yes, you may go, to buy a bunch of roses!

Pick up her tail and away she goes, away
    she goes, away she goes ;
Pick up her tail and away she goes, to buy
    a bunch of roses.

      —The children of Hexham Workhouse
             (Miss J. Barker.)

II. Queen Mary, Queen Mary, my age is sixteen,
    My father's a farmer on yonder green ;
    He has plenty of money to keep me sae braw,
    Yet nae bonnie laddie will tak' me awa'.

    The morning so early I looked in the glass,
    And I said to myself what a handsome young
        lass ;
    My hands by my side, and I gave a ha, ha,
    Come awa', bonnie laddie, and tak' me awa'.

—Berwickshire, A. M. Bell, *Antiquary*, xxx. 17.

III. My name is Queen Mary,
    My age is sixteen,
    My father's a farmer in Old Aberdeen ;
    He has plenty of money to dress me in black -
    There's nae [no] bonnie laddie 'ill tack me
        awa'.
    Next mornin' I wakened and looked in the
        glass,
    I said to myself, what a handsome young lass ;
    Put your hands to your haunches and give
        a ha, ha,
    For there's nae bonnie laddie will tack ye awa'.
          —N. E. Scotland (Rev. W. Gregor).

IV. My name is Queen Mary,
    My age is sixteen,
    My father's a farmer in yonder green ;
    He's plenty of money to dress me in silk [fu'
        braw'],
    For there's nae bonnie laddie can tack me
        awa'.
    One morning I rose and I looked in the glass,
    Says I to myself, I'm a handsome young lass ;
    My hands by my [1] edges, and I give a ha, ha,
    For there's nae bonnie laddie t' tack me awa'.
          —Cullen (Rev. W. Gregor.)

Mrs. Gomme says ' The Scottish game is played
by girls. The players join hands, form a circle
with one in the centre, and dance round singing.

[1] I.e. 'anches = haunches !

At the words " 'ill tack me awa'," the centre player chooses another one, and the two wheel round. Then the singing proceeds. At the exclamation " ha! ha! " the players suit the action to the words of the line. In the Cullen game the girls stand in a row with one in front, who sings the verses and chooses another player from the line. The two then join hands and go round and round, singing the remaining verses.'

Mrs. Gomme gives two tunes. Her first two versions are sung with hardly a note's variation to the first of the two Golspie tunes which I print on p. 199: that is what I call the ' Green gravel ' tune. Her last three versions are sung to ' Sheriff-muir,' which I print on p. 198.

I need not add much to my previous notes. ' Sae braw ' for ' in silk ' occurred to me years ago, and I suggested it on p. 199. But we find ' in silk ' in the *Green gravel* rime, and ' sae braw ' may be an alteration to get a rime to ' awa'.' On the other hand the original ought to have rimed, and ' in silk ' may have been an alteration made in some place where ' sae braw ' was not understood. But we may be dealing with lines borrowed from different games, and I prefer to suspend judgement.

The lines beginning ' Father and mother ' in version I. have a Golspie parallel which will be found on p. 129.

Mrs. Gomme's 2nd vol. (article ' Rosy Apple, Lemon and Pear ') gives 5 versions of ' Roses in and roses out.' Two I quote in full.

Maggie Littlejohn, fresh and fair,
A bunch of roses in her hair;
Gold and silver by her side
I know who is her bride.
Take her by the lily-white hand,
Lead her over the water;
Give her kisses,—one, two, three,—
For she's a lady's daughter.
Roses up, and roses down,
And roses in the garden;
I widna give a bunch of roses
For twopence ha'penny farthing.

—Rev. W. Gregor.

Roses up, and roses down,
And roses in the garden;
I widna gie a bunch o' roses
For tippence ha'penny farden.
So and so, fresh and fair,
A bunch o' roses she shall wear;
Gold and silver by her side,
Crying out, "[1] Cheese and bride."
Take her by the lily-white hand,
Lead her on the water;
Give her kisses,—one, two, three,—
For she's her mother's daughter.

—Fraserburgh (Rev. W. Gregor.)

The other three are from Berwickshire, Cullen
(Rev. W. Gregor), and Nairn (Rev. W. Gregor).
Only Nairn agrees with Golspie in having ' in ' and
' out,' not ' up ' and ' down.'

[1] I. e. "She's the bride"!!!

Mrs. Gomme adds 'In the Scotch versions the players all stand in a line, with one in front, and sing. At the end of the fourth line the one in front chooses one from the line, and all again sing, mentioning the name of the one chosen (Fraserburgh). At Cullen, one child stands out of the line and goes backwards and forwards singing, then chooses her partner, and the two go round the line singing.'

The game is obviously a marriage-game, and 'Rosy apple, lemon, and pear' are a corruption of something like 'Rosy, [1] happy, merry, and fair' (*or* 'maiden fair'). 'Give her kisses, one, two, three' is doubtless an allusion to the custom (in England at any rate) of kissing the bride in the vestry after the marriage. In 'Additional notes to the contributions' (p. 343) I have proposed a complete restoration of this rime.

So far as our game is concerned, it is only in the 5 Scottish versions of it that I find the stanza 'Roses—farden.' But it also occurs in strange guise in 2 of the 48 versions of 'Sally Water' which will be found in Mrs. Gomme's 2nd vol.

> A bogie in, a bogie out,
> A bogie in the garden,
> I wouldn't part with my young man
> For fourpence halfpenny farthing.
> —Long Eaton, Nottingham (Miss Youngman).

[1] A child might confuse '*appy* = *happy* with *appy* = child's language for *apple*.

A beau in front and a beau behind,
And a bogie in the garden oh!
I wouldn't part with my sweetheart
For tuppence (two) ha'penny farthing.

—London (Mrs. Merck.)

The stanzas beginning ' I can wash a sailor's
shirt ' and ' I can chew tobacco ' are paralleled in
a long set of verses from Rosehearty, on the other
side of the Moray Firth, communicated by the
Rev. W. Gregor to Mrs. Gomme's 2nd vol. (article
' Sailor Lad '). They run thus:

A sailor lad and a tailor lad,
   And they were baith for me;
I wid raither tack the sailor lad,
   And lat the tailor be.
What can a tailor laddie dee
   Bit sit and sew a cloot,
When the bonnie sailor laddie
   Can turn the ship aboot.

He can turn her east, [1]and he can turn her
   west,
   He can turn her far awa';
He aye tells me t' keep up my hairt
   For the time that he's awa'.

I saw 'im lower his anchor,
   I saw 'im as he sailed;
I saw 'im cast his jacket
   To try and catch a whale.

[1] 'And' spoils the metre.

He skips upon the planestanes,
  He sails upon the sea;
A fancy man wi' a curly pow
  Is aye the boy for me,
  Is aye the boy for me;
A fancy man wi' a curly pow
  Is aye the boy for me.

He daurna brack a biscuit,
  He daurna smoke a pipe;
He daurna kiss a bonny lass
  At ten o'clock at night.

I can wash a sailor's shirt,
  And I can wash it clean;
I can wash a sailor's shirt,
  And bleach it on the green.
    Come a-rinkle-tinkle, fal-a-la, fal-a-la,
    Aboun a man o' war.

It is clear that the stanza beginning ' He daurna '
is *meant* for the tailor, and Dr. Joass suggests that
' He ' is emphatic. Otherwise we must suppose
that lines referring to the tailor have been lost, or
else included in a corrupt form in the previous
stanza. In its original form it may have mentioned
the sailor as the one who ' is aye the boy for me '
and the tailor as the one who ' is no the boy
for me.'

L 2

[Johnie Johnson took a notion]

Johnie Johnson took a notion
For to go and sail on sea:
There he left his own dear ¹Maggie
Weeping at a willow tree.

'Hold your peace, my own dear Maggie;
Hold your baby on your knee;
Drink the health of a jolly ²jolly sailor
—I'll come back and marry ³thee.

'I will buy you beads and ⁴earings,
I will buy you diamond stones,
I will buy you a horse to ride on
When your true love's⁵ dead and gone.'

'What care I for beads and earings?
What care I for diamond stones?
What care I for a horse to ride on
When my true love's⁵ dead and gone?'

Take some one out at 'Hold your peace, my
own dear Maggie.'   [A. C.]

Dr. Joass suggests that these verses have been
learnt by grown-up fisher-girls from others of their

¹ B. C. has 'Mary' here and below.
² B. C. omits the second 'jolly' (not so well).
³ In B. C.'s version 'you' wrong).
⁴ So A. C. and B. C., here and below. It probably represents
actual pronunciation. And how many South-British say *ear-rings*?
⁵ B. C. has 'is' (not so well).

sex, at places like Fraserburgh and Peterhead
(whither Golspie fishermen take their families for
the herring-fishery), and have been overheard by
their younger sisters.

According to Scottish law children are legiti-
mated by the subsequent marriage of their parents.
'Johnie Johnson' contains no words which imply
that the singer is a woman, but the Northumbrian
song 'Bonny Bobby Shaftoe' does, and they refer
to a belated marriage as if it had been considered
no discredit at the time and place, and in the rank
of life, to which the singer belonged. The tune and
the words to it will be found in Bruce and Stokoe's
Northumbrian Minstrelsy, p. 115.

The last two verses remind one of the last two
of 'There she stands a lovely creature' (Newell,
p. 55). 'It is an old English song,' says Mr.
Newell, 'which has been fitted for a ring-game by
the composition of an additional verse, to allow the
selection of a partner.'

'Madam, I have gold and silver,
  Lady, I have houses and lands,
Lady, I have ships on the ocean,
  All I have is at thy command.'

'[1] What care I for your gold and silver,
  What care I for your houses and lands,
What care I for your ships on the ocean—
  [1] *All I want is a nice young man.*'

[1] These two lines appear in perverted form in 'Lady on the
mountain' (Mrs. Gomme, i, pp. 320-22).

[Here comes gentle(s) roving]

Here comes [1] gentle [2] Rover,
[3] Rover, Rover ;
Here comes gentle [2] Rover
[4]—Sugar, cake, & wine.

' Ladies will you taste them,
Taste them, taste them,
Ladies will you taste them
Before you go away ?

We'll first go round the kitchen,
Kitchen, kitchen ;
We'll first go round the kitchen,
And then go round the hall.

We'll take away the fairest,
Fairest, fairest ;
We'll take away the fairest,
The fairest of them all.

Pretty girls you must come in,
Must come in, must come in ;
Pretty girls you must come in,
And help us with our dancing.'

[B. C.]

B. C. tells me that at the 4th stanza the speaker
takes a girl out of the line, and that the two,

[1] This should certainly be 'gentles,' i. e. gentlemen.
[2] M. S. ' roving' (rightly).
[3] M. S. ' ro-ro-roving' instead of this line.
[4] M. S. ' with sugar-cake and wine' (much better'.

joining all four hands, dance round before the rest,
reciting the last stanza. They then begin again
together, taking a 3rd girl out at the 4th stanza—
and so on till every girl has been taken out.

There are certain resemblances between this and
A dis, a dis, a green grass (Chambers, p. 139).
The latter contains the following lines :—

> Come all ye pretty, fair maids,
> And dance along with us.
>
> For we are going a-roving,
> A-roving in this land ;
> We'll take this pretty fair maid,
> We'll take her by the hand.

The rime goes on

> Ye shall get a duke my dear,
> And ye shall get a drake ;

—the point of which is that in some dialects ' duke '
(*dook*) is very like either *duke* or *duck*. And there
is a Shropshire version of the rime in which 'duck'
is given (Jackson and Burne, p. 511).

There is a children's rime ' common through the
Middle States ' (Newell, p. 49) which begins

> We are three *ducks* a-roving (thrice).

Of this there is a New York variant (*ib.*) which
begins

> Forty ducks are riding (! ! !)

—while from Concord, Massachusetts, we get the rime (*ib.* p. 48)

    ' Here comes a duke a-roving,
       Roving, roving,
    Here comes a duke a-roving,
       With the ransy, tansy, tea!
    With the ransy, tansy, tario!
       With the ransy, tansy, tea!
    [1] Pretty fair maid, will you come out,
    Will you come out, will you come out,
       To join us in our dancing?'

Another variant is known in Dorset (Udal, p. 222) —the following are extracts from it :

    ' Here comes the Duke of Rideo—
       Of Rideo—of Rideo—
    Here comes the Duke of Rideo,
       Of a cold and frosty morning.'

      *   *   *

    ' I'll walk the kitchen and the hall,
       And take the fairest of them all;
    The fairest one that I can see
    Is Miss —— (*naming her*)
    So Miss —— come to me.'

      *   *   *

    ' Now we've got this pretty girl—
    This pretty girl—this pretty girl—
    Now we've got this pretty girl,
       Of a cold and frosty morning.'

      *   *   *

           (Symondsbury.)

      [1] = Prithee?

Apparently this is the same as a rime which, as given at Chirbury in Shropshire (Northall, p. 384), began

'Here comes three Dukes a-riding.'

The *gentle* $\left.\begin{array}{l}\textit{Rover}\\\textit{roving}\end{array}\right\}$ clearly represents a variation which began 'Here comes [three] gentles roving.'

In a Lancashire version of 1820–30 the first line seems to have been followed by a burden which 'evidently represented a flourish of trumpets' (Northall, p. 384)

With a rancy tancy, terry boy's horn,
With a rancy tancy tee

—which we find in an American version, quoted above, as

With the ransy, tansy, tario!
With the ransy, tansy, tea!

As 'tansy tea' was a favourite drink of our ancestors, these last words seem to have been taken to represent it, and when 'tansy tea' went out of use (or from a desire to substitute something more luscious) 'sugar-cake and wine' took its place!

If this conjecture is correct, the second stanza in the Golspie version would be of a later origin. It may have originally had *taste it* for *taste them*. The last line, 'Before you go away,' would then have rimed with the last line of the previous stanza 'With the ransy, tansy tea'—for 'tea,' as we know, was formerly pronounced nearly as 'tay.'

There is also in Mrs. Gomme's book (i, p. 293) a Derbyshire game-rime, reported by Mrs. Harley, beginning

Here comes one jolly rover, jolly rover, jolly rover,

and containing the lines [1]

So through the kitchen and through the hall,
I choose the fairest of them all.

As regards the last stanza in the Golspie rime, three of the versions of *A dis, a dis, a green grass* given by Mrs. Gomme [2] contain something corresponding to it, for instance the following heard by her in London (i, p. 160):

Will you come?
No!
Naughty miss, she won't come out,
  Won't come out, won't come out,
Naughty miss, she won't come out,
  To help us with our dancing.

Will you come?
Yes!
Now we've got our bonny lass,
  Bonny lass, bonny lass,
Now we've got our bonny lass,
  To help us with our dancing.

Here 'bonny lass' suggests a North-country descent for the lines. The two similar versions are

---

[1] See also (at end 'Pretty little girl of mine' in her 2nd vol.
[2] See also 'Pray, Pretty Miss' in her 2nd vol.

from Middlesex and from Liphook in Hants, but each gives the same suggestion of origin, the former in ' bonny lad,' the latter in ' bonny lass.'

[Mother, the nine o'clock bells are ringing]

' *Mother, the nine o'clock bells are ringing;*
Mother, let me out;
For my sweetheart is waiting;
He's going to take me out.

He's going to give me apples,
He's going to give me pears,
He's going to give me a sixpence
To kiss him on the stairs.'

I would not have his apples:
I would not have his pears:
I would not have his sixpence
To kiss him on the stairs.

And then I took his apples,
And then I took his pears,
And then I took his sixpence,
And kissed him on the stairs.   [B. C.]

At once mercenary and hypocritical!

On ' going to take me out ' Dr. Joass remarks ' Not local,' and there is no peal of bells in Golspie. ' On the stairs ' suggests some place up on a cliff, with steps down to the sea.

For a very funny Cheshire variant (or parody ?) see 'Additional notes to the contributions,' p. 344.

[Green grass set a pass]

Green grass set a pass,
A bunch of [1] *yellow roses,*
A red rose out upon my breast,
And a gold ring on my finger.

[E. I. O.]

E. I. O.
My very bonnie Bella, oh !
I kissed her once, I kissed her twice,
I kissed her three times over.

[Hop, Hop, the butcher's shop]

Hop, Hop,
The butcher's shop
—I cannot stay no longer ;
For, if I stay,
Mamma will say
I was playing with the boys down yonder.

[J. S.]

J. S. tells me that the speaker takes another girl
out of the line when delivering the 2nd stanza, and
hops at the beginning of the 3rd.

With ' I kissed her once,' &c., compare the fol-

[1] M. S., who gives this 1st stanza only, has ' loving silver,' which
is much more likely, first as giving a partial rime to ' finger,' and
secondly as presenting a difficulty to the understanding—which
difficulty was got over by substituting ' yellow roses.' *Loving-
silver* doubtless = the plant *silver-marriage,* otherwise *penny-bridal*
or *penny-wedding.* The English ' penny ' was always a silver coin
before the reign of George III.

lowing from a boys' game called 'Johnny Rover'
(Mrs. Gomme, i, p. 286):—

> A [I] warn ye ance, A warn you twice;
> A warn ye three times over.

This also is North-Scottish, being reported from
Keith by the Rev. W. Gregor.

Compare, too, the following (in Mrs. Gomme's
2nd vol.) from a variety of the game of 'Queen
Anne,' as played at Bocking in Essex:—

> I grant you once, I grant you twice,
> I grant you three times over.

There is likewise a Dorset children's rime (Udal,
p. 252),

> 'I owed your mother
> A pound of butter;
> I paid her once—
> I paid her twice—
> I paid her three times over.'

'Hop' perhaps originally meant Hob, the name
of the butcher (diminutive 'Hopkin').

[Green peas, mutton pies]

Green peas, mutton pies,
Tell me where my Bella lies.

[I love Bella, she loves me]

I love Bella, she loves me,
And that's the lass that I'll go wee [1].

[J. S.]

---

[1] = wi'.

These are written, and doubtless played, as a single set. But the first couplet reads as if Bella were supposed to be dead, and I suspect that *Green peas, mutton pies* is a mere variation on *Green grass set* (or *put?*) *a pass* (see above, p. 156), which might *possibly* = 'Green grass, set (put) apart,' i. e. 'Green grass, which I part with my hands.'

[Here's a poor widow from Babylon]

Here's a poor widow from Babylon
—Six poor children all alone :
One can bake, and one can brew,
And one can do the lily gollo.

[1] *Please take one out.*

This poor Bella, she is gone,
Without a father—[2] *on her hand*
Nothing but a guinea gold ring :
Good bye, Bella, good bye.   *[J. S.]*

J. S. tells me that this is played as follows. A girl acts the widow, and *behind* her are other girls (number immaterial) acting the children. She advances, repeating the rime up to 'Please take one out.' After these last words have been spoken, one of the line of girls *in front* takes one of the widow's children and says 'This poor Bella &c.,'

---

[1] These words are sung twice.
[2] J. S. has no stop. One version from Belfast and another from the Isle of Man see pp. 163-4) have 'Without a farthing in her hand,' which may be right.

after which the widow's child goes into the line,
and the girl who took her out becomes one of the
widow's children—the game beginning again.

Halliwell (p. 72) gives the following as part
of 'a game called "The Lady of the Land," a
complete version of which has not fallen in my
way:'—

> Here comes a poor woman from baby-land,
> With three small children in her hand:
> One can brew, the other can bake,
> The other can make a pretty round cake.
> One can sit in the garden and spin,
> Another can make a fine bed for the king;
> Pray, ma'am, will you take one in?

Elsewhere (p. 229) he tells us that 'One child
stands in the middle of a ring formed by the other
children joining hands round her. They sing—

> Here comes a poor woman from Babylon,
> With three small children all alone:
> One can brew, and one can bake,
> The other can make a pretty round cake.
>
> One can sit in the arbour and spin,
> Another can make a fine bed for the king.
> Choose the one and leave the rest,
> And take the one you love the best.

The child in the middle having chosen one in the
ring of the opposite sex, the rest say,—

Now you're married we wish you joy;
Father and mother you must obey:
Love one another like sister and brother,
And now, good people, kiss each other!'

Halliwell gives another version of this marriage-
game into the variations of which I need not enter.
Chambers (p. 136) says 'The girls in the ring
sing as follows:

Here's a poor widow from Babylon,
With six poor children all alone;
One can bake, and one can brew,
One can shape, and one can sew,
One can sit at the fire and spin,
One can bake a cake for the king;
Come choose you east, come choose you west,
Come choose the one that you love best.

The girl in the middle chooses a girl from the
ring, naming her, and singing:

I choose the fairest that I do see,
[Jeanie Hamilton], ye'll come to me.

The girl chosen enters the ring, and imparts her
sweetheart's name, when those in the ring sing:

Now they're married, I wish them joy,
Every year a girl or boy;
Loving each other like sister and brother;
I pray this couple may kiss together.

Here the two girls within the ring kiss each
other. The girl who first occupied the circle then

joins the ring, while the girl who came in last enacts the part of mistress; and so on, till all have had their turn.'

A version known in Philadelphia is given by Newell (p. 56), of which the first line is

' There comes a poor widow from Barbary-land '

with variations 'from Sunderland,' 'from Cumberland.'

There are two very amusing Dorset versions given by Mr. Udal (pp. 227–8), in which the game becomes one of servant-hiring. The first of these begins

    ' Here comes the lady of the land,
      With sons and daughters in her hand;
      Pray, do you want a servant to-day?'

while the second begins

    ' There camed a lady from other land,
      With all her children in her hand—
      Please, do you want a sarvant, marm?'

The variations in the ending of the first line are perplexing, and versions given by Mrs. Gomme (i, pp. 315–6) also supply Sandy Row (Belfast), Sandalam (Forest of Dean), and Sandyland or Sandiland (Ballynascaw School, co. Down). I believe ' Barbary-land ' to be the original[1]. In such

---

[1] There is also a New England children's dialogue beginning ' How many miles to Barbary-cross?' (Newell, p. 154), but there Barbary-cross must surely be a corruption of *Banbury*-cross. And

M

words as *barb* the *a* was often pronounced as in *hat* or *carry*. From ' Bărbary-land ' would come ' babby-land' (Halliwell, ' baby-land ') and Babylon. A nurse might explain Barbary-land as ' Sandy-land,' and from the latter might arise ' Sandalam,' ' Sandy Row,' ' Sunderland,' ' Cumberland,' ' other land.'

There is one striking peculiarity in the Golspie version. What is ' the lily gollo'? I propose this solution. The French *galop* is under all circumstances pronounced as if it had no *p*, and the accent is on the last—*galò*. Now ' le grand galop ' (= gallop) and ' le petit galop ' (= canter) are common terms in French, indeed ' les granz galoz' is found as early as the 12th cent. (Littré). And I suggest that *petit galop* was introduced as a riding-term in the 16th century and became (first perhaps ' petty galò(p),' and then) in child's language ' lilly galò ' (' lilly '= ' little '). So that ' do the lily gollo ' would mean ' do the canter.'

Of the versions given by Mrs. Gomme three show traces of ' lilly galò.' [1] They are

> One can make the winder go—Belfast (W. H. Patterson)

the game of ' Barley break ' (= Barley brig ?) sometimes begins ' How many miles to Barley-bridge?' (Halliwell, p. 217), while sometimes Banbury or Babylon is the place named (Newell. pp. 396-7).

[1] The first two, like ' lily gollo,' point to the pronunciation of ' brew ' at the end of the previous line as ' brow ' (an ancient form of it) ; the third is a variety which arose in some place where ' brew ' was pronounced *broo*.

One can make a lily-white bow—Ballynascaw School, co. Down (Miss C. N. Patterson)

The other can make a lily-white shoe—Forest of Dean, Gloucester (Miss Matthews)

In those versions in which the previous line ends with *bake* instead of *brew*, ' bow ' and ' shoe ' have been changed to ' cake,' and so we get

And one can make a lily-white cake—Isle of Man (A. W. Moore)

And one can bake a lily-white cake—Tong, Shropshire (Miss R. Harley)

from which such further variations as ' The other can make a [1]pretty round cake ' naturally arise.

As regards the last stanza in the Golspie version, we have [2]the following parallels in Mrs. Gomme's book (i, p. 315)

Now poor Nellie she is gone
Without a farthing in her hand,
Nothing but a guinea gold ring.
Good-bye, Nellie, good-bye!

—Belfast (W. H. Patterson).

[1] ' Pretty ' (and in another version ' wedding ') suggests an original '*petty* galo.'

[2] There is also a similar stanza in a Sheffield version of ' Green gravel' (i, p. 175) : it is obviously borrowed from the ' Poor widow ' game, for the next stanza begins ' Now this poor widow is left alone.'

[1] Now poor —— she is gone
Without a farthing in her hand,
Nothing but a gay gold ring.
Good-bye! Good-bye!
Good-bye, mother, good-bye!

—Isle of Man (A. W. Moore).

[When I was a lady]

When I was a lady,
A lady, a lady—
When I was a lady,
Oh! then, oh! then, oh! then,
It was hey oh! this way,
This way, this way;
It was hey oh! this way,
Oh! then, oh! then, oh! then.

When I got married,
Got married, got married—
When I got married,
Oh! then, oh! then, oh! then,
It was hey &c.

When I got a baby,
A baby, a baby—
When I got a baby,
Oh! then, oh! then, oh! then,
It was hey &c.

[1] Apparently the first 4 lines are spoken by the mother, the last by the daughter.

When my baby cried,
Cried, cried—
When my baby cried,
Oh ! then, oh ! then, oh ! then,
It was hey &c.

When my baby died,
Died, died—
When my baby died,
Oh ! then, oh ! then, oh ! then,
It was hey &c.

When I had a bustle,
A bustle, a bustle—
When I had a bustle,
Oh ! then, oh ! then, oh ! then,
It was hey &c.

When my bustle fell,
Fell, fell—
When my bustle fell,
Oh ! then, oh ! then, oh ! then,
It was hey &c.   *[J. S.]*

J. S.'s transcript of this was not sufficiently full : the above is given partly from that and partly from her recitation. She tells me that at ' hey oh ! this way ' the girls introduce some action (e. g. rocking a baby) suggested by the earlier part of the stanza.

In Jackson and Burne's ' Shropshire folk-lore '

are the following parallels (p. 514) together with another less interesting :—

' Girls stand in a circle, not taking hands, but *acting* and singing as they move round.

" When I was a naughty girl, a naughty girl,
    a naughty girl,
When I was a naughty girl, a-this a-way
    went I!
And a-this a-way, and a-that a-way,
And a-this a-way, and a-that a-way,
And a-this a-way, and a-that a-way,
    And a-this a-way went I!"

The series differs in different places.

" When I was a good girl, etc. a-this a-way
    went I (walks demurely).
When I was a naughty girl (puts finger on lip).
When I went courting (walk two and two, arm
    in arm).

When I got married (holds out her dress).
When I had a baby (pretends to hush it).
When the baby cried (whips it).
When the baby died (cries)."   BERRINGTON.

" When I was a naughty girl (pretends to tear
    her clothes).
When I went to school (pretends to carry a
    book-bag).
When I went a courting (walks in pairs, side
    by side).

When I got married (the same, arm in arm).
When I had a baby (hushes it).
When the baby fell sick (pats it on the back).
When my baby did die (covers her face with
a handkerchief, see p. 301).
When my husband fell sick (pats her chest).
When my husband did die (cries and ' makes
dreadful work ').
When I was a widow (puts on a handkerchief
for a widow's veil).
Then I took in washing (imitates a laundress).
Then my age was a hundred and four, and
a-this a-way went I, etc. (hobbles along
and finally falls down)."

MARKET DRAYTON.'

In Miss M. H. Mason's ' Nursery Rhymes and
Country Songs ' is the following version (p. 42).
It may be the original of all, or it may have been
altered from one of the others. But in any case it
suggests that ' lady ' in the Golspie version is
a corruption of ' maiden[1].'

1. When I was a maiden, O, then, and O, then,
   When I was a maiden, O, then!
   Lovers many had I as the stars in the sky;
   And the world, it went very well then, and
   O, then !
   The world, it went very well then.

---

[1] For a much more comical (Shropshire) corruption of ' maidens '
see p. 175.

2. I got me a husband, O, then, and O, then!
   I got me a husband, O, then!
   He was peevish and cross, as I found to my
      loss,
   And the world it went very ill then.

3. My husband fell sick, O, then, and O, then!
   My husband fell sick, O, then!
   My husband fell sick, and would take no
      physic,
   And the world it went very ill then.

4. My husband did die, O, then, and O, then!
   My husband did die, O, then!
   My husband did die, and rejoiced was I!
   And the world it went very well then.

5. I got me another, O, then, and O, then!
   I got me another, O, then!
   I got me another, but worse than the other,
   And the world it went very ill then.

6. He too did die, O, then, and O, then!
   He too did die, O, then!
   He too did die, and the mischief take I,
      If ever I marry again!

In 'The Thistle' (p. xxix) Mr. Colin Brown
says 'Who has not admired the graceful movements of rows of little girls marching and counter-
marching to the sweet melody . . . When I am
a lady, a lady, a lady, When I am a lady, a lady

am I.' Mr. Brown being a lecturer in Anderson's College, Glasgow, I presume these words to have been the beginning of another Scottish version of the Golspie rime.

[Here's three sweeps, three by three]

Here's three sweeps three by three. First of all there is a number of girls that stands in a row. There are other three girls in front of them. There is another girl at the back of the row of girls. The three girls sings [1] *...*

[J. S.]

Here's three sweeps, three by three,
And [2] *on by the door they bend their knee:*
' Oh ! shall we [3] *have lodgings here O ! here oh !*
Shall we [3] *have lodgings here ?'* [4] *' No.'*

[4] *Here's three bakers, three by three, etc.* '*No.*'

[4] *Here's three Kings, three by three, etc.* '*No.*'

Here's three Queens, three by three, etc. [4] '*Yes.*'

---

[1] This is good old English grammar, although not grammar which is now in fashion. In South England the plural of verbs was made in -*eth* (*we singeth*), in Middle England in -*en* (*we singen*), in North England and Scotland in -*es, -is,* and later in -*s* (*we singes, singis,* or *sings*). Thus 'the kye comes hame' should never be altered to 'the kye come hame.' Even Shakspere says 'those springs on chaliced flowers that lies' (where 'lies' is proved by the rime). See also p 97. note 1.

[2] Corrupted from ' And down '?

[3] J. S. ' get.'   [4] J. S. omits.

[1] [Take your daughter safe and sound]

Take your daughter safe and sound,
And in her pocket no thousand pound,
And on her finger no [2] guinea-gold ring,
And she's not fit to walk with a Queen.

[3] *Here's your daughter safe and sound,*
And in her pocket a thousand pound,
And on her finger a guinea-gold ring,
[4] *And she is fit to walk with a Queen.*

[M. S.]

J. S. tells me that the answers 'No' and 'Yes' are given by the girl standing behind the three speakers. At the last stanza but one they take a girl out of the line and, when the rime is finished, this girl becomes one of the three speakers, the Queen who took her out filling her vacant place in the general line. The rime is then recommenced.

The only parallel which I have seen to this rime in its entirety comes from Charlestown in West Virginia, and is printed by Newell (p. 46):

'On one side of the room a mother with her daughters. On the other three wooers, who advance.

---

[1] These lines are part of the same game.
[2] Here and in the next stanza the hyphens are M. S.'s. J. S. does not give this stanza, but writes 'guinea gold' in the next.
[3] J. S. 'Take.'   [4] J. S. 'She is fit to be a Queen.'

" Here come three soldiers three by three,
  To court your daughter merrily;
  Can we have a lodging, can we have a lodging,
  Can we have a lodging here to-night ? "

  Sleep, my daughter, do not wake—
  Here come three soldiers, and they sha'n't
    take;
  They sha'n't have a lodging, they sha'n't have
    a lodging,
  They sha'nt have a lodging here to-night."

Three sailors and three tinkers follow, with like
result. Then come three kings, and the case is
altered:

" Wake, my daughter, do not sleep—
  Here come three kings, and they *shall* take ;
  They *shall* have a lodging, they shall have a
    lodging,
  They shall have a lodging here to-night."

  ' (To the kings)—

" Here is my daughter safe and sound,
  And in her pocket five hundred pound,
  And on her finger a plain gold ring,
  And she is fit to walk with the king."

(The daughter goes with the kings; but they
are villains in disguise : they rob her, push her
back to her mother, and sing)—

" Here is your daughter *not* safe and sound,
   And in her pocket *not* five hundred pound,
   And on her finger no plain gold ring,
   And she's not fit to walk with the king."

(The mother pursues the kings, and tries to catch and beat them).'

Mr. Newell (p. 233) refers to a Faroese game ' in which the suitors, after rejection as thralls, smiths, etc., are finally accepted as princes, with the expression " take vid " (literally, " take with "), be welcome, which may explain the peculiar use of the word " take " in our rhyme.'

But the two final stanzas may be borrowed from some other game. The last of them is found in the English hiring-game referred to on p. 161. In one Dorset version (Udal, p. 227) the mother, after letting her child as a servant, says

   I leave my daughter safe and sound,
   And in her pocket a thousand pound,
   And on her finger a gay ring,
   And I hope to find her so again.

In another (p. 228) she says

   I leaves my daughter zafe and zound,
   And in her pocket a thousan pound,
   And on her finger a goulden ring,
   And in her busum a silver pin.

As the mistress in the hiring-game ill-treated her servant, very possibly the last stanza in the

American rime (the last but one in the Golspie one) was borrowed from a version in which the mistress made this reply to the mother when the latter returned to see her daughter. But young women with a thousand pound in their pocket do not often go out to service, and the stanzas were probably borrowed into the hiring-game. I also find in 'We are three brethren come from Spain' as given by Chambers (p. 143) the lines

Are all your daughters safe and sound?
*　　　　*　　　　*
In every pocket a thousand pounds
*　　　　*　　　　*
On every finger a gay gold ring

while in the same rime as given in *Gammer Gurton's Garland* (1783), quoted by Northall (p. 383), we have

Here comes your daughter safe and sound,
Every pocket with a thousand pound,
Every finger with a gay gold ring,
Please to take your daughter in.

As regards the descriptions of the ring, it seems to me that 'guinea-gold ring' is probably right. I take this to mean not a gold ring costing a guinea, but either a ring of gold of the quality of a guinea, or (still better) a ring made of Guinea gold. The guinea itself, when first coined in 1664, was so called from being made of gold brought from Guinea.

2. Games in a ring.

In the following games you skip round hand in hand to air of rhyme. [A. C.]

[Water, water, wallflowers]

Water, water, wallflowers,
Growing up so high:
We are all young maidens,
And we shall all die

— Excepting Maggie Stuart.
She's the youngest of us all:
She can dance, and she can sing,
And she can [1] knock us all!
Fie! fie! for shame again!
She'll turn her back to the wall again.

When they mention the name of the girl, it is supposed that she is the youngest, and she has to turn her back to the wall. [A. C.]

This is a very widely-known game, and the variations of the first line are very many. It has been confused with a rime addressed to 'Sally, Sally Water(s)' (*or* 'Walker')—for which see Northall (pp. 375-8) and Mrs. Gomme's 2nd vol. Mr. Newell (pp. 67-8) says that in New York it is 'Water, water, wild-flowers,' in Philadelphia 'Lily,

---

[1] I. e. thrash.

lily, white-flower.' Either 'Wall-flowers, wall-
flowers' (Shropshire)[1] or 'Wally, wally wallflower'
(Dorset[2] and Surrey[3]) may be the original.

In Berrington, Shropshire, the 3rd and 4th lines
run 'We all shall have the measles, and never,
never die!' This is partly due to *maidens* having
been mistaken for *maz(e)ls* (the old pronunciation
of *measles*).

The following is a Shropshire form of the game
(Jackson and Burne, p. 513):—

'The players form a ring and move round.

Chorus. 'Wall-flowers, wall-flowers, growing up
so high!
We shall all be [4] maidens, [and so] we shall all
die!
Excepting *Alice Gittins*, she is the youngest
flower,
She can hop, and she can skip, and she can
play the hour!
Three and four, and four and five,
Turn your back to the wall-side!'

Or—

'She can dance and she can sing,
She can play on the tambourine!
Fie, fie! fie, for shame!
Turn your back upon the game!'

Alice Gittins turns her back to the inside of the

---

[1] Jackson and Burne, p. 512.   [2] Udal, p. 215.
[3] Allen, p. 84.   [4] Miss Burne explains this as 'old maids.'

ring and continues the game facing outwards, and
they repeat the dance and song, naming the *next
youngest* girl, and so on till all the party have their
backs to the middle, when they go through them
all again, till every girl faces inwards again.'

I believe that this really *is* a game of 'old maid,'
and that 'Alice Gittins' is condemned to turn her
back to the wall-side as an indication that she will
be a 'wallflower,' i.e. unable to find a partner.
At Symondsbury in Dorset they say instead 'Turn
your back to overshed'—whatever that may mean
(Udal, p. 222).

[Hilli ballu]

[1] *Hilli* [2] *ballu ballai!*
Hilli [3] *ballu ballight!*
Hilli [4] *ballu ballai!*
Upon a Saturday night.

Put all your right feet out,
Put all your left feet in,
[5] *Turn them a little, a little,*
And [6] *turn yourselves about.*

[7] *Chu! Hilli ballu etc.*

[1] J. S. always writes 'Hilly,' not 'Hilli.'
[2] B. C. 'ballu balla.' J. S. 'bill lo bill la.'
[3] So B. C., but J. S. 'bill lo bill light.'
[4] B. C. 'ballu balla.' J. S. 'bill lo bill la.'
[5] B. C., J. S., and M. S. have 'shake.'
[6] So J. S. and M. S., but B. C. always 'twirl.'
[7] After 'Upon a Saturday night' M. S. says 'You cry Chu and
turn the other way saying the same verse. (2) Hillibilubila, etc.

Put all your right hands in,
Put all your left feet out,
Shake them a little, a little,
And turn yourselves about.

Chu ! Hilli ballu etc.

[1]*Put all your noses in,*
Put all your noses out,
Shake them a little, a little,
And turn yourselves about.

Chu ! Hilli ballu etc.

Put all your right ears in,
Put all your left ears out,
Shake them a little, a little,
And turn yourselves about.

Chu ! Hilli ballu etc.

[1]*Put all your neighbours in,*
Put all your neighbours out,
Shake them a little, a little,
And turn yourselves about.

Chu ! Hilli ballu etc.

At 'Put all your etc.' you do it, and swing
round at ' Turn etc.' The first verse is repeated

put all your left feet in, put all your right feet out, shake them
a little a little, and turn yourselves about.'

' Chu ' is pronounced *tshŏŏ*.

[1] J. S. omits these stanzas.

N

after every other verse.   At 'Chu,' instead of skipping round to the right, skip to left.

[A. C.]

The directions given in the game seem to vary at the pleasure of the speaker.   For B. C. gives :—

in stanza 1   Put all your right hands in,
Put all your left hands out,

and in stanza 2   Put all your right feet in,
Put all your left feet out,

M. S. describes the above game thus :—

' There are two forms of the following game

(1) Hillibilubila !
Hillibilubilite !
Hillibilubila !
Upon a Saturday night.

You cry Chu *and turn the other way, saying the same verse.*

(2) Hillibilubila ! *etc.*
Put all your left feet in,
Put all your right feet out,
Shake them a little, a little,
And turn yourselves about.'

This rime is not in Chambers, who, however, gives one called Hinkumbooby, containing very similar drill-orders, and played in much the same way.

Halliwell (p. 226) calls the game 'Dancing looby' and writes the first stanza as follows:—

> Now we dance looby, looby, looby,
> Now we dance looby, looby, light,
> Shake your right hand a little
> And turn you round about.

' Children,' he says, ' dance round first, then stop and shake the hand, &c., then turn slowly round, and then dance in a ring again.'

In ' The Baby's Bouquet ' Walter Crane gives music (p. 54) to the following words:—

> Now we dance looby, looby, looby
> Now we dance looby, looby light
> Now we dance looby, looby, looby
> Now we dance looby as yesternight
> Shake your right hand a little
> Shake your left hand a little
> Shake your head a little
> And turn you round about.

Mrs. Gomme (i, p. 353) gives a number of versions, but none except Chambers's ' Hinkumbooby ' from Scotland. The following are quotations from some of them.

I.   Here we dance lubin, lubin, lubin,
        Here we dance [1] lubin light,
    Here we dance lubin, lubin, lubin,
        On a Saturday night.
      *   *   *
—Oxford and Wakefield (Miss Fowler)

IV.   *   *   *
Here we come dancing looby,
Lewby, lewby, li.
      *   *   *
—Eckington, Derbyshire (S. O. Addy)

V.   How do you luby lue,
    How do you luby lue,
    How do you luby lue,
    O'er the Saturday night?
      *   *   *
—Lady C. Gurdon's Suffolk *County Folk-lore*,
p. 64.

VI.   Can you dance looby, looby,
    Can you dance looby, looby,
    Can you dance looby, looby,
    All on a Friday night?
      *   *   *
—Addy's *Sheffield Glossary.*

---

[1] A version containing 'loobin light' was once current in Golspie, but seems to have died out : see p. 184.

VII. Here we dance luby, luby,
Here we dance luby light,
Here we dance luby, luby,
All on a Wednesday night.
—Ordsall, Nottinghamshire (Miss Matthews)

VIII. Here we go lubin loo,
Here we go lubin li,
Here we go lubin loo,
Upon a Christmas night.
—Epworth, Doncaster (C. C. Bell)

IX. Here we go looby loo,
Here we go looby li,
Here we go looby loo,
All on a New-Year's night.
—Nottingham (Miss Winfield)

X. Here we come looby, looby,
Here we come looby light,
Here we come looby, looby,
All on a Saturday night.
—Belfast (W. H. Patterson)

XI. Here we come looping, looping [louping ?]
Looping all the night;
*   *   *
—Hexham (Miss J. Barker)

I suspect that the Golspie version reveals the origin of all these variations.

From Chambers (p. 13) we find that there was

a cradle-song known in Scotland in 1621 as *Baw lula low* or *Balulalow*, and that at a later time *Baloo-loo* or *Bal-lu-loo* was sung to crying children [1]. Among particular words sung to babies we also find *Hushie-ba, Bye, Hush and baloo, Hush-a-ba, And hee and ba* (*id.* pp. 14, 15). Chambers likewise gives *He-ba-laliloo!* as the title of 'the simplest of the lullaby ditties of the north' (p. 12).

In reference to this last name Chambers says ' It has been conjectured by the Rev. Mr. Lamb, in his notes to the old poem of *Flodden Field*, that this is from the French, as *Hè bas ! là le loup !* (Hush! there's the wolf); but the bugbear character of this French sentence makes the conjecture, in my opinion, extremely improbable.' Nevertheless I am convinced that the Rev. Robert Lambe was so far right that the name represents a French phrase *hé, bas là ! le loup !* or something very near to it.

For some time before the Reformation French influence is well known to have been very great in Scotland. It is also well known that wolf-hunting, which flourishes to this day in France, survived in Scotland to the beginning of the 18th century. Now [2] Littré gives ' ha, là bas ' as a cry used at

---

[1] In ' Bishop Percy's Folio Manuscript,' iii, p. 516 a song is quoted from a MS. copy of 1658 beginning ' Baloo my boy lye still and sleepe,' and with this refrain to the 1st verse :—

La loo, Ba loo, la loo, la loo, la loo, la loo, la loo,
Baloo, baloo, Baloo, baloo ; Baloo Baloo.

A tune ' Baloo' was known in London in 1611 (Beaumont and Fletcher, *Knight of the Burning Pestle*, Act ii, Sc. viii).

[2] Under *Là* he writes ' Terme de chasse. Là haut, là bas ! lorsqu'on est dans un fond, et que les chiens montent une côte ou

certain times in the chase. And I suggest that
hullabaloo = ha, là bas! loup! (which was, of
course, pronounced *hàlàbàlōō* [1]), that *Baw lula low*
(or *Balulalow*) = *Bas! loup, là! loup!* (pronounced *bàlōōlàlōō*), and that *He-ba-laliloo =* [2] *Hé,
bas là! le loup!* (pronounced *hébàlàlŭlōō*). I suggest that these hunting-cries, possibly introduced
into songs, and at any rate uttered by the huntsmen
to definite musical notes, were adapted as lullabies
because of their resemblance to the [3] lulling-cries *ba*
(= bye) and *lulli.*

And I would point out how much this theory
accounts for. It explains 1) the resemblances and
divergencies of the forms referred to, (2) the reason
why we do not get *Balulalow* and *He-ba-laliloo* in
the lullabies of South Britain (because we had no
wolf-hunting), (3) the reason why a children's game
should begin with Hillibalu (because it was a jovial
cry), and (4) the reason why the noun *hullabaloo*
comes to have its meaning.

Jamieson's Dictionary gives *Hilliebalow* as the
Roxburghshire and *Hullie-bullow* as the Fife form

---

un rocher, on dit, en leur parlant : il va là haut, ha, là haut ! et
quand on est sur une montagne et que les chiens descendent, on
dit : il va là bas, ha, là bas !'

[1] The *p* in *loup* is silent even before a vowel, and had become
so before the 16th cent.

[2] 'Hé . . . sert principalement à appeler. Hé ! venez ici' (Littré).

[3] Cf. 'lullaby,' 'bye ! baby,' ' go to bye-bye,' and the following
(quoted in ' The Century Dictionary '):—

> Lully lulla thow litell tine child ;
> By, by, lully, lullay, thow littell tyne child.
> Coventry Mysteries (ed. Halliwell, p. 414).

of this last word, together with an English form *Hillie-bulloo.* The English use of the word would of course have been derived from Scotland if my theory is correct, and the first three letters in it would have been originally *hal,* then *hul,* and last *hil*: I point out elsewhere (p. 123) that the *u* of *but* and the *i* of *bit* are interchangeable in Scots English.

Hilliebaloo and *Hullabaloo* have perhaps left traces of their initial syllables in the ' Here we ' and ' How ' of the English versions quoted.

The ' light ' at the end of the 2nd line seemingly arose thus. The 1st line once ended in ' low ' (cf. *Baw lula low*). But ' low ' is a North-English word meaning [1] ' flame ': so that it suggested the use of the synonym ' light ' when the cry was repeated.

The above version seems to have been learnt by the Golspie children about the middle of 1891, from young folk named Munro who lived in Edinburgh but sometimes spent their holidays in Golspie.

It is curious that the four writers should write the last syllable of the first line as *la* (3) or *lai* (1), and that six months later they should all pronounce it to me as *lee.* Did *là* become *là-ĭ, la-ēē,* and so *lee ?*

---

[1] And *lillylowe* (= *lilly* or little lowe) is ' the child's expression for fire or light ' (F. K. Robinson, *Whitby glossary*).

[Hull many an auld man]

Hull many an auld man,
An auld man, an auld man,
Hull many an auld man,
A dip, a dip a day.
The auld man is jumping in the sky
With his bonnie ¹*crucie wife, a dip a dip*
a day.

This is the one I choose, Oh !
I choose, Oh ! I choose, Oh !
This is the one I choose,
A dip, a dip a day.   *[J. S.]*

This singular rime must anciently have run thus:

> Holl monie an' auld mone,
> An' auld mone, an' auld mone,
> Holl monie an' auld mone,
> At dip, at dip, o' day.
> The auld mone is jumping in the sky
> With his bonnie crusie wife
> At dip, at dip, o' day.
>   &c.

Holl = 'hollow,' 'concave' (Jamieson's Dictionary).
Mone = 'moon,' which was so spelt at least as late
as the end of the 14th cent. and rimed with words
in -one. *Monie* = 'moon-ie,' its diminutive.

The old moon and his wife (the little concave
moon) are 'the new moone wi' the auld moone in

---

¹ J. S. thought this meant 'dear,' and said it was not a Golspie
word. It = *crusie*, i. e. 'lively.'

hir arme' (Ballad of Sir Patrick Spens, F. J. Child's *English and Scottish Popular Ballads*, iii, p. 20). They can often be seen clearly a little after sunset, i. e. 'at dip o' day.'

When I asked J. S. what the rime meant, she said 'The moon.' But when I asked her how she explained the man *and his wife*, she was only able to suggest the moon and the stars, which was not satisfactory.

It is possible that the lines also refer to a curious optical phenomenon, of which a recent instance occurred at about 7.50 p.m. on Sept. 1, 1895, and is the subject of descriptions in letters to *The Times* of Sept. 6 and following days. The moon then appeared to various persons in various places as 'all wobbly' (Southampton), 'jumping up and down' (Mortlake), 'skipping about in the sky' (Guernsey). Dr. Buchan tells me that this would be caused by wind interposing between us and the moon strata of air differing sharply in humidity or temperature, so that the 'index of refraction' would be changed, and the image of the moon, or parts of it, raised or depressed. The same kind of effect can be produced by looking at objects through hot air rising from a stove (letters in *The Times* of Sept. 10). One of the correspondents (*ib.*) noticed the same thing at Croydon on the evening of Sept. 6.

J. S. tells me that the game is played as follows. Two girls go out of the ring and then return to the middle of it, and dance, while the others walk round. They end by each taking another girl out, and the girls so taken out repeat the performance -- the first two joining the ring in their stead.

[Four in the middle]

Four in the middle of the soldier's[1] *joy, etc.*

[M. S.]

M. S. tells me that they dance in a ring, repeating these words, ' Four—joy,' until they are tired of them, when they change to another rime. Mr. A. M. Dixon, the postmaster of Golspie, tells me that ' the soldier's joy ' is the name of a country dance in which there are four in the middle, who cross hands and swing round. Sir John Stainer adds that this is the Chain in the old ' Lancers.'

3. 'Mrs. Brown.'

This was not among the game-rimes sent in to me, but, having seen the game played in Golspie, I have asked A. C. to write the lines down for me, and have expanded the three words *Mrs., pony,* and *Meroonie* to suit the way in which they are sung.

The game is played in this way. Two girls stand facing each other, each with her hands raised and linked in the hands of the girl opposite, in this position ∧. They then begin to sing the verses, to the tune of the last two lines of ' Not for Joe[2].'

---

[1] Or *soldiers'*. M. S. does not write any apostrophe.

[2] A song of about 1867.

At the syllable *Mis-* the players bring their hands smartly on to the leg above the knee. At the syllable *-sis* they clap them in front of their chests. At *Brown* they link them as at first. At *went* they bring them down again on to the leg, at *to* they clap them again, and so on, but the positions are (or should be) regulated so that the first and third always coincide with accented syllables.

Any number of couples will play this game at the same time, and the effect is exceedingly amusing.

I have indicated by the three signs ∧ ∨ ‖ the positions which, I think, should be used throughout, ∧ being the linking of the hands, ∨ the bringing them down, ‖ the clapping. When a syllable is not marked it is included in the previous sign.

[Mrs. Brown]

Mis-sis Brown
∧　∨　‖　　∧
Went to town
　∨　‖　∧
Riding on a po-o-ny.
　∨ ‖　∧ ‖ ∧ ‖ ∧
When she came back
　∨　　　‖　∧
With a [1] *Dolly Varden hat,*
　　∨　　　‖　　∧
They called her Miss [2] *Meroo-oo-nie.*
　　∨　　‖　　∧　　‖ ∧ ‖ ∧

---

[1] The 'Dolly Varden' style of dress came in about 1872.

[2] I have heard this sung as if written Malo-o-ney, or Molo-o-ny, which seems much more likely.

[Where have you been?]

'Where have you
∨　∥　∧
Been all the time?'
∨　∥　∧
'¹Down in the valley
∨　∥　　∧　∥
Courting Sally.'
∧　∥　∧

[Oh! what a cold you have got!]

Oh! what a cold
∨　∥　∧
You have got:
∨　∥　∧
Come with me
∨　∥　∧
To the doctor's shop².
∥　　∧　∥　∧

¹ Also sung　　'Down in the valley a-
　　　　　　　　∨　∥　　∧ ∥
　　　　　　Courting Sally.
　　　　　　∧　∥　∧ ∥
　　　　　　—Down in the valley a-
　　　　　　∧　∥　　∧ ∥
　　　　　　Courting me.'
　　　　　　∧ ∥　∧

But 'me' should probably be 'she,' which I believe I have either heard sung or seen in print.

As Dr. J. G. Soutar observes, 'valley' (not 'glen' or 'dale') indicates an English origin.

² A term obviously referring to a dispensary in a big town. There is no 'doctor's shop' in Golspie.

[Oh! dear, doctor, shall I die?]

'*Oh! dear, doctor, shall I die?*'
V || ∧ V || ∧
'*Yes, my lady, and so must I.*'
V || ∧ || ∧ || ∧

[There was a man]

There was a man, a man indeed;
   V || ∧   V || ∧
He sowed his garden full of seed.
   V || ∧ || ∧ || ∧
When the seed began to grow,
  V || ∧ V || ∧
'Twas like a garden full of snow.
    V || ∧ || ∧ || ∧
When the snow began to melt,
  V || ∧ V || ∧
'Twas like a ship without a [1] belt.
    V || ∧ || ∧ || ∧
When the ship began to sail,
  V || ∧ V || ∧
'Twas like a bird without a tail.
    V || ∧ || ∧ || ∧
When the bird began to fly,
  V || ∧ V || ∧
'Twas like an eagle in the sky.
     V || ∧ || ∧ || ∧
When the sky began to roar,
  V || ∧ V || ∧
'Twas like a lion at my door.
    V || ∧ || ∧ || ∧

[1] ? Central ribs. Prof. Joseph Wright in the English Dialect Dictionary gives it as Cheshire, but says it is only found in this verse, and queries the meaning as 'rudder' or 'rudder-lines.'

When my door began to crack,
V　‖　∧　V　‖　∧
'Twas like a stick upon my back.
V　‖　∧　‖　∧　‖　∧
When my back began to bleed,
V　‖　∧　V　‖　∧
It's time for me to die indeed.
V　‖　∧　‖　∧　‖　∧

[*A. C.*]

With *Oh! what a cold you have got!* compare
the following from the English Midlands, ' Said
when a child coughs in a lackadaisical manner '
(Northall, p. 311):—

" O, my dear, what a cold you've got,
Come with me to the brandy-shop ;
There you shall have something hot
To cure that very bad cold you've got."

With *Oh! dear, doctor* compare the following
' Repeated when a child says "Oh, dear " as a sigh-
ing phrase ' (Northall, *ib.*):—

" ' O, dear, Doctor, I shall die.'
' Yes, pretty maid, and so shall I.' "

There was a man begins with an old saying
given in another form by W. W. M. on p. 239.
Halliwell (p. 141) says ' The earliest copy of the
saying, " A man of words and not of deeds," I have
hitherto met with, occurs in MS. Harl. 1927, of the
time of James I.'   He also refers to James Howell's
Proverbs, 1659, where we have (p. 20)

A man in words and not in deeds,
Is like a Garden full of weeds.

Of the entire set of lines Halliwell has found
a version 'written towards the close of the seventeenth century, but unfitted for publication, . . . on
the last leaf of MS. Harl. 6580.'   He says they
were 'converted into a burlesque song on the
battle of Culloden,' which he quotes thus:—

> Double Dee Double Day,
> Set a garden full of seeds;
> When the seeds began to grow,
> It's like a garden full of snow.
> When the snow began to melt,
> Like a ship without a belt.
> When the ship began to sail,
> Like a bird without a tail.
> When the bird began to fly,
> Like an eagle in the sky.
> When the sky began to roar,
> Like a lion at the door.
> When the door began to crack,
> Like a stick laid o'er my back.
> When my back began to smart,
> Like a penknife in my heart.
> When my heart began to bleed,
> Like a needleful of thread.
> When the thread began to rot,
> Like a turnip in the pot.
> When the pot began to boil,
> Like a bottle full of oil.
> When the oil began to settle,
> Like our Geordies bloody battle.

On p. 28 he gives an ordinary version of the
lines, beginning

> A MAN of words and not of deeds
> Is like a garden full of weeds;

and ending

> And when your heart begins to bleed,
> You're dead, and dead, and dead indeed.

TUNES OF THE GAME-RIMES

O

TUNES OF THE GAME-RIMES

—◦—

No tunes were sent in; but Mr. A. M. Dixon, the accomplished postmaster of Golspie, has been so extremely kind as to take them down for me. First of all M. S. sang them to him, and he wrote down the notes. · These I copied over the rimes themselves, played them, and jotted down certain queries. Then A. C., B. C., J. S., and M. S., sang in Mr. Dixon's presence and mine, and he made any necessary alterations or additions in his manuscript. Lastly, Sir John Stainer has very kindly read them. So that they ought to be pretty accurate. But of course slight variations are to be heard from different singers. Some of them are due to the fact that one girl's version contains a word less (in which case a repeated note is dropped) or one word more (in which case a repeated note is inserted).

'Scottish' tunes may be broadly divided into [1] four classes : — (1) those of the native Gaels (2) those seemingly borrowed from the Irish Gaels (3) those of the Lowlanders (4) those borrowed from England or the continent. Of the first class

[1] In each of these classes there may be a combination of various ancient strains. For instance, the native Gaelic might include tunes of which the ultimate origin was Pictish, Dalriad Scottish (of Irish settlers in the West), or Norse (in Caithness, Sutherland, and the Western Isles). And the Lowland might include tunes originally derived from the Galloway Picts or the Strathclyde Welsh.

I may perhaps take as a specimen the tune ' [1] Bodhan aridh m' braigh Rannoch,' ' The Shealing in the Braes of Rannoch ' (No. 54 in Capt. Simon Fraser's collection); of the second ' Robin Adair ' (an inferior variety of ' Eileen Aroon '), or ' John Anderson, my jo ' (a variety of the ' Cruiskeen Lawn ' theme [2]); of the third 'At setting day '; of the fourth ' Jenny's bawbee ' (altered from ' Polly, put the kettle on '). If I may judge of the native Gaelic tunes from some played to me by Dr. Joass, as old ones, from the 1816 edition of Capt. Fraser's collection and those known to me in the later edition [3] of it, they have a distinct (and attractive) national character, though Irish tonality or Lowland rhythm is occasionally met with in them. The Lowland tunes I suspect to be, in the main, of one family with the old tunes of the

[1] 2nd ed., ' Bothan airidh 'm braighe Raineach.'

[2] As is the Welsh ' Yn nyffryn Clwyd,' perhaps older than either.

[3] This contains 232 airs, many of which are very late, while most are so florid as not only to hinder me from trying to play them but also to convince me that (in their present form at least) they have no claim to antiquity. And when I took the simplest and slowest airs—and charming some of them are—I found so much resemblance to some English and Welsh tunes, and so much else in rhythm and style that is open to suspicion, that I hardly knew what to give as a specimen Gaelic tune. The one I have chosen above was played to me by Dr. Joass. The extent to which Fraser has altered some of his airs in his 2nd edition—and, as far as I have seen, always simplified them—suggests to me that between the two editions he had received older and simpler copies or had struck out embellishments of his own.

The articles—at which I have barely glanced—on ' Scotish music ' in Grove's *Dictionary of Music* should be read by any one beginning a study of the subject.

English counties nearest the Border: but Fraser enumerates as Highland 25 airs to which Burns and others have set English words, e. g. 'Coming through the Rye.'

Among the tunes to which these game-rimes are sung, many are familiar as those of Lowland or English songs; but there are others to which the knowledge of a good many hundred old airs supplies me with no parallel. In none of these do I find anything 'Scottish,' except perhaps a note here or there which may be a modern alteration, and I suspect that, like so many of the rimes themselves, they are of purely English origin. I hope that all collectors of children's game-rimes will for the future try to collect the tunes likewise— as Mr. Newell, the American collector, and Mrs. Gomme have done. They will thus preserve many interesting old melodies which in course of time would otherwise have been lost, and will doubtless throw light on their origin and migration.

FATHER AND MOTHER, MAY I GO?

Fa-ther and mo-ther, may I go, May I go, May I go,

Father and mother, may I go a-cross the banks of ro-ses?

This is the 18th cent. English tune 'Nancy Dawson [1].'

[1] I had written 'Boys and girls come out to play,' a tune which begins in the same style. That learned musician Mr. G. E. P. Arkwright has pointed out the slip of memory.

The words are also sung to the (less pretty) tune of ' Sheriffmuir,' like the remaining rimes in the set, *As I went down yon bank, oh !* and *My delight's in tansies.* I give the alternative air as sung to these last-mentioned words : Englishmen of my own age will remember its being sung about 1865 to a comic song called ' Kafoozalem.'

MY DELIGHT'S IN TANSIES

And my de-light's in   tan - sies ; My de-light's in   pan - sies ;
? Some de-light   ? Some de-light

My de-light's in a   red red rose, The   co-lour of my Mag-gie, oh !

Heigh oh ! my   Mag-gie, oh ! My   ve - ry bon - ny   Mag-gie oh !
? bon-ny

All the world I would not give For   a kiss from my Mag-gie, oh !
? wor-(u)ld   I wad gi'e For   ae

My name is Queen Mary is sung to two tunes. A. C. and J. S. sing it to ' The Campbells are coming.' The second air, which M. S. sings, and which has a likeness to the modern tune called ' The bonnets of Bonnie Dundee ' in the first few lines, is really the English ' Green gravel ' tune.

The ' Bonnie Dundee ' tune may be, in part at least, of the same origin. ' It was known in Edinburgh about fifty years ago as " The band at a distance." . . . Many years afterwards a celebrated contralto of our time being in Scotland, heard the

air, and adapted it to Sir Walter Scott's stirring
words. . . . The air is believed to be of Scottish
parentage, but nothing more exact is known con-
cerning it ' (*The popular songs of Scotland*, ed.
by G. F. Graham and J. Muir Wood, p. 373).
There is a certain likeness in its beginning and
that of the German song ' Mein Schatz ist ein
Reiter.'

MY NAME IS QUEEN MARY

1st tune.

My name is Queen Ma - ry, My age is six - teen; My
fa - ther's a far - mer On yon - der green. He has
plen - ty of mo - ney to dress me in silk, But
? sae braw
no bon - nie lad - die Will tak me a - wa.

2nd tune.

My name is Queen Ma - ry, My age is six - teen; My
fa - ther's a far - mer on yon - der green. He has plen - ty of
mo - ney to dress me in silk But no bon - nie lad - die will
? sae braw
tak me a - wa.

With this latter tune compare the following versions of the 'Green gravel' tune, given by Mrs. Gomme (i, pp. 170, 171). To the Madeley version there is a long second part which I omit.

—Madeley, Shropshire (Miss Burne).

—Sporle, Norfolk (Miss Matthews).

—Lancashire (Mrs. Harley).

[I'll] take her by the lily white hand, Roses in and roses out, and *I've a lad at Golspie* are sung to the following.

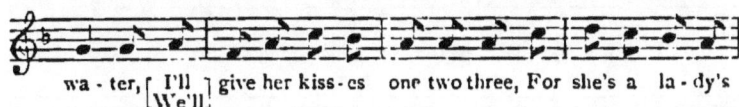

[I'LL] TAKE HER BY THE LILY WHITE HAND

I'll / We'll take her by the li-ly white hand, I'll / We'll lead her o'er the wa-ter, [I'll / We'll] give her kiss-es one two three, For she's a la-dy's daugh-ter.

Or

daugh-ter.

Mr. G. E. P. Arkwright tells me that his mother learnt this tune from a servant, she thinks at Richmond in Surrey, as part of the following game-rime [1].

Spoken.

 Q. Who's there?

 A. Poor Peg full of sorrow and care.

 Q. What does poor Peg want?

 A. A sheet to put Tom in.

 Q. What? is Tom dead?

 A. Yes.

 Q. When did he die?

[1] For a 1679–83 version, and a conjectural restoration, see pp. 345-6.

I can wash a sailor's shirt

Sung.

Quick.

Oh yes-ter-day in the morn-ing gay Poor Tit, poor Tom &

I, I, I, We heard a bird sing in a bush Poor

Tom was like to die, Sing right and do no wrong. Poor

Tom was a right hon-est man, man, man, [1] So we'll take this cup and

drink it up And so shall ev - 'ry one ——

I can wash a sailor's shirt, I can chew tobacco, and *May be I'll get married* are sung to the following.

I CAN WASH A SAILOR'S SHIRT

I can wash a sai - lor's shirt, I can wash it clean;

I can wash a sai - lor's shirt, And bleach it on the green.

Johnie Johnson is sung to the following, which is suspiciously like 'The Grecian bend,' a comic song of about 1867.

[1] From here to the end is part of the Devonshire song 'A nutting we will go ' which is the original of 'The low-back'd car ' (S. Baring Gould's *Songs of the West*, p. 178).

JOHNIE JOHNSON

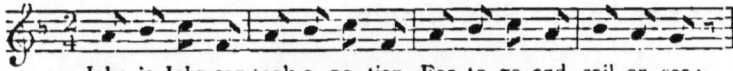

John-ie John-son took a no-tion For to go and sail on sea:

There he left his own dear Mag-gie Wee-ping at a wil-low tree.

The following are the tunes of *Here comes gentle(s) roving* and *Mother, the nine o'clock bells are ringing*. Both appear to me to be either English or German.

HERE COMES GENTLE(S) ROVING

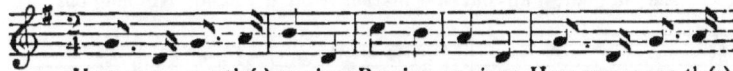

Here comes gen-tle(s) ro-ving, Ro-ving, ro-ving; Here comes gen-tle(s) Ro-ro-

ro-ving, With su-gar-cake and wine.

MOTHER, THE NINE O'CLOCK BELLS ARE RINGING

Mo-ther, the nine o'clock bells are ring-ing; Mo-ther, let me

out; For my sweet-heart is wai-ting; He's going to take me out.

Green grass set a pass seems to be spoken, not sung, while *E. I. O.—Hop, Hop—Green peas, mutton pies*—and *I love Bella* are recited on one note (say the lower F).

Here's a poor widow is a compound of ' Nancy Dawson ' and ' Sheriffmuir.'

HERE'S A POOR WIDOW

Here's a poor wi - dow from Ba - by - lon —Six poor chil-dren

all a - lone: One can bake, and one can brew, And one can do the

(Repeat these 2 bars.)

li - ly gol - lo. Please take one out. This poor Bel - la,

she is gone, With - out a fa - ther — on her hand No-thing but a

guinea-gold ring : Good bye, Bel - la, good bye.

When I was a lady is sung to the tune of ' There's nae luck about the house,' the air being repeated to eke out each verse. The tune of Miss Mason's version (see p. 167) is quite different. So is that of Mr. Colin Brown's (see p. 168).

WHEN I WAS A LADY[1]

When I was a la - dy, a la - dy, a la - dy, When
 (mai-den) (mai-den) (mai-den)

I was a la - dy, Oh! then, oh! then, oh! then.
 (mai-den)

[1] ' Lady ' is a mistake for ' maiden ' : see p. 167.

Here's three sweeps, three by three and *Take your daughter safe and sound* are sung to the following.   It seems to me related to the French 'Tremp' ton pain, Marie' (Weckerlin, *Chansons de France pour les petits Français,* p. 9).

HERE'S THREE SWEEPS

Here's three sweeps, three by three, And on by the door they ? down
bend their knee : 'Oh! shall we have lo-dgings here O(h)! here Oh!
shall we have lo-dgings here ?'   'No.'

Water, water, wallflowers is sung to the following, which sounds rather like a hymn-tune.

WATER, WATER, WALL-FLOWERS

Wa - ter, wa-ter, wall-flowers, Grow-ing up so high :
We are all young mai - dens, And we shall all die— Ex - ? all shall
cep-ting Mag-gie Stu-art. She's the young-est of us all :
She can dance, and she can sing, And she can knock us all !
Fie! fie! for shame a gain! She'll turn her back to the wall a-gain.

Hilli ballu has the following air, which is repeated to eke out each stanza.

HILLI BALLU

Hil - li bal - lu bal - lai!   Hil - li bal - lu bal - light!

Hil - li bal - lu bal - la!   Up - on a Sa - tur-day night.

This is practically the same as one of the tunes
given by Mrs. Gomme (i, p. 352) for this rime :—

—Doncaster (Mr. C. Bell).

Sir John Stainer thinks that the Doncaster tune
should be

and so on.

Hull many an auld man (Holl mon-ie an' auld
mone) is sung to the same tune as *When I was*

a lady ('There's nae luck about the house'), and *Four in the middle of the soldier's joy* to the following, which is altered from 'Polly, put the kettle on.'

FOUR IN THE MIDDLE OF THE SOLDIER'S JOY

Four in the mid - dle of the sol-dier's joy, sol-dier's joy

sol-dier's joy; Four in the mid-dle of the sol-dier's joy,

sol-dier's joy, sol-dier's joy.

Mrs. Brown is sung to the air of the last two lines of 'Not for Joe.'

MRS. BROWN

Mis - sis Brown Went to town Ri - ding on a po - o - ny.

When she came back With a Dol - ly Var - den hat, They

called her Miss Me - roo-oo - nie.

The tune of *See the robbers passing by* is given on p. 342: it is only 'Sheriffmuir' again.

SONGS ABOUT GOLSPIE

P

SONGS ABOUT GOLSPIE

—••—

My hope of getting some good old folk-songs and the tunes of them was not fulfilled. But the following particulars, by W. W. M., of songs about the place are worth preserving :—

There are only three songs relating to Golspie and its inhabitants which I can remember at present. They are 'A memory of Golspie,' 'The Golspie men at the Dunrobin review,' and 'Coming down Dunrobin Glen.'

'A memory of Golspie' describes a walk along the Links which stretch along the shore towards the western side of the village. Then the writer mentions other places, indeed I may say all the places of interest about the village, such as Culmaily Burn, the Ferry Wood, the Churchyard, Ben Braggie, and Ben Braggie Wood (or the Big Wood, as it is more commonly called), Dunrobin castle and gardens, the Museum, &c.

'The Golspie men at the Dunrobin review' was written by a schoolmaster who once lived in Golspie. He speaks of the strength and bravery

P 2

of the Golspie men, and of [1] *how they were once
beaten in a trial of strength by the Rogart men.*

*' Coming down Dunrobin Glen' describes the
march of the Rogart men down Dunrobin Glen
on one of the occasions when they visited Golspie.*

I shall mention the first two verses of [2] *' A
memory of Golspie' to show what it is like, but
it is too long to tell the whole of it. The first
two verses are*

*(1) Let us wander once again
O'er the links along the shore :
Hand in hand we'll walk as then
And be lovers as of yore.*

*(2) On the sweetly scented braes
Where we gathered the wild thyme
We'll recall the happy days
When our love was in its prime.*

[W. W. M.]

---

[1] Was this schoolmaster born in Rogart? or did he describe
some mere trick by which the strength and bravery of Golspie
were for once deprived of victory ?

[2] W. W. M. says that he has seen the song printed in a newspaper. If all of it was as good as the specimen, I am sorry not
to be able to give it entire.

NUMBER-RIMES

NUMBER-RIMES

The three rimes originally contributed were all sent by A. G., and by him alone. He tells me that they are used only in ' Hide and seek.' The reciter of the verses points to a different player at each word, and the player pointed to at the last word is counted out. The process is repeated till only one player is left—who has to go and look for the others, who have meanwhile been hiding themselves.

This class of rimes is the subject of a considerable work, 'The counting-out rhymes of children—their antiquity, origin, and wide distribution—a study in Folk-lore—by Henry Carrington Bolton ' (London, Elliot Stock, 1888). Mr. Bolton has collected (with the help of American children) no fewer than 464 such rimes used by speakers of English, and 419 used by speakers of other languages.

> *One, two, three, four,*
> *Mary at the cottage-door,*
> *Eating cherries off a plate ;*
> *Five, six, seven, eight.*   *[A. G.]*

This is exactly Mr. Bolton's no. 423, which he gives as a girls' rime from two places in the United States, Newport (Rhode Island) and Philadelphia.

> *Scinty, tinty, my black hen,*
>   *She lays eggs for gentlemen :*
> *Gentlemen come here to-day*
>   *To see what my black hen doth lay.*
>
>   *[A. G.]*

A. C. has since given me

> *Zeenty, teenty, my black hen,*
>   *She lays eggs for gentlemen,*
> *Sometimes nine, sometimes ten*
>   *—Zeenty, teenty, my black hen.*
>
>   *[A. C.]*

She pronounces ' zinty, tinty ' and says the first word is sometimes pronounced ' sinty.'

Halliwell (p. 107) has a rime identical with A. C.'s except that ' Higglepy Piggleby ' take the place of ' zeenty, teenty.' And he has another (p. 102) identical with A. G.'s except that the strange words are ' Hickety, pickety ' and that ' every day ' takes the place of ' here to-day.'

Mr. Bolton gives the following :—

799. Mitty Matty had a hen,
       She lays white eggs for gentlemen.
       Gentlemen come every day,
       Mitty Matty runs away.

Hi! ho! who is at home?
Father, mother, Jumping Joan.
O-U-T out,
Take off the latch and walk out.

Ireland.

800. Mitty Mattie had a hen,
She laid eggs for gentlemen,
Sometimes nine and sometimes ten.

Georgia.

801. Hickety, pickety, my black hen
She lays eggs for gentlemen;
Gentlemen come every day,
To see what my black hen doth lay.
Some days five and some days ten,
She lays eggs for gentlemen.

Connecticut.

We shall see by and by that the 'Scinty tinty'
of the Golspie version means 'One, two'—these
doubtless being the number of eggs laid. The
numbers 'nine' and 'ten,' or 'five' and 'ten,' in
some of the other versions are possibly due to
'ten' being suggested as a rime by 'hen' and
'gentlemen.'

'One, two' seems also to be the original meaning of 'Higglepy, Piggleby,' 'Hickerty, pickerty,'
'Hickety, pickety,' and 'Mitty Matty' (-ie). These,
together with 'Hickory, dickory' (Bolton, 774)
and 'Zickety, dickety' (773), are relatives of 'Inky,
pinky' (685), 'Ink, pink' (703), 'Ink, mink' (702),

'Inty, minty' (567), and 'Hinty, minty' (556). And in the following rime (704)

Hink, spink, the puddings stink,
The fat begins to fry;
Nobody at home but jumping Joan,
Father, mother and I.

we get 'Hink, spink' in connexion with 'home,' 'father,' 'mother,' and 'jumping Joan' where another rime has given us 'Mitty Matty.'

Scinty tinty heathery beathery bank fore littery over dover dicky dell lamb nell san tan toosh.

[A. G.]

This is one of a very large number of rimes which are founded on the names of the numbers 1 to 20 in Welsh, probably the extinct Welsh of the old kingdom of Strathclyde. These numbers are in some cases still easily distinguishable: for instance in the above rime 'beathery'= the modern Welsh 'phedair a'='4 and,' while 'dicky'=the modern Welsh 'deg'='10.' In other cases the connexion can only be traced by the help of inter-mediate forms: thus between 'bank fore' and the Welsh 'phump a' (pronounced *fimp a*)='5 and' we get the Renfrewshire form 'bamf a.' And the ordinary causes of corruption have been assisted by the desire of those who adopted these numbers to give them rhythm and rime. In the above specimen we get no fewer than four couplets :—

Scinty	heathery	over	dicky dell
tinty	beathery	dover	lamb nell

In many cases, moreover, the Welsh number
has been lost altogether, and either a gap is left
or else the gap is filled with some other word.

Mr. Bolton's book contains few of the varieties
of this class of counting-out rimes. But Mr. A. J.
Ellis has collected and discussed a great many in
a paper of his entitled 'The Anglo-Cymric Score,'
published in the Transactions of the Philological
Society for 1877-9, pp. 316-72. Mr. Ellis's conclusions were carried a good deal further by
Mr. Henry Bradley in a review of that paper.
The reader who desires further information as to
Mr. Ellis's views, Mr. Bradley's, and my own will
find it on pp. 301-5.

As very few Scottish versions of the rime have
been printed, I add the following:—

> (1) Zeeny, meeny, mitty, mat,
>   Dumma dee, dumma dat,
>   Anty, panty, peela, rôz [1],
>   An, van, tōōsh.

This was learnt (I should suppose as early as
1815) at Glasgow (or Hamilton near Glasgow) by
Miss Margaret Dick, who recited it to me in
1893. It is very corrupt and I cannot spend time
over it, but Mr. Bolton's no. 642, which comes from
Montreal, is very like it.

> (2) Zinty, tinty, hĕthery, mĕthery,
>   Bankful, eetry, dickit doc, dan, tōōsh.

This was learnt (I should suppose as early as

---

[1] Pronounced as the word 'rose.'

1850) at Inverness by Miss Joass, who recited it
to me in 1892.

> (3) Eenerty, feenerty, fickerty, feg,
>   El, del, dômun, eg,
>   Ĭrky, bĭrky, stōry, roc,
>   Ăn, tăn, tŏŏsh, joc.

This was learnt about 1863 at Forfar by Mr. G.
Shepherd, now of Edinburgh, who recited it to me
in 1896.   The *-y* in the first three words is more
marked (perhaps owing to the previous *t* being
sounded high up) than in the third line.   The *ĭ*
in *ĭrky*, *bĭrky*, is sounded as in *pin*, and not as in
South-English *irk*, *birk*.   In *dômun* the *o* is
sounded as in South-English *dome*, and in *stōry*
apparently as in South-English (=*stawry*).

This rime differs very little from Bolton's 866.

> (4) Sinkty tinkty hĕthery bĕthery banks fōr
>   littery
>   Ôver dòver dicky del lammy nel sang tang
>   tŏŏsh.

This was learnt (about 1871?) at Golspie by
Dr. J. G. Soutar, who recited it to me in 1896.   It
is almost the same as A. G.'s rime on p. 218.

In these two Golspie versions *Scinty, tinty,
heathery, beathery, bank fore* and *Sinkty tinkty
hĕthery bĕthery banks fōr* are corrupted from
Welsh (or Cumbrian) words meaning 'One and,
two and, three and, four and, five and.'   'Six and'
is missing, *fōr* being apparently supposed to

represent 6. *Littery, ôver, dôver, dicky* are corrupted from words meaning 'seven and, eight and,
nine and, ten.'

Del(l), lamb (lammy), nel(l) I have never seen
except in these two Golspie versions. I take them
to be corrupted from *eleven, twelve*: a version from
Kirkpatrick-Durham in Kirkcudbrightshire has
'levem (Ellis, p. 53), and *twell* is old Scots English
for *twelve*.

San(g), tan(g), toosh is an ending paralleled in
almost all the Scottish rimes of this kind, but in
none of the English. Compare those just quoted
from Miss Dick, Miss Joass, and Mr. Shepherd.
Mr. Ellis (p. 42) gives *rahn, tahn, toosh* from
the end of a Roxburghshire rime. Mr. Bolton's
nos. 699 and 760, both from Edinburgh, have *Am,
pam, push*, and *Ant, tant, tooch*; his 866, also
Scottish, has *An, tan, toosh*. And Mr. Gregor
(p. 173) gives *An tan toust* from the S. side of
the Moray Firth.

I have not the least doubt that these words are
borrowed from some French counting-out rime,
perhaps introduced into Scotland as early as the
16th cent. They probably represent the words
'Vont-en tous,' i. e. 'All go away,' pronounced
(except for the peculiar sound of the *n*'s) *Von(g)-
tàn(g) tōoss* [1]. For the French counting-out rimes

---

[1] Littré: 'au pluriel, l's se lie: tou-z animaux; tou-z y sont;
quelques-uns font sentir l's du pluriel même devant une consonne:
tous' viendront; ils y sont tous'.' Note that he writes not *touz*
in these last cases but *tous'*, i. e. apparently *tōoss*.

numbered 62, 68, and 71 in Mr. Bolton's book contain the direction 'va t'en' or 't'en va' ('go away'), while 69 ends with 's'en va' ('goes away') and 79 with 'vont' ('go').

And I may here note that the same verb 's'en aller' with 'tous' has invaded many of the American counting-out rimes, having doubtless been learnt from the French either of Canada or of Louisiana. Mr. Bolton's no. 689 (from Connecticut, 1835) ends 'High, zon, tuz' and his 625 (from Pennsylvania) has 'I, pon, tus': these are doubtless the French 'Aillent s'en tous' ('Let all go away'), pronounced very much as if written in English *Ay zàn(g) tōōss*.

RIMING INSCRIPTIONS
IN BOOKS

RIMING INSCRIPTIONS IN
BOOKS

—•—

If I by chance should lose this book,
And you by chance should find it,
Remember Willie is my name,
And Munro comes behind it.

[W. W. M.]

Black is the raven,
Blacker is the rook,
But blackest is the [1] *person*
Who steals this book.

[W. W. M.]

With this latter compare the following, ' much in
vogue at Rugby ' (Northall, p. 103),

Small is the wren,
Black is the rook,
Great is the sinner
That steals this book.

---

[1] The original must have been much more forcible—? ' craven.'

MISCELLANEOUS RIMES

MISCELLANEOUS RIMES

—*+*—

[Eel-e, eel-e-ot]

Eel-e, eel-e-ot,
Make a sailor's knot,
And I will let you to
Your water-pot.   *[M. S.]*

Chambers (p. 200) says 'Boys, finding an eel,
will say to it:

> Eelie, eelie, ator,
> Cast a knot upon your tail,
> And I'll throw you in the water.

So in Peeblesshire; but in the Mearns:

> Eelie, eelie, cast your knot,
> And ye'll get back to your water-pot.

The object, after all, being to cause the animal
to wriggle for their amusement.'

M. S. knew nothing about the lines except that
she had heard them from her father, a reporter.

[Golspie is a bonny place]

Golspie is a bonny place,
A bonny set of people,
White stones at every door,
And a church with a steeple.

[W. W. M.]

If the last two statements were ever correct, they
are not so now. There is no church with a steeple,
and some of the doorstones are not artificially
coloured at all, while many others are blued.

The fact is that ' people '-and-' steeple ' rimes are
applied to a great number of places and are apparently transferred without scruple from one to
another. In Northall's ' English folk-rhymes ' I find
that Essex, Lancashire, Middlesex, Northants, Rut-
land, Salop, and Westmorland have each 1 place
which is thus distinguished, while Herefordshire
has 2, Sussex and Yorkshire 3, and Lincolnshire 7.
The following examples will suffice.

Ugley in Essex (p. 25):
Ugly church, ugly steeple,
Ugly parson, ugly people.

Cowarne in Herefordshire (p. 28):
Dirty Cowarne, wooden steeple,
Crack'd bell, wicked people.

Weobley in the same county (p. 29):
Poor Weobley, proud people,
Low church, high steeple.

Ashton in Lancashire (p. 33):

> Proud Ash'on, poor people;
> Ten bells, un' un owd crackt steeple.

Legsby in Lincolnshire (p. 42):

> A thack church and a wooden steeple,
> A drunken parson and wicked people.

Beswick in Yorkshire (p. 83):

> A thatched church, a wooden steeple,
> A drunken parson, and wicked people.

Raskelfe (pronounced Rascall) in the same county (p. 90):

> A wooden church, a wooden steeple,
> Rascally church, rascally people.

It is also a common assertion that the ' people ' of a place sold their bells to build (or repair) their ' steeple.'

I have found no really complimentary rime (such as the Golspie one) in Mr. Northall's book.

[I, when I think of what I are]

> *I, when I think of what I are* [1]
> *And what I used to was* [2],
> *I find I fling myself awa'* [3]
> *Without sufficient cause.*   [M. S.]

---

[1] ' I are ' is East English, but apparently not Scots English.

[2] ' Used to was,' which I have heard as jocular English from my childhood, is perhaps a mere comic invention.

[3] Only Scots English. The rime is not in any real dialect.

[Napoleon was a general]

Napoleon was a general;
He had ten thousand men.
He marched them up to the top of a hill,
And he marched them down again.
When he was up he was up,
And when he was down he was down,
And when he was half-way up
He was neither up nor down.   *[M. S.]*

Northall gives the following as a juvenile rime in Warwickshire, adding that ' It is also sung as a catch ' (p. 99):

O, the mighty King of France,
Duke of York,
With his twenty thousand men,
He marched them up a very high hill,
And he marched them down again ;
And when they were up, they were up, up, up,
And when they were down, they were down,
And when they were half way up, I say
They were neither up nor down.

Halliwell (p. 3) gives the following :

(1) The king of France went up the hill,
     With forty thousand men ;
     The king of France came down the hill,
     And ne'er went up again.

(2) The king of France with twenty thousand men,
     Went up the hill and then came down again ;

The king of Spain, with twenty thousand
   more,
Climb'd the same hill the French had climb'd
   before.

(3) The king of France, the king of France, with
   forty thousand men,
Oh, they all went up the hill, and so—came
   back again !

The first of these versions he finds in print in
1642 in 'Pigges Corantoe, or Newes from the North,'
where it is called 'Old Tarlton's Song'—Tarlton
being identified with the writer of that name who
died in 1588.

The version I learnt as a child (from a West-
Midland mother) was something like ' King Pippin
he marched up the hill And then marched down
again,' and I think I have seen King P. alluded to
in books as the hero of this feat of arms.

[Rain, rain, rattle-stone(s)]

Rain, rain, rattle stone;
   Don't rain on me;
Rain on John O'Groat's House
   Far out at sea.   *[M. S.]*

Chambers (p. 184) gives this as
   Rain, rain, rattle-stanes,
      Dinna rain on me ;
   But rain on Johnnie Groat's house,
      Far owre the sea.

He adds ' Sung during a hail-shower.' ·This version is apparently purer than the Golspie one in every single particular wherein the two differ except as regards ' But ' at the beginning of the 3rd line, which may or may not have been in the original lines.

' Johnnie Groat's house ' is of course not ' out at sea ' in the ordinary sense, but if the rime was made by people living on the Moray coast it might be so described. If ' owre the sea ' is right, they must almost certainly have been the makers of it.

'Johnnie Groat's' is right and not 'John O'Groats.' The name of the family was Grot. ' In the year 1496 John Grot (according to local tradition one of three brothers named Malcolm, Gavin, and John) had from William earl of Caithness a grant of lands in Dungsby' (*Origines Parochiales Scotiæ*, ii. pt. ii, p. 814). We also hear of John Grot in Dongasby in 1525, and of a John Grot in the same parts in 1547, while [1] 'A writer in 1726' calls the house itself ' the dwelling house of Grott of Wares ' (*ib.*).

Richard Franck, writing in 1658 his ' Northern memoirs ' (which he did not publish till 1694), says ' More North in an Angle of *Cathness*, lives *John a Groat*, upon an Isthmus of Land that faceth the pleasant Isles of *Orkney*' (p. 177). This *a* may be an attempt to translate a supposed Latin *de*. For in the 1793 Statistical account of Scotland, viii, p. 167, we are told by the Rev. John Morison, D.D., that ' In the reign of James IV of Scotland, *Malcolm, Gavin* and *John de Groat*

---

[1] Reference is made to ' Macfarlane's Geog. Collect.'

(supposed to have been brothers, and originally from Holland,) arrived in Caithness, from the south of Scotland, bringing with them a letter, written in Latin, by that prince '—after which comes the ridiculous story of the [1] 8-sided meeting-room with 8 doors, built by a John de Groat to prevent the 8 Groat families from squabbling about precedence at their annual celebration ! ' The particulars above mentioned were communicated to John Sutherland, Esq. of Wester, above 50 years ago, by his father, who was then advanced in life, and who had seen the letter wrote by James IV in the possession of George Groat of Warse.' But Malcolm and Gavin are not the names one expects in people 'originally from Holland.'

When staying at the modern Johnnie Groat's house in 1894, I walked over to the kirkyard of Canisbay, which contains many names of the family from *Grot*'s of 1550 and thereabouts down to Helen Groat in 1850, and I saw no *de* Groat, no *a* Groat, and no *o'* Groat. But the force of tradition is such that, when I mentioned this to a parishioner of Canisbay parish who enters that same kirk-yard once a week, he told me where I should find a tombstone of Finlay *de* Groat. I walked over again to Canisbay, and found only that of Findlay Grot who died in 1601.

---

[1] A room, or house, in that situation might very well have been built 8-sided to diminish the power of the wind to blow it down. Dr. Joass tells me that Highlanders often round off the corners of their houses and of their roofs with this object.

In 1760 Bp. Pococke writes ' we came to " Johnny Grott's House," which is in ruins, and from a quondam inhabitant of that name gives the appellation to this angle of Scotland ' (*Tour through Sutherland and Caithness*, ed. by D. W. Kemp, p. 26).

And Burns, in a poem printed in 'The Kelso Chronicle' on Sept. 4, 1789, writes

Hear, Land o' Cakes, and brither Scots,
Frae Maidenkirk to Johnnie Groat's!

The right pronunciatio' of Groat might be doubtful from Burns, who often rimed very loosely; but the quotations of 1726 and 1760 show that it is properly *Grot*, not *Grote*.

Mr. Henderson gives the following from Sunderland (p. 24):

' Rain, rain, pour down
Not a drop in our town,
But a pint and a gill
All a-back of Building Hill.'

PROVERBS, PHRASES, SIMILES

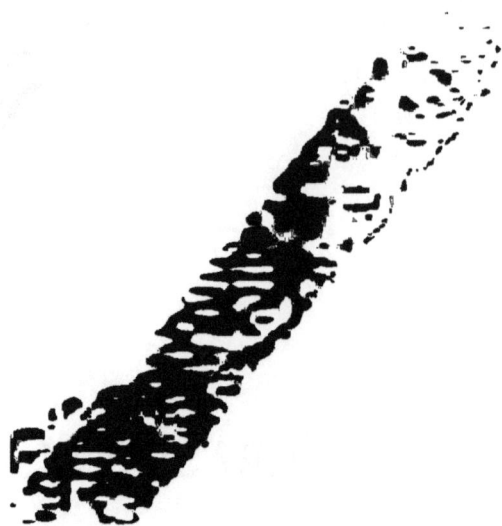

PROVERBS, PHRASES, S[...]

PROVERBS IN RIME

A man of words and not of deeds
Is like a garden full of weeds.

See pp. 190–92.
[W. W. M.]

Birds of a feather
Flock together.   *[W. W. M.]*

Early to bed, early to rise,
Makes a man healthy, wealthy, and wise.
[W. W. M.]

PROVERBS IN PROSE

Barking dogs seldom bite.   *[A. G.]*

Be sure your sin will find you out.
[W. W. M.]

Fools and bairns should never see [1] have
finished work.   *[A. G.]*

Fools make feasts and wise men eat them.
[A. G.]

[1] = half.

It is an ill wind that blows nobody good.
[M. S.]

Look before you leap. *[W. W. M.]*

Small fish are better than none. *[A. G.]*

'Small fish is better than no fish,' means that *we should content ourselves with any kind of fish in the scarce season.* *[M. S.]*

There is no use crying over spilt milk.
[J. S.]

It is no good crying after spilt milk. *[M. S.]*

There's no rest for the wicked. *[W. W. M.]*

Two heads are better than one, although it be a sheep's head. *[A. G.]*

This seems to convey a compliment to sheep's heads *when cooked.*

PHRASES

These, like the Similes, were written in answer to a request for 'sayings.' Various other phrases were given, but they were all in ordinary South-British use.

Come in if your feet are clean.
[J. S., M. S.]

M. S. adds 'a jocular welcome to an acquaintance.' It doubtless arises out of the common practice among Scottish children of the poorer classes, in Golspie and elsewhere, of walking about the streets barefoot.

He is early up that ne'er gangs doon.

[*M. S.*]

M. S. adds ' that the speaker has not been in bed.'

It is like to be wet.   [*W. W. M.*]

This I give, of course, merely as an example of ' like to be,' which is good English and common in folk-speech, but not at present in fashion.

Stand aside, and let a better man than yourself pass.   [*J. S.*]

I remember something like this as a jocular saying among boys in England: cf. ' Make way for your betters.'

Thanks no pay.   [*M. S.*]

M. S. adds ' means Cash is preferable to thanks.'

SIMILES

When I asked for ' sayings,' I meant proverbs and the like. This was not fully understood, and the proverbs which have come in are few in comparison with the similes : indeed the first two prize-winners sent in no proverbs at all, but a large number of similes. These, however, seem to me of sufficient interest to print, and at the end of the list I have added a few remarks on it.

R

As black as the ¹*crook* [B. C.]
  „   „   „ *night* [A. G.]
  „   „   „ *soot* [A. C.]
  „   „   „ *a sweep* [A. C.]
  „   „   „ *the* „   [B. C.]
  „   „   „ *tar* [W. W. M.]
  „ *busy* „ *a bee* [B. C.]
  „ *cold* „ *ice* [A. C., B. C., W. W. M., A. G.]
  „   „   „ *lead* [A. C., J. S.]
  „ *cute* „ *the* ²*mischief* [B. C.]
  „ *dark* „ *pitch* [B. C., W. W. M.]
  „   „   „ *tar* [A. G.]
  „ *fast* „ *a hare* [A. C.]
  „ *fat* „ *a ram* [B. C.]
  „ *happy* „ *the day is long* [B. C.]
  „   „   „ *a king* [A. C., B. C.]
  „ *hard* „ *iron* [B. C.]
  „ *hot* „ *fire* [B. C.]
  „   „   „ *the fire* [W. W. M.]
  „ *light* „ *day* [A. G.]
  „ *light* „ *a feather* [B. C.]
  „ *neat* „ *a pin* [A. C.]
  „ *old* „ *the hills* [W. W. M.]
  „ *poor* „ *a church rat* [J. S.]
  „ *quiet* „ *a mouse* [A. C., W. W. M.]
  „ *red* „ *fire* [A. C., B. C.]
  „ *rich* „ *a* ³*jeu* [B. C.]
  „ *sharp* „ *a needle* [A. C.]

---

¹ The iron rod which hangs down from inside a chimney, with a hook at the end, on which a cooking-pot can be hung.
² I. e. Devil.   ³ I. e. Jew.

As soft   as porridge [A. C., B. C.]
,, strong,, a horse [W. W. M.]
,, swift ,, the wind [B. C.]
,, warm ,, fire [A. G.]
,.   ,,   ,, a pie [A. C., B. C.]
,, white ,, a ghost [A. C., B. C., A. G.]
,,   ,,   ,, snow [A. C., B. C.]

Nearly all these similes, I suppose, will be familiar to those who, like myself, have been brought up almost entirely in South or Middle England, and many of them may have been acquired from books.

To me the following are unfamiliar :—' As black as the crook ' (which the New English Dictionary gives as Scottish), ' As black as *the* sweep ' (instead of ' *a* sweep '), ' As black as tar ' (I should say ' as pitch '), ' As cold as lead,' ' As dark as tar ' (I should say ' as pitch '), ' As hot as *the* fire ' (I should say ' as fire '), ' As poor as a church rat ' (I should say ' church mouse '), ' As soft as porridge,' ' As warm as a pie.'

The use of ' tar ' as well as ' pitch ' as a symbol of darkness is perhaps due to Golspie being a place of many fishing-boats. The omission of ' As black as a coal ' might be explained thus : coal has probably been little used in Golspie until recent times —its place having been held by peat. The omission of ' As heavy as lead ' and ' As white as a sheet ' is also noticeable. But I find that all **three** of these similes are used in Golspie.

BELIEFS ABOUT WEATHER

BELIEFS ABOUT WEATHER

—·—

If the hens in any yard were seen picking their feathers, it is a sure sign of rain. [A. C.]

So on the other side of the Moray Firth ' If hens and ducks preen themselves with more than usual care, foul weather is regarded as certain ' (Gregor, *Folk-lore of N.-E. of Scotland*, p. 142).

Dr. Buchan tells me that the increased amount of moisture in the air does actually occasion certain uncomfortable feelings in the birds which cause them to act in this way.

That birds flying low was a sign of rain.
[B. C.]

This, Dr. Buchan says, is correct as regards some birds, swallows for instance.

Dr. Joass observes that at such times insects fly low because the upper air is too rare, and that birds which feed on insects pursue them at this lower level.

THE PLACE AND ITS PEOPLING

at some point where it is not covered with vegetation or alluvium, you will see that here also in most places, from foot to summit, the soil consists

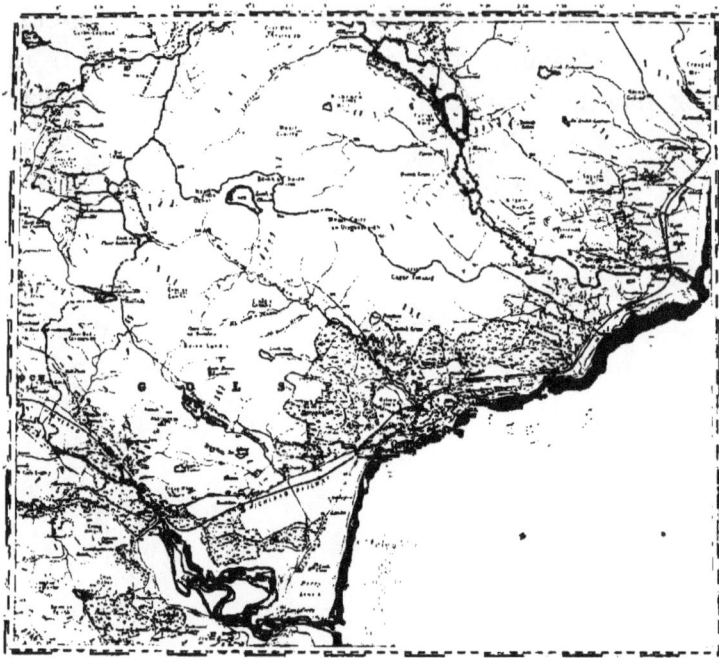

THE PLACE AND ITS PEOPLING

The lie of the land. The village of Golspie lies in a bay on the E. coast of Sutherland, only some 3 or 4 miles south of the S. point of Norway. It is built on a narrow plain which is continued both to the N. and the S. At the back of this plain rises a very low terrace. And off this low terrace (sometimes almost from its edge, sometimes a little more inland) springs a range of mountains. The mountain immediately at the back of the village is called Beinn a' Bhraghaidh (see p. 19— commonly pronounced Ben (a) Vraggie).

The forming of the land. Walking along this narrow plain you may observe that just below the grass is nothing but sand and pebbles : indeed, S. of the village you will find sandy hillocks between which lie large numbers of stones obviously thrown up by the sea. So you will conclude that at one time the sea must have rolled over the site of Golspie.

If you next look at the slope of the low terrace at some point where it is not covered with vegetation or alluvium, you will see that here also in most places, from foot to summit, the soil consists of sand and pebbles. And you will conclude that at one time the sea must have rolled not only over the plain below but over all the ground on which this low [1] terrace stands, until the waves washed against the now buried base of the mountains beyond.

If you have spent a shilling in buying, and a very few hours in carefully reading, Geikie's delightfully simple [2] Primer of Geology, you will know why the sea does not still do so. First the land which now forms the low terrace was heaved up from under the sea : then the plain on which Golspie stands was also heaved up, and the sea driven back still further, to its present limit. I am told by Dr. Joass that these upheavals took place after the separation from Norway and after the great Ice Age.

There is one other feature of the landscape to which I must call your attention. Dunrobin Park and the hamlet at Backies are separated from Golspie and the hamlet at Golspie Tower by a glen

---

[1] This terrace is in fact what geologists know as the 100 ft. beach, and the plain below what is sometimes called the 20 ft. beach. These are traceable round great part of the Scottish coast, but are not always of those same heights : see Geikie's *Scenery of Scotland*, pp. 380, &c.

[2] One of Macmillan's Science Primers. An intelligent reader of that little book (supposing him to have read no geology before) will find his understanding and appreciation of landscape immensely increased. And, if in going to fresh regions he will take with him the best book on their scenery (for instance, Geikie's *Scenery of Scotland*), he will find himself a still greater gainer. I speak from experience.

THE WATERFALL

called Dunrobin Glen, down which runs the beautiful stream known as Golspie Burn. For miles from its beginning up in the mountains this glen is a broad upland dale, down which a glacier once rolled into the sea those masses of puddingstone of which fragments are so plentiful on Golspie beach. As the age of snow and ice passed away, the glacier melted into a wide river, which at last dwindled away into Golspie Burn. Before shrinking to its present size, however, this river cut itself a ravine through the terrace which had been heaved up from under the sea ; and the mouth of this ravine was widened by the sea running up it, until the upheaval of the plain on which Golspie stands drove the sea back. So it is that at this point a fairly broad delta of gently sloping ground has been cut for several hundred yards out of the heart of the ancient beach-terrace.

Did all these changes happen before or after the district was first inhabited ? Well, an immense number of implements, and flakes, of the Later Stone Age have been found on Golspie Links. Consequently, the lower of the two old beaches must already have been deserted by the sea when these implements came there.

The climate and the soil. The climate is, for Scotland, comparatively dry and mild. The yearly rainfall is only about $\frac{1}{5}$ as much again as that of London, there is little frost near the sea, and the mountains shield you from the N. and N.W. winds.

And, although the natural soil is little more than

sand mixed with decayed vegetation and with whatever the burns bring down from the mountains,
careful tillage has made it highly productive. Walk
along the roads, and look at the [1] oats, the barley,
the kitchen-crops around you, and you will as-
suredly never dream that you are within 60 miles
of Johnnie Groat's house. As for trees and flowers,
they flourish right royally, and you will seldom see
a richer garden than that to which my eyes are
lifted as I write [2].

The first inhabitants. If the peopling of the
neighbourhood began in man's earliest days, no
doubt its inhabitants dwelt—some of them at least
—in *caves* on the mountains and sea-shore. There
are natural caves on Beinn a' Bhraghaidh (one) and
above Backies (two). There are also two natural
caves in the old cliff-side at Strathsteven, with the
rock worked into footholds beneath them ; and the
larger of the two is obviously used as a temporary
dwelling even at the present day. This latter cave
has had ledges cut in its sides and basins scooped
in these ledges, and at its further end are smaller

---

[1] On Aug. 18, 1769, Pennant saw at Dunrobin 'a very fine field
of wheat, which would be ripe about the middle of next month.
This was the last wheat which had been sown this year in *North
Britain*' (*Tour in Scotland*, 1st ed., p. 146). It is still grown
sometimes between Golspie and the Fleet—and in one spot in the
parish of Loth, even further north.

[2] South-British gardeners may perhaps take one hint at least
from Golspie. The tall crimson loose-strife (*lythrum roseum*)
which grows beside many of their streams is here cultivated as
a garden-flower, and at Dunrobin is grown in large beds which
produce a brilliant effect.

openings at a higher level, which look as if they
had been contrived as sleeping-berths: but whether
these adaptations were made 3000 years ago or 300
I cannot tell.

After the caves would probably come the [1]*weems*.
Weems are round pits, about 4 to 8 feet across, and
they were doubtless covered with boughs of trees.
They are always found in small groups, and one
such group, containing charcoal and shells, and
with flint instruments close to it, has been found as
near as Kilmaly.

After the weems would come the *hut-circles*.
A low circular wall was built of two parallel rows
of boulders, filled in with smaller stones and covered
with turf. Against the inner side of this seem to
have been propped trunks, sloping inward so that
their tops met in the centre. These of course
would be covered with branches or turf to keep
out wind and rain, except that at the top a space
may have been left unroofed for the escape of
smoke. The inside diameter of such circular walls
is about 30 ft., and a gap is left in them facing the
morning sun: no doubt a corresponding gap was
left in the circle of tree-trunks, and this was the
way the hut received most of its daylight. Remains
of such hut-circles are found as near as Beinn a'
Bhraghaidh and Kilmaly. At whatever time they
were first invented, they were in use as late as the

---

[1] *Weem* probably represents a South-Lowland form of *wame*
(belly, 'womb'), used metaphorically (as we speak of the belly
of the earth).

Iron Age, since iron implements have been found among them.

Perhaps the [1] *earth-houses* are later than the hut-circles. These, like the pit-dwellings, are called 'weems' in some parts of Scotland, and no doubt they were developed from the pit-dwellings. They consist of low narrow underground galleries, walled and roofed with boulders. One was found on the slope of the 100 ft. beach, in making the new grave-yard at Golspie. Another still exists near Kilmaly-craigton, just beyond Kirkton, and its shape, that of a ⊥ with entrance at both ends, is more developed than is commonly the case. Objects as late as the Roman period have been found in some Scottish earth-houses.

Later, probably, than any of these forms of dwelling are the [2] *Duns, Brochs, 'Pictish towers,' or 'Picts' houses.'* On the map you will see one (called Carn Liath, 'Grey Cairn') about $1\frac{1}{4}$ mile E. N. E. of Dunrobin (on the edge of the higher of the two ancient beaches), a second about a mile N. W. of Dunrobin, and a third at Backies about $\frac{3}{4}$ mile N. W. of the second. No doubt, as Dr. Joass suggests, this was intended as a line of towers from the coast to the upland dale of Dun-robin Glen. Apparently there was a fourth such tower on the site of Dunrobin itself, where remains

---

[1] See Anderson's 'Scotland in pagan times—the Iron Age,' pp. 282–307.

[2] *Dun* is the old Sutherland name for such structures: it signifies in Gaelic a mound or fort. *Broch* is the Gaelic *brugh*, a large house.

similar to those found in such towers have been discovered in excavating.

[1] Brochs are circular buildings of unhewn and uncemented stone, narrowing in outside diameter as they rise, and with a central court open to the sky. The only perfect specimen of them, on the isle of Mousey (one of the Shetlands), is 45 ft. high, but some seem to have been a little higher than this. They have very thick walls, in the width of which (about 15 ft.) are contained a number of rooms level with the ground, while above them are galleries reached by a spiral staircase — which, like the galleries themselves, is contained within the thickness of the walls. The rooms and galleries are lit by openings through the inner wall into the central court. This court was normally about 30 ft. across, and in it we often find one or more wells or walled pits. Entrance was to be had only by a narrow passage containing a barred door, or pair of doors, and guardchamber.

The kindness of Dr. Anderson and his publisher Mr. David Douglas allows me to reproduce here three woodcuts from Dr. Anderson's ' Scotland in pagan times—the Iron Age,' pp. 175, 178, and 187, which will give a fair idea of the outside appearance, interior architecture, and outlying defenses of a broch.

[1] On the subject of Brochs see papers by Petrie, Joass and Aitken, Anderson, and Sir H. Dryden in *Archaeologia Scotica,* vol. v, pt. 1 (1873) – also Anderson's 'Scotland in pagan times— the Iron Age,' pp. 174-259. Dr. Joass's paper contains (besides much other valuable matter) a full illustrated description of Carn Liath and the remains found there.

In the section on p. 259, the white space at the foot of the righthand wall represents the entrance-passage. Fronting us are the doors of two out of three rooms built in the thickness of the wall and entered from the centre court : above the doors are window-holes. At the bottom of the lefthand wall is the section of a fourth room, from one end of which rises the staircase. Each of the 5 horizontal dotted

The Broch of Mousey, Shetland (Anderson).

lines represents the roof of one gallery and the floor of the gallery above it. 'These galleries, situated in the heart of the wall, are six in number. Each begins about 3 feet 9 inches in front of the stair, and goes round the whole tower till it comes against the back of the stair, which closes it at that end, so that entrance to the gallery or exit from it can only be obtained by stepping across the space intervening between the end of the gallery floor and the steps of the stair. . . . None of the galleries exceed 5 feet 6 inches in height or 3 feet 2 inches in width ' (Anderson, p. 179). The narrow strips with 5 bridges across them in the centre of the right- and lefthand walls are a section of

¹ *Section of the elevation of the Broch of Mousey* (Anderson, from Plan by Sir H. Dryden).

¹ I had better explain this term to those who have no knowledge of building-terms. The ' elevation' of a tower is that part which is elevated above ground: it does not include the foundations. ' Section' means ' cutting,' and a section of the elevation is a plan of what we should see if we were able to cut the tower in two from the top to the ground, and to look at one of the two pieces from inside. If our section went down to the bottom of the foundations,

these galleries with their floors. The 17 little black openings which run up the inside of the court, on the left side, looking like a pile of black hats, are windows lighting the galleries. The white openings in the right- and lefthand walls are sections of similar tiers of windows, but the lefthand tier has lost some of its lintels. There is a fourth tier of this kind which lies outside the section.

No broch has been found anywhere out of Scotland and the neighbouring isles [1]. The round towers of Ireland, besides bearing evidence of ecclesiastical origin, are always limebuilt and sometimes contain hewn stone. But the idea of a house with chambers inside its wall is found in Ireland, Wales, and Cornwall as well as in Scotland.

In the Balearic isles, the Italian isles of Sardinia and Pantellaria, and in the ' heel ' of Italy are more or less similar structures [2], all of them in districts which were once exposed to the possible ravages of Etruscan or Carthaginian pirates. And, since about the year 369 the Atecotti, who lived between the Forth and the Tyne, ' were enrolled in the Roman army and stationed on the continent ' (Rhŷs, *Celtic Britain,* p. 93), I fancied at one

it would be not a 'section of the elevation' but a 'vertical section,' that is, a cutting straight down. If instead of cutting down through the tower we cut across it, all the way round, as we might cut off the top of a round cake or an egg, that would be a 'horizontal section' or cutting along a level.

[1] See *Arch. Scot.* v. pt. i, p. 163 (Dr. Anderson's paper).

[2] Anderson, 'Scotland in pagan times—the Iron Age,' p. 206. Anderson refers to the existence of multitudes of similar towers in the Caucasus.

time that the germ of the idea had been brought back from the Mediterranean by some returned native soldier. But there is nowhere on the continent any building which does not differ from the broch in very important particulars, and the broch can be accounted for as a development of pre-existing native structures. In its shape, its diameter, and the lean-to of its sides it agrees with the hut-circle ; the long low narrow entrance and the long low narrow galleries (Anderson, p. 207) are like an earth-house ; ' the circular wall, with chambers in its thickness . . . is common . . . in Scottish beehive houses ' (Anderson, pp. 206-7).

The relics found in the brochs show that their latest inhabitants, at any rate, were in a comparatively advanced state of civilization, and in one case Roman coins, but not later than the empress Crispina (A. D. 180-192), have been discovered. The situations, moreover, in which we find them show that they were built for the protection of the people who cultivated the arable land along the coasts and up the valleys.

S. of the Great Glen of Scotland (the line of the Caledonian Canal) only 3 brochs had been found up to the year 1883, though probably the grassy mounds ' which exist abundantly in the valleys of the Forth and Teith for instance [1] ' conceal many more [2]. But the mainland of Invernessshire

---

[1] Anderson's ' Scotland in pagan times—the Iron Age,' p. 191.

[2] Mr. Kidston, the well-known geologist, who lives at Stirling, tells me that he knows of four not far from there.

contains 6, of Ross 10, of Sutherland 60, and of Caithness 79! The Orkneys contain 70, the Shetlands 75, the Isle of Lewis-and-Harris 38, the Isle of Skye 30, and the Isle of Raasay 1! It is plain that, whenever and against whatever foes brochs were *first* built, it was against foes from the northern seas that they were *chiefly* built.

The brochs contain no wrought flints, and they do contain bronze— so that they are later than the Stone Age. They also contain a very little iron. The relics found in them 'are characteristic of the Celtic area and of post-Roman times' (Anderson, p. 259). But were they first built against Saxon pirates or Norse pirates, and how long did their building continue?

No chronicle, Irish or Norse, mentions the building of a broch, but we have Norse evidence [1] that the broch at Mousey was already in existence about A. D. 900. Add that the brochs have yielded up no Anglo-Saxon or Carolingian coins, and no inscriptions— although there are Pictish inscriptions (both in Ogams and in Roman letters) dating back apparently to the 7th century.

As to the time when the earliest brochs may have been built as a defense against Saxon attacks, we find that the British coasts had begun to be attacked at least as early as A. D. 287, since Carausius, who then assumed rule in Britain, had before that 'risen to be the head of a fleet intended to

---

[1] *Egills Saga*, c. 32, 33 ; *Mém. de la Soc. Roy. des Ant. du Nord,* 1850–60, p. 127—both referred to in *Arch. Scot.* v. pt. i, p. 158.

repress the Saxons and other German tribes who now ravaged the coasts of Britain and Gaul [1].' We know also that in A. D. 369 a Saxon fleet retreated before Theodosius to the Orkneys [2]. But the broch at Cockburn Law, Berwickshire, must have been erected after the end of the Roman occupation of that part of Scotland, which was almost continuous from A. D. 78 to A. D. 391 : during the occasional inroads of Picts and Scots there would have been no building of forts against Saxon attacks, nor is it till after Roman rule had ceased in Britain that we hear of the Saxons as attacking the Picts and Scots. And it is pretty certain that before the end of the 6th century, or at any rate the middle of the 7th, Cockburn Law would have been part of the Anglian kingdom of Bernicia.

The fortifications of Cockburn Law are on 'a natural platform projecting from the shoulder of the hill over the valley of the Whitadder water, about 250 feet above the bed of the stream' (Anderson, p. 186), and are 10 miles from the sea. This suggests that they were built when the invaders were already masters of the seacoast, or at least were accustomed to raid 10 miles inland [3]. And it recalls an extraordinary fact—that although there are 75 brochs in Shetland, 70 in Orkney, 79 in Caithness, 60 in Sutherland, 6 on the main-

---

[1] Rhŷs, *Celtic Britain*, p. 92.   [2] *Ib.*, p. 93.

[3] The diameter is abnormal, and so is the size of many of the stones (Anderson, p. 188). Dr. Joass also tells me they are tooled, and he regards this as a *late* broch.

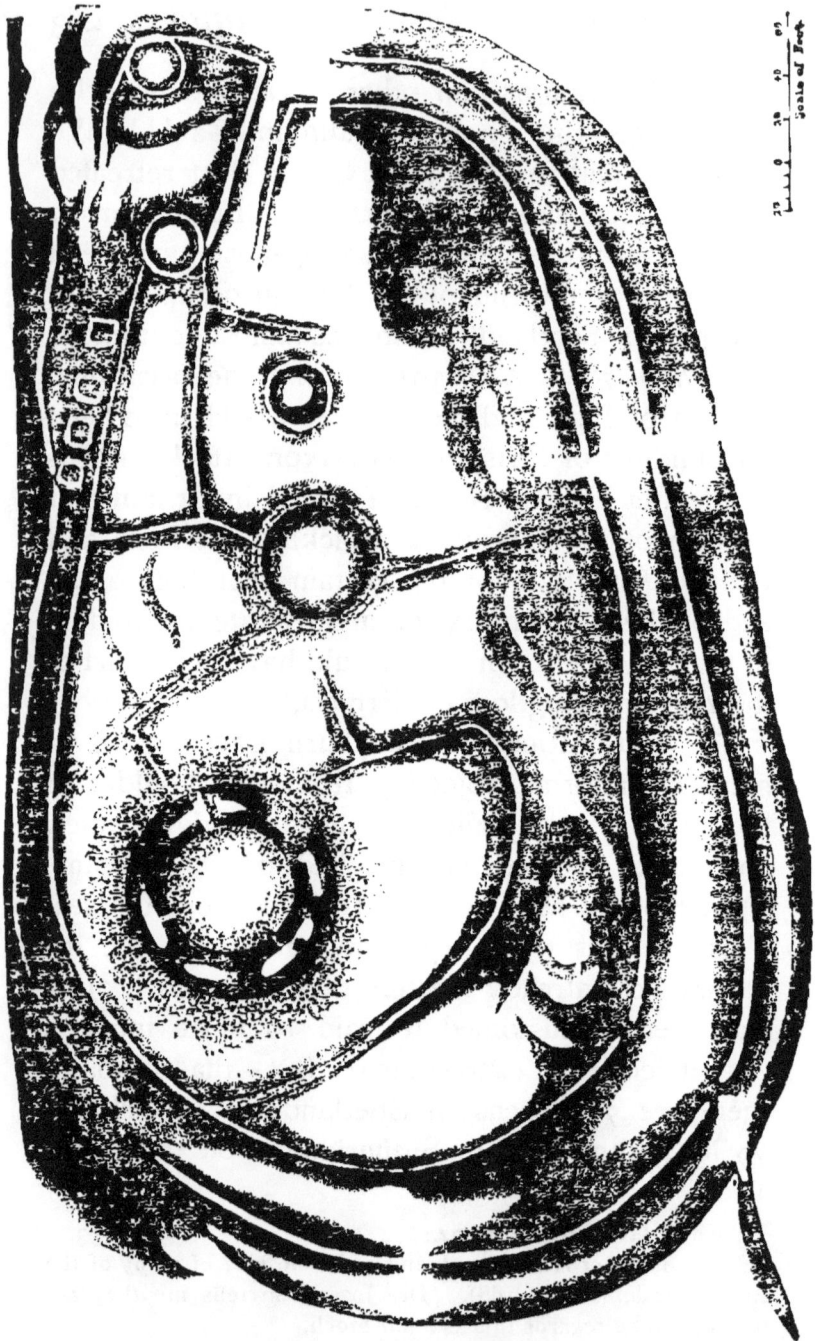

General plan of Broch and its fortifications on Cockburn Law, Berwickshire (Anderson).

land of Ross, and 10 on that of Invernessshire, there is not one yet discovered in the seaboard counties of Nairnshire, Elginshire, Banffshire, Aberdeenshire, Kincardineshire, Forfarshire, Fife, Linlithgowshire, Lothian, or Haddingtonshire! Of the remaining counties on the E. coast of Scotland S. of the Moray Firth Perthshire has 1 (inland), and Stirlingshire 4—but these two are only washed by the upper waters of estuaries—while Berwickshire has none except that on Cockburn Law.

What natural explanation can be given of these extraordinary differences? I believe one is to be found in the statement of Geoffrey of Monmouth[1] that, at the time when the kings of Britain caused Art(h)ur to be crowned over-king, the Saxons had 'subjugated to themselves all the part of the isle which is extended from the river of Humber as far as the Caithness sea,' i.e. the Moray Firth. Arthur was crowned about the beginning of the 6th century, the *Annales Cambriæ* apparently placing his great victory over the Saxons at the Badon Mount in 516 and his death in 537, while Geoffrey puts his death in 542, and Gildas, who apparently wrote not later than 547, refers to him as if he were dead[2].

In other words I suggest that, whether or not

---

[1] Subjugaverant etiam sibi totam partem insulæ, quæ a flumine Humbri usque ad mare Catanesium extenditur.—Giles's edition. ix. § 1. On Geoffrey and the Old Breton chronicle he translated, see my letter in *The Academy* of Apr. 11, 1896.

[2] See my letter in *The Academy* of Oct. 12, 1895.

isolated brochs were built earlier, and whether or
not the practice was continued later, the great
majority were built in the late 5th or early 6th
century, after the Saxons had conquered the seaboard from the Humber to the Moray Firth, and
were built to protect the rest of North Britain
against their devastations.

The first names we possess for the inhabitants
of these regions are furnished by the Greek geo-
grapher Ptolemy, who flourished about A.D. 126–
161, and who gives a list of the tribes inhabiting
North Britain. He says (ii. § 11) that the last of all
were the [1] Κορναύιοι, a name which in Latin would be
written Cornavii, and obviously means those who
dwelt in the northern *horn* of the isle (Gaelic *corn*,
'horn'): these are placed by Rhŷs and Kiepert in
Caithness.   Next to them (§ 12) along the E. coast
came the Λοῦγοι (= Latin *Lugi*) and Δεκάνται (= Latin
Decantae), but, while Rhŷs places the Lugi along
the Golspie coast and the Decantae to the south
of them, Kiepert continues the Decantae N. from
Ross across the Dornoch Firth and Loch Fleet—
which seems to me less likely.

[1] In the Greek and Latinized forms of this (and the names
mentioned in connexion with it) the final diphthong or vowel is
a Greek or Latin termination.   All we know of the Gaelic names
is that they were Cornav-, L(o)ug-, Decant-, Smert-.   Holder
(*Alt-Celtischer Sprachschatz*) derives *Cornavii* from the stem of an
original *cornu*, gen. *cornav-os*.   The name of the Decantae seems
to come from a Keltic stem *dec-*, related to the stem of Latin
decentes, Greek δοκοῦντες, and may mean ' illustrious,' ' comely,'
or ' decorated.'

In the 2nd century, then, the people of the Golspie coast seem to have been called Lougoi or Lugi, a name of which we do not know the meaning[1], though there are *loug-* and *lug-* stems in Keltic. The inhabitants of some of the highlands behind (but beginning at what distance from the coast we cannot tell) seem to have been called (Ptolemy, ii. § 12) Σμέρται (= Latin *Smertae*), which looks as if it meant 'the smeared people'; for we have in Highland Gaelic the participle *smeurta* 'smeared' and in Irish Gaelic *smeartha* with the same meaning—both pointing to an earlier *smerta*.

Why should these Sutherland highlanders be called by such a name? Well, in those days the climate was much more wooded than it is now, and therefore probably wetter and colder. Now the North Britons of the 2nd century probably had not much clothing[2], and n the northernmost highlands they may have smeared themselves with whale-oil or the oil of other marine animals, as a protection against wet and cold. In 1793 it is said of Golspie, 'Seals and porpoises are on the coast; sometimes small whales are seen near it; and there are instances

---

[1] In Highland Gaelic *lug-ach* = 'bowlegged,' and *lug-an* = 'a crooked person': Mr. Macbain derives them from a root meaning *bend*. Did the Lugi carry coracles and creels on their backs, and get the name from a bent position in walking?

[2] The Greek historian Herodian, writing in 218, describes the North Britons against whom the Romans marched in 208 as being tattooed and wearing iron ornaments, but not knowing any use for clothing (iii. 14. § 7). This last statement is incredible: perhaps they stripped for battle, and so gave occasion for his belief.

of some being driven on shore ' (*Statistical account of Scotland,* ix. p. 27). Even now a whale occasionally appears off Golspie.

Kilmaly. But the first people hereabouts whom we find living together in a place possessing a distinct name are probably the people of Culmalin or Kilmaly. This (Gaelic) name indicates a church ('cell,' Latin *cella,* pronounced *kella*) dedicated to a saint named Malin. We have already seen that there are weems, hut-circles, and an earth-house (probably of much earlier date) at Kilmaly.

Who was St. Malin? His name is unknown in that form. But I believe I have found him in the celebrated Irish saint commonly known as Moling, who died in 697, and who is called Maling in a manuscript so near to his own time as the 8th century[1]. The change of Maling to Malin is exactly paralleled in the modern names Mullinakill, where one tradition places his birth, and St. Mullins (originally Tigh-Moling), where he founded a monastery (Smith and Wace, *Dict. of Christian biography,* iii, p. 930).

St. Maling died 'in Britonen,' 'among Britons,' and the kirk may have been dedicated to him soon after his death by some missionary successor of St. Columba. But the Columban monks were expelled from Pictish into Scottish soil (Argyll and

---

[1] A MS. at the Monastery of St. Paul in Carinthia: see Windisch, *Irische Texte,* p. 317. Maling is probably the correct form, corrupted into Moling because the honorific prefix *Mo* 'my' was commonly attached to the names of ecclesiastics: thus Cua became Mochua.

thereabouts) in 717, and we don't know when they returned or whether they returned at all. The foundation of the kirk is more likely to be due to the Culdees at a much later period. It has been said that the see of Dornoch, which is only 6 miles off, was founded by Malcolm III, about 1066, but evidence of this is not forthcoming[1]. Ecclesiastical land, however, was held at Kilmaly when the Kilmaly Ogam-stone was carved, and that (as I shall presently show) may be put with much probability about 1070.

The Kilmaly Ogam-stone is the most ancient record which exists relating to any part of the parish of Golspie. It used to be at Kilmaly, but is now in the museum at Dunrobin. I give photographs of both sides of it, and you will see that the side which has the figure of a man has strokes cut round the righthand edge and along the top. These strokes are letters of a peculiar alphabet used in the early middle ages by the Irish and the Picts, and by those branches of either race which were settled in N. and S. Wales, Devon, and Cornwall[2].

This alphabet is called the Ogam alphabet, and the separate letters Ogams. I should like not only Golspie people but everyone in Scotland N. of the Forth to be able to recognize Ogams when he sees them; for there can be no serious doubt that the number of Ogam inscriptions yet found in Scotland,

---

[1] *Orig. paroch. Scotiæ*, ii. pt. ii, p. 598.

[2] An Ogam-stone has also been found at Silchester in Hampshire, an important place in Romano-British times.

Orkney, and Shetland is far short of that which we may reasonably expect to discover. And so I shall borrow from my own book ' The vernacular inscriptions of the ancient kingdom of Alban ' enough not only to explain the Kilmaly Ogam-stone, but to enable the reader to identify Pictish Ogams wherever he may see them.

The Ogam alphabet is not found outside the British isles, and was employed only by those peoples whose occupation of them preceded the Roman invasion—probably only by those of Gaelic race. A great number of inscriptions in it have been discovered in Ireland; smaller numbers in Scotland, the Shetlands and Orkneys, the Isle of Man, Wales, and England. But none have been found in Scotland S. of the Forth, or on the west side of it where the Irish colonists called Scots planted themselves.

The alphabet consisted of strokes—almost exclusively straight strokes—written on a ¹ line commonly called the stem-line—which is normally

¹ This line may run along a natural edge of the stone, but I know of no case where the edge certainly takes the place of a stem-line. Such an instance was supposed to be found in the Kilmaly stone, but a microscope shows me parts of a faint stem-line in a photograph taken by Mr. A. M. Dixon for the Earl of Southesk. Where (as sometimes happens) the stem-line is hardly more than a scratch, and where (as invariably happens) it has been exposed to the weather of 700 to 1200 years, it cannot always be detected at a glance upon a deeply pitted or abundantly veined stone. The same remark applies to the ' ties ' which sometimes join the tops or bottoms of strokes forming part of the same letter, and to the ' rulings' upon or below which the letters were sometimes written.

straight, but in one instance (the Carden Moor stone at Logie Elphinstone) circular. The more ordinary characters were as follows

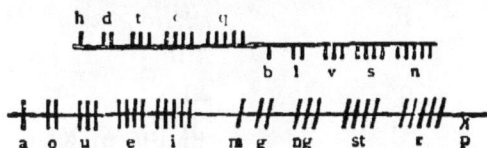

According to Irish tradition, ⊓ represented *f*; but it is found in places where an ancient Irish initial *v* would be expected, and, as such a *v* ordinarily passed into *f* in later Irish, the value of its sign might similarly change. Its value in Pictish inscriptions is always *v*, *w*, or *u*.

The following are the types of Ogams found in Pictish inscriptions

English equivalent	Ogam character
A	┼ or ┿ or ↗ or ↙
B	⊤
C (hard)	⊔⊔⊔
D	⊥⊥
E	⧢ or ⇶ or ↗↙ or ✳
G	⧸⧸
H	⊥
I	⧢
K	⊔⊔⊔
L	⊤⊤
M	⊁
N	⊓⊓⊓
O	╫ or ⇉ or ⇇
P	✗

English equivalent	Ogam character
Q	⠇⠇⠇⠇
R	ﬀﬀ
S	⊤⊤⊤⊤
T	⊥⊥⊥
U	ﬀ (or ⊤⊤⊤ *w*)
V } W }	⊤⊤⊤
ᚦ	ꜱ
HO	ᚶ
IA	ﬀﬀﬀﬀ
MA	ƒ
OE	⊤⊢
OI	⊖ or ⊕
RR	⨯⨯⨯⨯
ST	ﬀﬀ
? UI	⏝

The question of the origin of all or any of the Ogam characters lies outside the object of this sketch: but it has long been pointed out that ⫿⫿⫿⫿⫿ represent [1] initial letters of the Old Irish numerals for 1, 2, 3, 4, 5. It is also obvious that the sign for *rr* is formed by crossing two *r*'s. The sign for *p* is either a modification of ⊤ *b*, or an angular form of the Roman P. The sign for ᚦ is obviously formed out of that for *d*. The modified form of *o* which I take

---

[1] *H-óin, dá, trí, cethir,* and some form of *cóic* spelt (like Latin *quinque*) with initial *q*.

to =*oe* is apparently meant to represent a combination of ╫ *o* and ╫╫ *e*. The two signs for *oi*
may represent a Roman *o* (sometimes written ◇ by
Irish scribes) with a Roman *i* (the stem-line laid
crosswise inside it. ▽ may represent a Roman
u with a Roman *i* (the stem-line) laid across the
top. And it will be seen that the combinations
for *ho, ia, ma* are made up of *h+o, i+a*, and
m+a.

The writing of consonants on Pictish Ogam-
stones usually slopes : above the stem-line the slope
is almost always \, and below the line /, and this
is so on the Kilmaly stone, except that the last
9 strokes above the line slant /. If you stand to
the right of it and read from the bottom upwards,
and then read along the top from right to left (as
if you were standing above it), you get the inscription correctly as follows

(foot)

a l l h h ä l l o ɛ ɛ ð d d m̄ q q ɳ u˙u v ʀ a

(top right corner)

ɛ ɛ e c c h

The thin dotted line is the stem-line, so faintly
scratched that probably you will not be able to
find it on the stone. There are three peculiarities
about the inscription : (1) Tacked on to the beginning of the first *q* is a small mark signifying the
omission of a vowel, as on the Shevack ('Newton')

T

stone. (2) The first strokes of the two *q*'s are higher than the rest. (3) Between the two *u*'s is a small straight stroke to show that they do not go together (*uu* being a frequent combination in Pictish). The number of double consonants is mainly due to the Pictish habit of doubling them after a short vowel.

Written with words separated, the inscription = *Allhhallorr èdd M'qq Nu Uvvarrecch*, or in our spelling *Alhallr, àit Mic Nu Uabharaich* ' Alhallr, place of Mac Nu the Proud (*or* the Bold)[1].'

Alhallr is not Pictish, but Norse: it is compounded of *al-* ' all-', 'completely,' and *hallr* 'slope,' and it correctly describes the character of the ground on or close to which the stone stood. So that the stone tells us that the Norsemen had been at Kilmaly, but that in some cases at least their homesteads were now occupied by Picts.

The man on the stone is M'cNu himself. Above him is a figure of frequent occurrence on Pictish stones; some varieties of it look like attempts to represent a whale or other marine animal. And in front of him is a fish. These animals may or may not be meant to show that his property extended to the shore, or that he was a fisherman. The object below him is probably a double brooch[2], indicating that the owner was a ' gentleman'; it is common on such stones, as are also combs

---

[1] At pp. 321–27 I have given a full account of each word in the inscription.

[2] See Stuart, *Sculptured stones of Scotland*, ii, p. ix, &c.

and mirrors. Above it to the right is a Z-shaped object across which is an inverted crescent: the latter may be a brooch, the former some kind of pin—these likewise are common on Pictish stones. The intertwined snakes [1] may also represent a bracelet, necklace, or badge: the snake is found on other Pictish stones, and sometimes with the Z-shaped ornament which I believe to be a pin [1]. The object at the very top of the stone may represent the top and front of a decorated casket [2]. In front of M'cNu's feet is something which may be a woollen glove with bent fingers: that is the best guess I have made at it. And he himself, with an axe in one hand and a knife in the other, is apparently attacking a wild cat or wolf.

On the other side of the stone is a cross of interlaced work, bordered with ornamented panels, and without any original inscription at all. But hundreds of years afterwards one of the Gordons (whose family then held the earldom of Sutherland) thought he would use this as a burial-stone; so he had cut round it the following unfinished inscription which Dr. Joass has copied for me:—IEIR · IS · THE · BURAL · PLEAC · OF · ROBERT · GORDON · ELDEST · SON · TO · ALEX · GORDON · OF · SUTHE. When he had got as far as the *e* in ' Sutherland ' something made him change his mind. Possibly people began to make a fuss because there was a cross on the stone, and to call him Papish!

[1] See Stuart, *Sculptured stones of Scotland*, ii, p. xi.
[2] Ib., plate 11.

Now comes the question *where* the stone was at Kilmaly. Stuart in his ' Sculptured stones of Scotland ' (i, p. 12) tells us that it was said to have come from Kilmaly kirkyard—which is ' Alhallr,' ' a complete slope,' with a vengeance. But an old man now dead, who lived at Backies, told Dr. Joass that he had helped to move this and another stone on the same day, and that this (which he seemed to regret not having broken, as Papish!) came not from the kirkyard but from a field about half a mile nearer the River Fleet, a field where (Dr. Joass tells me) traces of buildings have been discovered, and just *under* the slope of the ' hundred-foot beach.' But the fact of someone trying to turn it into a burial-stone makes it much more likely that the account Stuart heard was correct, and that the stone came from the kirkyard.

At any rate it was (like every stone with a cross and Pictish inscription yet found on the mainland of Scotland), simply a boundary-stone of property belonging to the neighbouring kirk. It is just possible that M'cNu was a tenant under the kirk, and that, while the inscription and the accompany-ing sculptures on the same side declare his tenant-right, the cross on the other side means that the kirk was ground-landlord. But there are stones in Perthshire (one at Doune, one at Greenloaning) where the tenant's name and the kirk's cross are on the *same* side of the stone. So that when we find them—as in the Kilmaly stone—on opposite sides, the presumption is that there is no tenancy at all, but that the kirk owned the land on the cross-side, and that the land on the other was private. Very possibly M'cNu *gave* the land on which the kirk was built, and the monks who built it, and who put up the boundary-stone between the properties, sculptured his portrait on it for him, with suitable accessories, as a trifling acknowledgement.

The date of the stone is probably not far off the year 1070. The Norsemen did not get to the border between Caithness and Sutherland till 875, and we have to allow time for them to spread down to Kilmaly, to occupy a farm there and give it a Norse name, and to be succeeded as occupants by a Pict. And there are so many points of resemblance common to this and the Scoonie and Dyke (' Brodie ') stones [1] that I regard all three as belonging to the same period. Now the kirk at Scoonie was given to the Culdees of Loch Leven by Bishop Tuadal, 1055–9 [2], and the Scoonie stone was very probably erected by them to mark the boundary of their property: so that I date it at about 1057. No inscribed Pictish stones later than these three are known to exist.

Dr. Joass tells me that there is beneath the waters of Loch Brora—on its N.E. side, below Gordonbush House—a stone which was broken up and thrown into it as having ' Popish tricks and capers '—to use his informant's phrase. Whether it bore an

---

[1] Nicholson, p. 24.
[2] Walcott, *Scoti-monasticon*, p. 357.

inscription or not, it is morally certain to have been nothing worse than the cross-marked and sculptured boundary-stone of land belonging to the ancient kirk of Columba (Kilcolumcille) hard by. Probably the same people who broke and threw it in, as a supposed relic of Roman 'superstition,' were themselves frightened if they saw the first lamb of the year with its tail turned towards them, and were ready to accuse the nearest old woman of witch-craft if their cows happened to fall short of milk!

The first mention of Kilmaly is in 1401, when the *n* had begun to be dropped and it is called Culmali: however, we find Culmalin in 1471. Culmaly occurs in 1512, Kilmale in 1532, Kilmaly in 1536 [1].

The kirk was the parish kirk of Golspie from the time when parishes were established [2] till 1619, when the chapel of St. Andrew at Golspie super-seded it as such. Kilmaly itself remains under two names—a group of cottages on the slope of the 100 ft. beach and the edge of a burn, keeping the old name [3], and a farmstead further along upon the plain (close to another burn), bearing the English name of Kirkton. At Kirkton are traces

---

[1] Kil- or Cil- was certainly the earliest form, though not recorded for Kilmaly so early as Cul-. The spelling still varies greatly, and the 1-inch Ordnance Map and W. W. M. (p. 211) use Cul-.

[2] They cannot be traced in Scotland before Alexander I (1107-24).

[3] There is also a Kilmaly-craigton on the hillside beyond Kirkton, but there are no houses there now.

of the ancient kirk, with the graveyard which belonged to it, and which was used as late as the present century. In the wall which divides this graveyard from the road is a modern slab containing the mistaken statement that the ashes of very many earls of Sutherland are there buried.

Strange to say, however, we do not know whether at the time of the Reformation the old kirk was dedicated to St. Maling or to St. Carden. For 'In 1630 there was a yearly fair held at Kilmaly called " Sanct Carden his fayre ",' and this suggests that the kirk had been dedicated to him. There was at the same time a Saint Carden's fair at Loth, 13 or 14 miles northward. In the *Dictionary of Christian biography* the Rev. James Gammack says 'There are many Cardenwells throughout Scotland,' and there are other Scottish place-names which may be compounded with the same saint's name. As Dr. Anderson suggests to me, it doubtless represents that of the semi-legendary 7th century saint Queretinius, Queritinus, Kiritinus, or Curitan, who is said to have been abbat of Rosmarkyn (Rosemarkie) in the adjoining county of Ross[1]. There may, indeed, have been an earlier and a later dedication at Kilmaly, one Columban, the other Culdee—as at St. Vigean's near Arbroath, which about the year 700 was dedicated not to Vigean but to Drostan (Nicholson, p. 10). In that case the Carden dedication would doubtless be the later (Culdee), partly because of

---

[1] There is a Kincardine only some 14 miles S.W. of Kilmaly.

the fair bearing his name, and partly because he seems to have been an apostle of Roman, not Columban, ideas. But it is equally possible that the fair on Carden's day was an institution borrowed from Rosemarkie or some other place where there was a dedication to him.

Golspie itself is mentioned in 1330, as the site of a chapel of St. Andrew's. It is then called Goldespy [1]. What does the name mean? That has never been made out within any measurable distance of probability: let me try to make it out now.

No derivation is of any great value which does not take the oldest known form of the name and explain every letter in it. And my belief is that the place was a settlement made by some Lowlander named Gold patronized by one of the first earls of Sutherland [2]. Adam Gold was bailiff of Montrose in 1296, and there was a John Golde at Haddington in 1335-6 [3]. Either form of the surname would naturally have had *Goldes* for a genitive in 1330. As for the *-py*, ' by ' is [4] early English for a place of abode, and we actually find the spelling Gollesby in 1499, and Golesby in 1539 [5].

---

[1] *Orig. paroch. Scot.*, ii. pt. ii, p. 650.

[2] Sutherland (Norse *Sudurland*) was the Norse name for the *southern* part of Catt; the northern part, the promontory or ness of Catt, they called Cathanes, now Caithness.

[3] *Calendar of documents relating to Scotland*, ii, 198.

[4] The New English Dictionary gives examples of it as a separate word from about 950 to about 1314.

[5] *Orig. paroch. Scot.*, ii. pt. ii, p. 677.

The Highlander's propensity for sounding *b* as *p* is so notorious that I need not cite instances of it; and the same tendency is found in the oldest Highland Gaelic known, that is, 'Pictish.' Gold may have been a merchant who carried on an export and import trade between the opposite shores of the Moray Firth, and he would naturally take up his station within easy reach of the protecting arm of a powerful noble [1].

The derivation just put forward is strongly supported by the case of the village of Canisbay on the N. coast of Caithness. The neighbouring *bay* is not so called, and apparently never was. The ending -*bay* is first found about 1640; in 1577 it is -*be*; before then it is always -*bi* -*by* -*bie* or -*bye*, the oldest known form of the name being Cananesbi in 1223–1245 (*Two ancient records of the bishopric of Caithness*, Bannatyne Club—facsimile at end). Now the church was 'apparently dedicated to Saint Drostan' (*Orig. paroch. Scot.*, ii. pt. ii, p. 792). Well, the chief foundation connected with that saint, a foundation of Pictish times, was at Deer in Aberdeenshire, and when we turn to the records of its history contained in the celebrated 'Book of Deer' we find that among those who had conferred lands on it (apparently after 1131–2) was Clan Canan (p. lvi). And I suggest that Cananesbi = Canan's settlement, and that one of Clan Canan, in founding a kirk there, naturally

---

[1] One finds that in 1527 there was a *port* of Dunrobin (Sir W. Fraser, *The Sutherland book*, iii. p. 79).

dedicated it to Saint Drostan. The *b* in that name
has not been changed to *p*, because the Gaels on
the N. coast of Caithness were either expelled or
absorbed by the Norsemen.

In 1401 we find *Bakys, Drommoy,* and *Dun-*
robyn mentioned [1].

At Bakys, now **Backies,** are some ancient sand-
banks, and Dr. Joass plausibly suggests the Norse
bakki ' bank ' as the origin of the name. He finds
· the Backies ' in a deed of 27 Nov. 1546 preserved
at Dunrobin (a precept of sasine in favour of one
Richard Sutherland). Mr. J. Hutt, of the Bodleian,
has pointed out another instance, about 1620, where
the plural pronoun ' them ' is applied to ' the
Backies ' (Sir W. Fraser, *The Sutherland book,*
ii, p. 347), and ' the Backies ' is still sometimes
heard. Lastly, I find the singular ' Backie ' in
a document of about 1630 (*ib.* iii, p. 193).

Drommoy, now **Drummuie,** on the slope of
the 100 ft. beach, apparently means ' ridge of the
plain,' from Gaelic *drom-, druim,* ' ridge', and *magh*
(locative-dative, *maigh*), ' plain.' *Magh,* Prof. Mackinnon tells me, ' undoubtedly yields ' Moy ',' which
is found as a place-name in Sutherland itself.

The derivation of Dunrobyn, now **Dunrobin,**
has never been satisfactorily made out, except that
the first part is of course the Gaelic *dùn* ' castle.'
It is commonly said to have been named from
a Robert, earl of Sutherland. But there was no

---

[1] *Orig. paroch. Scot.,* ii. pt. ii, p. 673.

DUNROBIN IN 1805

Robert before the 6th earl, who did not succeed before 1370 and is said to have died in 1442. There was almost certainly a castle at Dunrobin before he was born : indeed Dunrobin seems to have been built over an old Pictish broch. And in 1556 we find the then Earl granting the chaplaincy of St. Andrew on condition of the chaplain 'doing the funeral rites (*exequias*) and other services according to the foundation of the chaplaincy, together with the service and worship (*seruitio et diuinis*) due and wont within the palace or fortalice of Dunrobin when possible besides the cure and service of the chaplaincy according to the same foundation ' (*Orig. paroch. Scot.*, ii. pt. ii, p. 651). This implies that the foundation-deed obliged the chaplain to officiate at the castle as well as in the chapel. Now the chapel of St. Andrew was founded at least as early as 1330, for in that year we have a charter dated there.

There was, moreover, not only a *Dun*robyn or *Dun*rabyn, but also a *Drum*rabyn. In 1512 we have an ' Instrument of Sasine in favour of John Sutherland, son and heir of the late John, Earl of Sutherland, in the Earldom of Sutherland,' printed by Sir William Fraser (*The Sutherland book*, iii, pp. 47–8). It mentions the castle 4 times—thrice as *castrum de 'Dunrabyn,'* once as *castrum de 'Dunrabin.'* But the document is witnessed by (among others) Dauid Stewart, constable of *Drum*rabyn (' constabilario de Drumrabyn '), and it is not likely that in so important a deed, and one in which the name of the castle is 4 times written correctly, this Drum should be simply a mistake for Dun [1]. The fact is that Dunrobin stands on a *druim*, a ' ridge,' which is a continuation of the Drummuic ridge, and on this ridge, between the castle and Golspie, traces of ancient houses have been found. It is the entire ridge which is clearly indicated by Drumrabyn, and we have to consider what *rabyn* is likely to mean in the name of the ridge as well as in that of the castle. I have exhausted my ingenuity in attempts at a really plausible Gaelic or Norse derivation for *-robin* and *-rabyn*. As Dr. Joass points out, various ' duns ' *are* named after persons, and if the name had only been Dunroibeirt or Dunraibeirt one would have had no doubts. But I can find very few traces of Robin as an old Scottish name, the forms being mainly Robert, Roby, Rob: and the odds are always heavy that a Robertson is of Scottish descent and a Robinson of English. Prof. Mackinnon would have expected Dùn Raibeirt, and suggests that, if *-robin* really = Robert, ' the name took its rise with those more accustomed to Scotch than Gaelic.' But then one has to suppose the same of *Drum*rabyn too, which seems very unlikely.

' In the midst of the court within the castle,' says Sir William Fraser, ' there is one of the deepest draw-wells in Scotland, all lined with ashlar-work, which was built and finished before the house was

---

[1] If the mistake be attributed to a copyist from dictation, let me say that *Dun* is properly pronounced *Dōōn*.

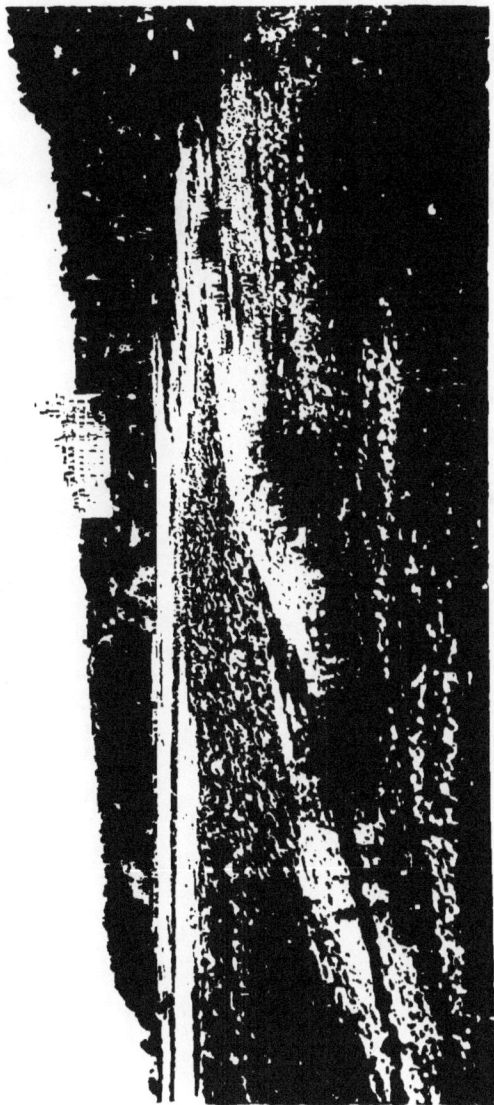

begun. The well was known as that of St. John '
(*The Sutherland book*, i, p. xxxi). This looks as if
there had been a chapel of St. John on Drumrabyn.
In that case it may have been one de endent upon
Kilcain (= Kirk of John) on Loch Brora, which
was only ½ a mile further than Kilmalin.

In 1456 we find mention [1] of the alehouse of the
tower of Gouspy. **Golspie Tower** was a castellated house which has been demolished for some
centuries: all that now remains of it is a small part
of one end, which stands at the corner of a road-
side garden [2]. But there are still cottages and
farmbuildings at the spot, which is about ¾ of a
mile from the sea, by the side of a burn, and on
the slope of an old beach above the 100 ft. beach.
There are other burnside cottages half a mile higher
up, on the edge of a still higher and older beach,
and these also bear the name of Golspie Tower.
The burn beside which the two hamlets stand is
now carried by a modern channel (partly underground) into Golspie Burn, between the Manse
and the Sutherland Arms. But at one time, when
it was a wide stream instead of a mere rivulet, it
entered the sea in a quite different direction, by
a mouth of its own cutting, broad and deep, through
the 100 ft. beach. If you walk past the School
toward Rhives, you will almost immediately come

---

[1] *Orig. paroch. Scot.*, ii. pt. ii, p. 677.
[2] This fragment was several feet higher until about a dozen
years ago, when it was reduced because it shut out light from
the cottage.

to the gap made by the stream and the sea in the
front of this beach, and you will descry a singular
inner gap—its broad bed a sown field, its deep
sloping sides still covered with grass and flowers.
This inner gap—called ' The Hollow Park [1] '—is the
end of the ancient course cut by the stream [2], and
such disused river-mouths are, I believe, so very
seldom to be met with that I have had a photograph taken of this one—which I here present.

[1] In Scottish use 'park'=simply an enclosed field, and is
even applied to an enclosed plantation of trees (see Jamieson's
Dictionary).

[2] The breadth of the stream at its *present* outlet is about a yard,
its normal depth less than 2 inches, the height of its dug banks
2 or 3 feet. In comparing with these dimensions those of its
ancient outlet, we must bear in mind that the soil of the banks of
the latter is very loose and liable to be washed away, that the
sea may have been the main factor in broadening the distance
between them, and that the stream, though apparently broad,
needs not have been deep. The result of a long walk up it is to
lead me to believe that it was everywhere much broader than at
present, but that it cut a deep channel only where there was
a marked fall in the land, and where consequently its own force
was considerably increased. Nor can I feel sure how far its
apparent breadth was due to floods, or to its having shifted its
course. The considerable length to which the old deep outlet
runs I should venture to explain thus : (1) the stream, falling over
the 100 ft. beach into the sea, cut a deep outlet in the soft edge
of the beach ; (2) the fall in its bed was thus carried continuously
further back, and its channel continuously deepened further back
in consequence.

The apparently much greater volume of this and Golspie Burn
in former times is to be explained partly by the fact that the
mountains were not so much wasted as they are now, and that,
being higher, they arrested more rain and snow than at present ;
partly by the fact that (in a later age) the country was more
wooded than it now is, and so likely to be wetter.

AN OLD BURN-MOUTH

A few words about **Rhives** (pronounced Rivz), the homestead where the Duke's factor resides. It is on the edge of the 100 ft. beach, by the side of a burn. It seems to be mentioned first in 1548[1], as Ruvis, while in 1563 we have it as Ruves, in 1566 as Ruiffis and Ruves[2], and in a map made by Herman Moll in 1714 I find Ruifis. I suspect that these forms are simply variant plurals of *roof*[3], and that the buildings at Ruvis were so named because they were timber-roofed at a time when the neighbouring houses were mere turf cabins.

The present village of Golspie consists chiefly of one long broad street of low stonebuilt houses. For a small part of the length of this street, the fronts of the seaward row are turned toward the sea, because at that part of the bay the fishing-boats put in. This seaward row is known as Fishertown.

At present Golspie proper has only four houses across the Burn; that is, two at the Mill, the Duke's solicitor's house, and a Lodge near the shore. But formerly there were other houses not far from the last mentioned.

The original village, indeed, seems to have been mainly on that side, where the last house (once the Inn[4]) was pulled down only in 1894. It

---

[1] *Orig. paroch. Scot.*, ii. pt. ii, p. 680.

[2] Fraser, *The Sutherland book*, iii, pp. 135, 137, 138.

[3] Dalrymple's 1596 translation of Leslie's History of Scotland speaks of ' the ruffe of ony hous,' and Jamieson's Dictionary gives ' ruiff-spar ' as = roof-spar.

[4] The Sutherland Arms was built in 1809-11, but has been much added to.

stood in an angle formed by two walls, about 60 yards E. of the Lodge, which was built in 1894, and to which its occupants removed. The longer of these two walls once formed the back of an entire row of houses.

Probably there were very few houses on the site of the modern village before 1808, when the transfer of crofters from the interior of Sutherland was begun [1]. In 1793 the population of the village was estimated at only 300, that of the entire parish at 1700 (*Statist. account of Scotland*, ix, p. 28), of whom 800 were males, 900 females.

The population of the parish [2], which consists of 19,690 acres (nearly 31 square miles), amounted at the 1891 census to 354 families, comprising 661 males and 790 females—1451 altogether. Since the 1881 census there had been a decrease in the number of families and of both sexes.

The population of the village [3] amounted at the 1891 census to 220 families, comprising 427 males and 508 females—935 altogether. Since the 1881 census there had been a decrease of 1, 3, and 18 under these three heads respectively. But since 1891 a number of new houses have been built or are in course of building.

Their occupations. The register of parishioners entitled to vote for county-councillors in

---

[1] 'In the year 1812, it was composed of a collection of black mud huts . . . It now consists entirely of a street, of neat, clean, well-built houses, with some excellent shops' (Loch, *Improvements on the estates of the Marquess of Stafford*, 1820, Append. p. 20).

[2] *Parliamentary papers*, 1892, vol. 76, p. 10.   [3] *Ib.*, p. 130.

1889-90 contained the names of 243 persons. Of these, 73 were women, whose occupation was not stated. An analysis of the occupations of the remainder gives the following results.

About $\frac{1}{3}$ were employed, in one capacity or another, on farms or estates.

About $\frac{1}{4}$ were tradesmen [1] or artisans.

About $\frac{1}{10}$ were engaged in professions or the public service.

About $\frac{1}{15}$ were engaged in fishing or fisheries.

About $\frac{1}{15}$ were crofters.

About $\frac{1}{25}$ were in the railway-service.

It must, however, be noted that this is an analysis of a list of ratepayers only, and that a considerable number of heads of families were not on the list through being in arrears of poor-rates. Consequently the proportion of the well-to-do classes was probably much less than the analysis indicates, and that of the fishermen in particular probably much greater.

Owing to names having been struck off for neglect to pay the county rate, or because the bearer had been exempted from its payment, subsequent lists show a much smaller number of voters, that for 1895-96 containing only 214, of whom only 37 were women.

Their races [2]. Very nearly $\frac{1}{4}$ of the 243 voters

---

[1] I have been obliged to group these classes together because the register does not show whether the voter is an employer or a mechanic, but only what his occupation is (e. g. painter).

[2] Probably the Highland element is larger than the register shows—for the reason already given.

bear names which are either certainly or probably
not of Highland origin. None of these names is
owned by as many as 5 voters, but there are 4
Watsons, 3 Burnetts and Nicols, 2 Andersons,
Bruces, Grays, Melvilles, Mitchells, Nobles, and
Smiths. No doubt much of the non-Highland
element came in originally in the retinue of various
Earls and Dukes of Sutherland. There is only
1 voter bearing a name which suggests at all recent
immigration from Scandinavia: that is Olson.

About ¾ of the rest, or ½ of the entire number,
consist of persons bearing one of the following
11 names

Sutherland	30
Mackay	18
Murray	15
MacDonald	10
Ross	9
Gordon	8
MacKenzie	8
Grant	6
Gunn	6
Matheson	6
MacRae	5
	——
	121

All these are names of clans.

Sutherland is the clan of which the Earls (Dukes)
of Sutherland have been the chiefs.

Mackay is a clan once specially connected with
Strathnaver in the north of the county.

The first earl of Sutherland came from Moray, and was for a time called 'de Moravia.' Perhaps *Murray* was the name borne by the dependents who accompanied him from Moray. Or it may have been given to later immigrants from the opposite Moray coast.

MacDonald is the name of several clans. That of MacDonald of the Isles, as having once been associated with the earldom of Ross, is the most likely stock for Golspie MacDonalds.

Ross is another clan associated with the extinct earldom of Ross. Just as part of the retainers of the Earls of Sutherland may have been called by the original family-name of Murray while part bore the later name of Sutherland, so part of the retainers of the Earls of Ross seem to have been called by the original family-name of MacDonald and part by the later name of Ross.

Gordon is the name of the family to which the earldom of Sutherland passed by marriage early in the 16th century. This family came from Aberdeenshire, and most of the Sutherland Gordons may be descendants of retainers brought from the former county.

MacKenzie is a clan once specially connected with Kintail in Ross.

Grant is a clan specially connected with Strathspey, in the shires of Elgin, Banff, and Inverness. Dr. Joass suggests that the prevalence of the name in Golspie may be due to the fact that in the last century a Sir James Grant occasionally lived in

Sutherland as the acting curator of the Countess-Duchess of Sutherland during her minority.

Gunn is a clan once specially associated with Caithness;

Matheson with Loch Alsh, opposite Skye; and *MacRae,* like MacKenzie, with Kintail in Ross.

Now let us sum up our results.

Of Sutherland origin are probably the Sutherlands and Mackays—total 48.

Of Caithness origin are probably the Gunns—total 6.

From Ross have probably moved up the Mac Donalds, Rosses, MacKenzies, Mathesons, and Mac Raes—total 38.

From the opposite side of the Moray Firth have probably come the Murrays, Gordons, and Grants—total 29.

Presumably, then, the great majority of the population take their origin in what we may call the head and neck of Scotland, and an appreciable part of the remainder from what we may call its shoulder. Both these regions were originally peopled by the Picts (not by the Scots); and, although the Pictish element in the shoulder of Scotland has been diluted a good deal by a Lowland element, and in the head and neck of Scotland by Scottish inflows from the southwest and Norse inflows from the east, I see no reason to doubt that the Pictish element is still numerically dominant here, and in almost all parts of the Highlands except Argyll and its borders.

The mere names of clans, however, only afford a *presumption* as to the race of the persons bearing those names.   A MacRae *may* be a descendant of the Rae from whom his clan takes its name : much more probably he is only a descendant of a retainer or tenant of some chief or sub-chief of the clan.   And in the latter case, although the chances are that he belongs to the original stock of the district in which the clan is settled, he *may* be of any other stock in the wide world— and very possibly *is* a Norseman or a Lowlander.   Dr. Joass tells me that he knows of a case in which persons coming to Lochaber in the retinue of a bride changed their names of Green and O'Brien to Cameron, because they settled on the lands of a chief of that name.

And, as an evidence of the need of caution in drawing conclusions from *partial* statistics, I may mention that in the voters' list current in August, 1896, the Sutherlands had fallen to 11 while the Mackays had risen to 21.   The Murrays had fallen to 9, and the MacDonalds to 4, while the Munros had risen to 7, and the Frasers to 5.   The Munros are an East Ross clan, and the largest Fraser clan is in Invernessshire.

Their languages.   The language of Sutherland in ancient times was Pictish, the oldest form of Highland Gaelic.   The influx of English-speaking settlers, and the teaching of English in schools, have naturally diminished the prevalence of Gaelic, and in 1891 only 707 parishioners out of 1451 spoke Gaelic in addition to English, and only 464 villagers out of 951 ; while the number of parishioners who spoke Gaelic alone was but 6, and of villagers but 5.

No sensible man who wished the Highlander to live in intimacy and friendship with the other races which inhabit these isles, or who wished to see him cultivated and prosperous, would do otherwise than wish him to speak and read English well. But I hope the day will never come when Gaelic will become extinct in the Highlands, as unhappily Cornish was allowed to become extinct in the 18th century. In it are imbedded no small part of the Highlander's history—the history of his settlements, the history of his descent, the history of his thought, the history of his culture. It is not only bad for a race to forget such things, but it is bad for science too: no study of a dead language can recover for us all of that knowledge which would have been transmitted by its preservation. Every Highlander, every Irish Gael, every Manksman, and every Welshman, should know and speak the speech of his fathers, and should see that his children also know and speak it. And every government should show for all such healthy developments of race-feeling that sympathy which is the best bond of union.

As regards the Golspie dialect of English, I have had scarcely any opportunities of hearing it freely spoken among the bulk of the people themselves. But I believe that it has very little of the ' broad

Scots' about it. It belongs, of course, to that class
of dialects, prevailing from the more Northern counties of England upwards, in which the *a* in such
words as *fame* is not pronounced with that ' vanishing sound ' of the *ĭ* in *pin*, and the *o* in such words
as *note* is not pronounced with that ' vanishing
sound' of the *u* in *pull*, which South-English
speakers incorrectly give; in which *r* is not habitu-
ally degraded; and in which *wh* is still rightly
sounded as [1] *hw*, and not as *w* without any *h* at
all. On the other hand it has its faults—for instance,
the obscure pronunciation of *ĭ* and *u* in such
words as *nit*, *nut*, which makes the vowels almost
or quite indistinguishable from each other[2], and the
pronunciation of such a word as *mountain* as if it
were *mount'n*.

The pronunciation of *village* varies: J. S. said
villaj (with *a* as in *villa*), but B. C. *villij*. The
natural pronunciation of *outside our house* in
this district would be *ootside oor hoose*. B. C.,
when asked to read a sentence in which those
words occurred *as if she were talking to other
young folk and not as if she were reading out
of a book*, said *outside our house*, but, when
questioned, admitted that she usually said *ootside
oor hoose*. That shows the influence of the
School on the pronunciation given to written

---

[1] Until about 1300 the *wh-* class of words were (correctly)
written with *hw-*. To say *wen* for *when* is historically as bad as
to say *en* for *hen*.

[2] ' Him' and ' it ' when unemphatic are often very nearly *um*
and *ut*, even in the mouths of the most highly educated.

words. But J. S. not only *read* the words as *outside our house*, she said that that is her ordinary pronunciation, and that she does *not* say *ootside oor hoose*. That shows the influence of the School on the pronunciation of daily life. But both B. C. and J. S. pronounced *saw* (from 'see') as *sà*, which apparently represents the old preterite *sah*, a form earlier than *sauh* and *saw*.

Oo is sounded long, and final *-ng* (whatever its origin) usually as *-ng*, not as *-n*.

May dialect-pronunciation long survive—at least until we have a standard pronunciation fixed by a competent and authoritative body and systematically taught. Much is to be learnt from it of the history of our language and of the right and wrong ways of pronunciation, and—speaking as a Southron bred—I regard it as an unmixed piece of good fortune for the future of English that the first and still joint editor of the New English Dictionary should be a Lowlander.

Their education. Almost every boy or girl over 5 years old and under 15 attends the district school; but few, especially of the boys, stop beyond the latter age.

There was a time—not so very long ago, but before the present Code was in force—when, I am told, as many as a dozen boys[1] in the school were reading Homer. They were mostly sons of poor parents, and some at least of them became members of the learned professions. The Code

---

[1] Some of them, however, the master's boarders.

made that state of things impracticable for the time. I do not blame it : its object rightly was to give the children the highest average training, and not to push on the cleverest at the almost unavoidable cost of the less clever. But it was a grievous pity, all the same, that here and elsewhere children whose education might be much further advanced, to the improvement both of their culture and of their prospects in life, should be kept back in order that time might be found to work up the duller ones to a lower standard. Fortunately Golspie School is now a Centre of Secondary Education, and Homer can once more be read, as well as Latin, French, German, and English classics. It is pleasant to add that of the contributors to this book A. C. and M. S. are now pupil-teachers in the School, and that B. C., who has stayed on simply as a pupil, is not only 'dux' of it but is distinguished in its prospectus and prize-list as 'First Girl over all the Counties in the Highland Trust Bursary Competition for 1895.'

APPENDIX

THE ANGLO-CYMRIC SCORE

The following passages are extracted from Mr. A. J. Ellis's paper.

' The use of this Score in England is various. There is evidence of its having been used for scoring sheep, because not only is this frequently traditionally affirmed . . . but one of my informants actually heard it so used at Helmsley Blackmore near Scarborough . . . There is evidence that it is used by old women to count their stitches in knitting . . . Most people, however, merely recollect it as a strange piece of gibberish, which they retail from memory, extending sometimes more than fifty years back, and in the process necessarily either forget or alter the words, to which they attach no value or importance, regarding them as an idle curiosity. The Score in fact seems to have descended to be a plaything, especially of girls and boys at school, used for the purposes of " counting out " . . . Besides schoolboys, nurses seized hold of the Score to amuse babies and keep them quiet, or give them something to do . . .

It would seem to have existed over the old Cum-

brian kingdom, and to have been thence exported
. . . The principal area of this score would appear
to be Cumberland, Westmorland, the N.W. of
Lancashire, and N.W. of Yorkshire, with the adjoining part of Durham. There are traces in Roxburghshire, Renfrewshire, Northumberland, Mid,
East, and South Yorkshire, which may be all more
or less importations from the other area. When
S. Lancashire, East Lincolnshire, Epping, and, still
more strangely, North American India contribute
their quota, we may be sure that the versions given
are entirely exotic' (pp. 6-9).

'The names of the numerals 1. 4, 5, 10, 15, 20
can all be easily connected with the Welsh, but
what is most important is that the structure of the
names for 16, 17, 18, 19 as [1] 1 & 15, 2 & 15, 3 & 15,
4 & 15, is peculiar to the Welsh among all known
Celtic languages and probably all known languages.
This makes it indisputable that the origin of the
Score is Welsh, unless the language of the Strathclyde kingdom, of which I know and have as yet
been able to learn nothing, is the same[2]. If it is,
the Score may have sprung up in Strathclyde, as
has been suggested. But the absolute divergence
of the names for 2, 3, 6, 7, 8, 9 from any Celtic
type, invalidates the hypothesis of indigenous
growth and confirms the notion of importation '
(p. 26).

[1] He means that the Welsh for 16 means ' 1 & 15 ' and so on.
[2] The paramount Welsh tribe of N. Wales descended from the
north about the beginning of the 5th century.

The remarks about the numbers mentioned in this last sentence do not stand investigation. It is very surprising that Mr. Ellis should not have seen that the commonest forms of 2 and 3 diverge from the natural type only in such a way as to show that they have been altered to make rimes to 1 and 4. The numbers 6-9 are much harder, but Mr. Henry Bradley, in a review of Mr. Ellis's paper (published in *The Academy* of May 17, 1879) has satisfactorily established the Keltic connexion of these also. The following passages are extracted from Mr. Bradley's review.

'The preceding scheme has, I trust, made it evident that all the differing forms of the " Anglo-Cymric " numerals from 6 to 9 may (with two or three trifling exceptions) be traced to one common original, which may be given as *haita, saita, ova, dova*. . . .

I have often heard people count in English in the following manner :—" One, and two, and three, and four," &c. This in modern Welsh (taking the feminine forms to agree with the word *dafad*, sheep) would be " Un, a dwy, a thair, a phedair, a phump," &c. Repeated in this way, the numerals up to ten would sound to an English ear something like " Een, a dwee, a thair, a fedder, a fimp ; whaik, a saith, a ooith, a now, a deg." Under the influence of rhyme, this might easily be corrupted into " Eena, deena, tethera, fethera, fimp ; haitha, saitha, ova, nova, deg." For the change of *nova* into *dova* (produced), probably, by the following *d* in the word for ten), we may compare the Slavonic word for nine, *devyat.*

My conclusion on the whole is, that these "Anglo-Cymric" numerals are entitled to be regarded as a genuine remnant of the British dialect of the north-west of England, and as proving that that dialect was nearly identical with the oldest known Welsh. It seems, however, possible that the Cumbrian Celtic may have had *dî*, two; *hech*, six; *ôth*, eight; and *növ*, nine; but this is venturing on somewhat unsafe ground.'

The following observations of my own are printed as they stood before I had seen Mr. Bradley's, except that in (5) I have added the words ' and *four*,' and that I have re-written (6) to express my meaning better.

(1) The period during which the Welsh numerals may have been introduced extends at least as far back as the 5th century.

(2) The border-country over which they may have crept is extended from the English channel to the Clyde: for the Welsh kingdom of Strathclyde took in the entire S.W. of Scotland.

(3) They may have been introduced at the most diverse times and places, and by persons of different nationalities. In one part they may have been learnt in the 5th century from Welsh people who continued to live as free men among their Saxon conquerors (as we are now coming to believe that they very often did live) or from

Welsh who were captured in war. In another part they may have been learnt in modern times from an English child.

(4) We have consequently to take into account

    (a) not only the modern Welsh forms of the numerals, but their ancient forms, and

    (b) the sound-changes which have been going on in the various dialects of English.

(5) As regards the Welsh names for *two* and *three* and *four* we have to take into account that they have both a masculine and a feminine form, and that as used by Welsh children in counting girls they would not be quite the same as when used in counting boys.

(6) We have to allow for the possibility that the Welsh conjunction [1] *ac* or *a* ('and') was used between some of the numbers, *ac* before vowels and *a* before consonants.

(7) We have also to allow for the fact that when *a* is so used in *late mediaeval or modern* Welsh it causes a following *t* to change to *th* (= *th* in *thin*), and a following *p* to change to *ph*.

---

[1] In the Renfrewshire specimen printed by Mr. Ellis *a* is actually given: we get in it *tether a mether a bamf a* &c., i.e. *3 and 4 and 5 and* &c. From *bamf a* has arisen the *bank fore* of the Golspie version. Again the fact that the Welsh *ugen* (pronounced *igen*) almost always appears in the English rimes in a form beginning with a *g* or *k*, as *gigam* or *o kick cm*, points to its having been preceded by the conjunction *ac*.

ADDITIONAL COUNTING-OUT RIMES

The following 8 additional rimes in italics have been furnished to me by A. C.

(1) *Ease, oze,*
Man's brose :
Out goes she (or *he*).

Bolton's no. 653 is

Eze, oze,
Manze, broze,
Eze, oze, out!

This is from Portland, Oregon, and he says ' Obviously of German origin.' His reason seems to be that ' Ose, Pose ' is found in a German rime (269). His 680 is from the West of Scotland and is

Ease, ose,
Man's nose ;
Caul parritch,
Pease brose.

[1] Is this also ' obviously of German origin ' ?

---

[1] The 3rd line in the German ends with ' Packedich,' which is suspiciously like ' parritch.' Neither Bolton nor Simrock gives the source of the German rime : may not that be the borrowed one ?

(2) *Eetly, otly,*
    Black botlie :
    Out goes she (or *he*).

Are we to compare ' Eel-e, eel-e-ot ' on p. 229 ?

(3) *One, two, three :*
    Out goes she (or *he*).

This = the first two lines of Bolton's 416.

(4) *One, two, three ;*
    Mother caught a flea.
Flea died : mother ⎱⎰ *Flea died : mother*
    cried ! ⎰⎱   *cried*
Out goes she (or *he*). ⎱⎰ ' *Out goes she* (or *he*).'

The alternative punctuations which I have given of the last two lines allow the reader a choice between pathos and sarcasm. A. C. put no quotation-marks.

This is very nearly Bolton's 413, given from 4 American states ; compare also 414. ' Nanny ' and ' Granny ' are variants given by Bolton. Doubtless there is another version with ' Mammy,' the missing link between these and ' Mother.'

(5) *Tick, tack, toe,*
    Round I go,
    And if I miss
    I stop at this.

Bolton's 854 (' used by boys in the south

of Scotland and in the Lake districts of England ') is

> Tit, tat, toe,
> Here I go,
> And if I miss,
> I pitch on this.

(6) *Eeny, meeny, [1]many moe,*
Catch a nigger by the toe:
If he's good, let him go
—Eeny, meeny, many, moe.

This is very nearly Bolton's 600-603, one of which is from Edinburgh. But in the 3rd line they all give 'If' (*or* 'When ') 'he hollers' (*or* 'squeals ' *or* 'screams '). None of them gives 'many' but three have 'miny.'

(7) *Zeenty, teenty, [2]heligo, lum,*
Peelty, polty, peel a gum,
Franc'is in, Franc'is out:
I.—O.—the Laird of [3] Peasle p—o—pipe.

'Herricum is found in Bolton's 684 (Derbyshire) and 'Elligo' in his 598 (Maine), while 'heligo, lum,' is a variation of 'hick-ary hum' (Bolton's 443, 'hickory, hum' 451). We get 'peelers gum' followed by 'Francis' in his 470 (Virginia), and

---

[1] Pronounced 'may-ny.'
[2] Pronounced with *e* as in *hell*.
[3] Pronounced as if written *Peezle P O pipe.*

'pela' in his 642 (Montreal), as well as 'peela' on p. 219 of this book.

> (8) *'Mr. Mundy, how is your wife?'*
> *'Very sick, and like to die.'*
> *'Can she eat*
> *Any meat?'*
> *'Yes, as much as you can buy.*
> *A plate of porridge very thin:*
> *A pound of butter you'll put in.'*
> *Bake a pudding, bake a pie*
> *—Stand you out by.*

The two following variants used south of the Moray Firth are given by Gregor (pp. 170, 173, 175).

> "'Mr. Mundie, [1] foo's yir wife?'
> 'Verra sick, an like t'die.'
> 'Can she eat ony butcher meat?'
> 'Yes; more than I can buy.
> Half a horse, half a coo,
> Half three-quarters o' a soo.
> She mak's her pottage very thin;
> A pound o' butter she puts in.'
> [2] Fite puddin, black troot,
>   Ye're oot."

> "'Mr. Mungo, [1] foo's yir wife?'
> 'Very sick an like t'die.'
> 'Can she eat any butcher meat?'
> 'Yes; more than I can buy.

---

[1] How's.   [2] White.

Half a sow,
Half an ox, half a quarter of a cow ;
She likes her porridge very thin,
A pound of butter she puts in.
I choose you oot
For a penny pie, put."

    " ' Mr. Murdoch, how's your wife ? '
    ' Very ill, and like to die.'
    ' Can she eat any meat ? '
    ' Yes, as much as I can buy ;
    She makes her porritch very thin,
    Pounds o' butter she puts in.'
    Black fish, [1] fite troot,
    Eerie, aarie, ye're oot."

What was the real name of this interesting
female ? All versions agree that it began with
Mu, but was it Mundie, Mungo, or Murdoch ? It
seems to me that the last is the form which best
explains the others : pronounced with a trilled
Scottish *r* it is not an easy name to ' catch ' in
a district where it is uncommon.

Mr. Udal gives the two following from Dorset
(*Folk-lore journal*, v, p. 253) :—

    (1) " ' Doctor, Doctor, how's your wife ? '
    ' Very bad upon my life.'
    ' Can she eat a bit of pie ? '
    ' Yes, she can as well as I.' "

---

[1] White.

(2) " ' [1] Gargy, Pargy, how's yer wife ? '
    ' Very bad upon my life.'
    ' Can she ait a bit o' pie ? '
    ' Ees, sa well as you or I.' "

The latter of these is used as a counting-out rime.

[1] Doubtless pronounced ' Jargey.' ' Jargey-pargey ' would = our old friend ' Georgey-porgey.'

¹GLOSSARY TO THE CONTRIBUTIONS

A. Corrupted from *at*, p. 185.

Allow . . . see. Allow to see, p. 69.

Am to. Am about to, p. 25.

An. And, p. 185.

Anyone is not. People are not, p. 98.

Are. (? Burlesque for) Am, p. 231.

Bairns. Children, p. 239.

Baps. (Corrupted from Paps?) Blows, p. 122.

Belt. Part of a ship, p. 190, where see note.

Blaws. Blows (verb), p. 240

Bothy. Rudely furnished shed, p. 15. Pronounced with *o* as in *bother*, but *th* as in *both*.

Brunny. Brownie (a kind of elf), p. 17. Pronounced *broony*.

Bullie Horn. Name of a game, p. 117.

Buttony. Name of a game, p. 118.

Byre. Cow-house, pp. 64, 65, &c.

Cans. Chimney-pots, p. 92.

Clapping. Knocking, p. 30.

Coocoo. Cuckoo, p. 62.

Decent. Good, p. 26.

Deil. Devil, p. 39.

Demanded. 'Was demanded . . . to come' = 'Was ordered . . . to come,' p. 81.

Done on. Done to, p. 80.

¹ By far the greatest part of these spellings, words, or phrases, needed no explanation, and those which did need any have already been explained by me. They are brought together here simply for the sake of those interested in the study of English.

Doon. Down (adverb), p. 241.

Far and few. Few and far between, p. 26.

[Full? Fill, p. 98, note.]

Gangs. Goes, p. 241.

Giggie. (?) Little gig (spinning-top), p. 120.

Go under. Undergo, p. 118.

Gollo. (?) Corrupted from French *galop*, 'gallop,' pp. 158, 162, where 'lily gollo' = *petit galop*, our 'canter.'

Got. Have got, p. 103.

Gowk. Fool, p. 109.

Gowking-day. April Fools' day, p. 109.

Greedly. Greedily, p. 17.

Guising. Disguising oneself, p. 99.

Happen one. Happen to one, p. 65.

Have. Half, p. 239.

Have . . . safe. Keep . . . safe, p. 103.

Hile-posts. Goal-posts, in game of Shinty, p. 116.

Hiles. Goals, in game of Shinty, p. 116.

Hilli ballu. [Hullaballoo], pp. 176, 182 84.

Hog(o)manay. New Year's eve, pp. 100, 104-8.

Horn. Nail of finger or toe, p. 66. See also 'Bullie.'

Housie meetie (mettie). 'Rounders,' p. 116.

Hull. Holl, i. e. hollow, concave, p. 185.

Is. (?) Are, pp. 84, 97.

Jeu. Jew, p. 242.

Kilpies. Kelpies (demon-horses), pp. 17, 24, 332.

Liftet. Lifted, p. 38.

Like to be. Likely to be, p. 241.

Lily. Little, pp. 158, 162.

Loving-silver. Name of a plant, p. 156, note.

Mains. Farm attached to a mansion, p. 40.

Make damage to. Do damage to, p. 103.

Man. Corrupted from *mon (e)*, i. e. *moon*, p. 185.

Manie. „ „ *monie*, i.e. *moon-ie*, ' little moon,' p. 185.

Milkhouse. Dairy, p. 80.

Mischevious. Mischievous, p. 93.

Mischief (The). Satan, p. 242.

No sooner than ... than. No sooner ... than, p. 26.

On the Christmas week. In Christmas week, p. 26.

„ one bed. With one bed, one-bedded, p. 27.

Paps. Blows, p. 122.

Porter Lodge (= Porter-lodge ?). Porter's Lodge, p. 40.

Pot. Hop-scotch, p. 115.

Presently. At present, p. 81.

Rodin-trees. Rowan-trees, mountain-ashes, p. 27.

's. Has (plural), p. 340.

Shiney. Ball, in game of Shinty, p. 116.

Skeby. Name of a game, p. 120. Pronounced *skĕĕby*.

Spague. Name of a game, p. 116. Rimes with *plague*.

The day. Next day, p. 15.

Thumble. Thimble, p. 121.

Till you take. Till you have taken, p. 27.

To bed. In bed, p. 27.

Trembulos. Tremulous, p. 38.

Waiting on. Waiting for, p. 29.

Was. (? Burlesque for) Be (infinitive), p. 231.

Wee. *Wi'*, i. e. *with*, p. 157.

¹ RIMES, GAMES, Etc.,

IN CHAMBERS'S 'POPULAR RHYMES OF SCOTLAND'

KNOWN TO A. C. OR B. C.

(before they had read that book)

†p. 19 I had a little pony &c.
†p. 20 This is the man &c.
†p. 24 The wife put on &c.
†p. 35 Katie Beardie had &c.
 p. 108 Pease-porridge &c.
 p. 109 Riddle me, riddle me &c.
†p. 114 Cripple Dick upon &c.
†p. 116 Put your finger in &c.
†p. 116 This is my lady's &c.
 p. 122 Who goes round &c.
†p. 123 How many miles &c.
†p. 136 Here's a poor widow &c.
†p. 139 A dis, a dis, a green &c.
†p. 154 The Gunpowder &c.
†p. 165 Get up goodwife &c.
 p. 182 Rain, rain &c.
†p. 184 Rain rain rattle-stanes &c.
 p. 371 Till May be out &c.
†p. 383 Some say the deil's dead &c.
 p. 379 A rainbow in the morning &c.
†p. 389 Some hae meat &c.
 p. 393 Multiplication is a vexation &c.

---

¹ I mark with a † all those which were unknown to me except from books : I had an English West-Midland mother.

¹RIMES

IN HALLIWELL'S NURSERY RHYMES

KNOWN TO A. C. OR B. C.

(before they had read that book)

¹ I mark with a † all that were unknown to me except from books.

†CLXXXI (p. 47) I'll sing you a song &c.

CCIX (p. 51) Little Nancy Etticoat &c.

CCXVIII (p. 52) Pease-porridge hot &c.

†CCXIX (p. 52) As I was going o'er Westminster Bridge &c.

CCXXVIII (p. 53) Elizab th, Elspeth, Betsy and Bess &c.

CCXXIX (p. 53) As I was going to St. Ives &c.

CCXL (p. 54) Matthew, Mark, Luke and John &c.

CCLIII (p. 56) There was an old woman who lived in a shoe &c.

CCLXV (p. 58) Old mother Hubbard &c.

†CCLXXVIII (p. 61) Who goes round my house this night? &c.

†CCCV (p. 66) There were two blackbirds &c.

CCCXIII (p. 67) Ride a cock-horse to Banbury cross &c.

†CCCXXVIII (p. 70) How many miles is it to Babylon?—&c.

†CCCXXIX (p. 70) Clap hands, clap hands! &c.

†CCCXXXVII (p. 71) Here sits the Lord Mayor &c.

†CCCXXXVIII (p. 72) Ring the bell &c.

†CCCLXXXI (p. 81) Dance, little baby &c.

†CCCXCI (p. 82) Rock-a-bye baby &c.

CCCXCIV (p. 83) Hush-a-bye baby &c.

CCCCVI (p. 85) Ding, dong, bell &c.

CCCCLXIV (p. 92) Jack Sprat could eat no fat &c.

CCCCLXXXV (p. 97) Jack and Jill &c.

†CCCCXCV (p. 99) The cuckoo's a fine bird &c.

†DXXXII (p. 103) Once I saw a little bird &c.

DLXXVIII (p. 108) I like little pussy &c.

A DICTIONARY OF THE KILMALY OGAM-STONE

For the satisfaction of students of language, and of everyone who knows Gaelic, I shall here explain fully all the words in this inscription, and shall illustrate them as far as possible from all the other Old Highland Gaelic (' Pictish ') inscriptions which are yet known.

Including the Kilmaly stone, there are 22 inscriptions, or, if we include a Latin postscript to one of them, 23. They are all cut on stones.

The following is a list of the stones and inscriptions in northward order [1].

Those marked * are in the National Museum of Antiquities, Queen st., Edinburgh. Those marked † are on properties within a few miles (at furthest) of their original site. **C** is within a few yards from

---

[1] See my work on 'The vernacular inscriptions of the ancient kingdom of Alban' (London, B. Quaritch, 15 Piccadilly, 1896), and my letter on 'Three unpublished Pictish inscriptions' in *The Academy* of May 23, 1896. The stones for which capitals are used, as **A**, are included in my book; those denoted by small letters (a[1], a[2], a[3], h) have become known to me since.

where it first stood; so, probably, is a^3 (which was found face downwards under the surface in 1822); while apparently **D** has never been moved.

All the inscriptions are in Ogam letters, except a^1, a^3, **C**, G^2, and G^3, which are in varieties of the Roman alphabet.

a^1. †The Annet Burn stone (Perthshire)—now at Doune Lodge.

a^2. †The Coillechat Burn stone (Perthshire)—now at Doune Lodge.

a^3. The Greenloaning stone (Perthshire).

A. *The Scoonie stone (Fife).

B. *The Abernethy fragment (Perthshire).

C. The St. Vigean's stone, near Arbroath (Forfarshire).

D. The Easter Aquhollie stone, near Stonehaven (Kincardineshire).

E. †The Aboyne fragment (Aberdeenshire)—now in the grounds of Aboyne Castle.

F. †The Carden Moor stone (Aberdeenshire)—now in the grounds of Logie Elphinstone, near Pitcaple.

G^1.
G^2.
G^3. } †The Shevack stone (Aberdeenshire)—now in the grounds of Newton House, near Pitcaple.

h. †The Burghead stone (Elginshire).

H[1].
H[2]. } †The Dyke stone (Elginshire)—now in the
H[3]. } grounds of Brodie Castle, near Forres.

I.   †The Kilmaly stone (Sutherland)— now in the museum in Dunrobin gardens, Golspie.

J.   *The Burrian stone (North Ronaldsha, Orkney).

K.   *The St. Ninian's stone (St. Ninian's Isle, Shetland).

L.   *The Culbinsgarth stone (Bressay, Shetland isles).

M.   *The larger Conningsburgh fragment (Mainland, Shetland).

N.   *The smaller Conningsburgh fragment (Mainland, Shetland).

O.   *The Lunasting stone (Mainland, Shetland).

*a*hta, **aihta, ehte**, &c. [Irish *áite*, *áit*, Highland, *áite*[1], *áit*, ' place,' ' dwelling']. Subs. (masc.), ' place,' or ' tenement.'

I. 2-*syllable forms*. (1) a[2], **ahtè** (doubtful). (2) M, **ehte** *Con Morr*—apparently in apposition with preceding loc.-dat. *èt*. (3) F, **ahta** (angled *a*'s)—in apposition with preceding loc.-dat. pl. (4) a[1], **aihta**. (5) G[2], **ættæ** *Æc Nun Vavr*.

The various endings are due to the word belonging to the Irish declension of stems in *ia*

---

[1] The normal Highland pronunciation I don't know, but sometimes it is *áihte*, in the North Highlands at any rate : so I learn from Dr. Joass, who suggested the identification to me.

Y

(for Irish *aite* made pl. acc. *aittiu*). In that declension terminal -*e* sometimes becomes -*æ* and sometimes -*a* : thus we have both *cumachte* and *cumachtæ*, *dalte* and *dalta*.

II. 1-*syllable forms*. (1) A, eht *arr bavonn* : D, (?) e(ht)—followed by unaspirated loc.-dat. pl. *Tedov* (?). (2) H³, ehht. (3) E, *n*èhht (on the *n* see Nicholson, Append. p. 88) followed by aspirated loc.-dat. pl. *Vrobbaccènnevv*. (4) O, *a h*-èhhtt (for prosthetic *h* see Nicholson, p. 44, under a). (5) O, ètt. (6) C, ett—followed by aspirated loc.-dat. sing. *Forcus*. (7) M, *d*'èt—loc.-dat. sing. governed by prep. *d*'. (8) a³, (perhaps) ait. (9) G¹, aedd *Aiq N'nn Vor*, where idd is a possible alternative reading (see Nicholson, Append. p. 69). (10) H³, edd *arr bavonn* : I, *Allhhallorr*, edd *M'qq Nu Uvvarrcech* [1].

In aedd (or idd), ètt, ett, and edd the doubling may be simply due to assimilation of the original *h* to the following dental : and in Irish we get the forms *aidde* (sing. nom.) and *aittiu* (pl. acc.). But in èhht, ehht, ehhtt this cannot be so, and we must suppose the *e* to be *ĕ*: it is the infected *a* written in Irish *ai*,

---

[1] In only one of these examples is the case quite certain, i.e. in II. 7, where it is governed by a preposition. In I. 5 and II. 9 it aspirates a following masc. gen. proper name (*Æc* and *Aiq = Mhæc* and *Mhaiq*), but so it might if it were a nominative. In II. 3. 6 it aspirates a following proper name, but possibly only in composition with it. In I. 2 the apposition with a preceding dat. is not quite certain, because the two lines may be two separate inscriptions.

and in Ulster pronounced *ĕ*. For the ordinary meaning of doubled consonants in these inscriptions is that the preceding vowel is short.

The word occurs in the 12th century Gaelic entries in the Book of Deer as *ét* in the place-name *étdanin*, i. e. ' place of two forks,' doubtless = ' place of two cross roads ' (for *nin*, ' fork,' see the dictionary to Windisch's *Irische Texte*).

The derivation of *àite* is unknown, but the forms with medial *h* show that it represents a*h-te*, *aih-te*, in which *-te* must be a suffix, and *h* arise from aspiration of some other consonant. Are we to connect a*h* and *aih* with Highland *àth* and Old Irish *áith*?[1] both of which now mean ' kiln ' but may perhaps once have meant merely ' fire[2].' Or are we to compare Old Irish *áed*, *áed*, ' fire,' and Modern Irish *aodh*,—taking our *h* to arise out of an older *dh* ?

Or, as initial Indo-European *p* is lost in native Gaelic words, should we turn to the root (*p*)*et*, ' stretch '[3]? which appears in Greek as *pet-*, in Latin as *pat-*, and from which Stokes and Macbain derive Gaelic *aitheamh*, ' fathom.'

Or are we to suggest (as I find Macbain has already) the same root as that of the Greek *pedon*, ' ground '? In that case also the *h* would

---

[1] *Th* is pronounced *h* both in Highland and in Irish.

[2] O'Reilly gives an Irish fem. *athan*, ' fire,' but he cannot be depended on.

[3] Cf. from root (*p*)*et*, ' fly,' O. Ir. *áith*, ' wing,' and *ette*, *ette* (= aith + te, Ascoli, *Glossarium*, p. xlix), ' wing.' Ascoli also holds that there is an O. Ir. *aith* (genitive *atho*), ' area, field.'

arise out of an older *dh*. Macbain compares early Irish *ed*, ' space,' Highland *eadh*.

Allhhallorr [Old Norse *al-* ' all,' ' completely,' and *hallr* ' slope [1] '] subs., ' all-slope,' ' complete slope'—Norse proper name of a Sutherland homestead subsequently occupied by a Pict.

Sing. nom. masc., **Allhhallorr, I**(*Allhhallorr edd M'qq Nu*). The *o* represents a vowel which was lost before Old Norse took literary form.

The doubling of the consonants is to be explained as follows.

The *o* was of course short, as it is lost altogether in Old Norse MSS.; but the inscription **L** *begins* with the word *crræscc*, where *r* is doubled without *any* vowel preceding it. The remaining double consonants indicate that the two *a*'s were short. Cf. Cleasby and Vigfusson, *Icelandic-English Dictionary*, p. 1, ' *a* and *á* . . . sound short if followed by two or more strong consonants (a double mute or liquid): thus the *a* and *á* sound . . . short in . . . *hǎll, lubricus*.'

èdd. See *ahta*.

[**Maqq**] [Old Irish (Ogams) *maqq-i*, *maq-i* (genitives); (MSS.) *macc, mac*; Highland *mac*]. Subs. masc., ' son,' used in proper names.

Sing. nom. Not found in our inscriptions unless we divided in **E** *Maqq Oi Talluorr*.

---

[1] I should have said the adjective *hallr* ' sloping,' but that my friend Prof. York Powell tells me a Norse homestead would hardly be named by an adjective without some accompanying substantive.

Sing. gen. (1) *unaspirated*, **Meqq**, K (*Les Meqq Nan*), L (*ann Berniases Meqqddrroi-ann*); **M'qq**, I (*edd M'qq Nu Uvvarrecch*).

Sing. gen. (2) *aspirated* (occasional after subs. or loc.-dat. sing.?), **Aiq**, G¹ (*aedd Aiq N"nn Vor*); **Æc**, G² (*ætæ Æc Nun Vaur*), h (*Æc Bœad*). Here *m* has been aspirated into *mh*, pronounced *u* or *v*, and this *u* or *v* has been dropped. So the modern Highlander for *Mac Mhic*—'son of Mac—' often says *Mac Ic*—.

B apparently has *qmi*=(*Meq*)*q* or (*Maq*)*q Mi* . . .

The doubling of the *q* in an inscription so late as the Kilmaly one is probably due to the short-ness of the preceding vowel. But in Old Irish, which does not seem to double consonants on this principle, it is probably due to the loss of a final *u*.

The mark which denotes the omission of the vowel in the Kilmaly stone is ⁄. It is only found here and in the genitive *N'nn* (**G¹**) where it represents the omission of an *u* (**G²** has *Nun*) or obscure vowel. In the Kilmaly stone of course it represents an omitted *e* or *i*. In each case it is attached to the foot of the first stroke in the following consonant—thus, in **G¹** ⫲ and in the Kilmaly stone ⫳.

Nu? nu? Found only in a man's name:—
  Sing. gen. **Nu? nu?**, I (**M'qqnu**).
Prof. Rhŷs called my attention long since to

the similarity between this and Mac Naue in the following passage of Adamnan's Life of Columba (*præf.* II):—'cuius pater Latine Filius Nauis dici potest, Scotica uero lingua Mac Naue.'

The person alluded to is stated in the genealogy given by Bishop Reeves, Adamnan's editor, to have been the son of a man named 'Nave' (rather Naue) or 'Noe.'

Assuming such an Irish name as Naue, it might pass into Nue as *aue* became *oa* and *ua*, or as *gau* became *gó* and *gú*. The reduction of a nom. *Nue* to *Nu* raises no difficulty, as we have abundant instances in Old Irish and Pictish of dropped -*e* in nom. and dat.

To take M'qqnu as literally='son of a ship,' i.e. sailor, or ship-builder [1] is tempting, but can the -*e* of the Old Irish gen. *naue*, *noe* be dispensed with?

[**Nu**]. The possible nominative of the following proper names:—

Sing. gen. **Nun**, G[2] (*Æc Nun*), **N'nn**, G[1] (*Aiq N'nn*), **Non**, D (*Vi Non*).

Cf. Old Irish *brú* nom. to the gen. *brunn* and *bronn*, *cú* nom. to the gen. *con*.

[**uvar**] [Old Irish *úabar*, Modern Irish and Highland *uabhar*]. Subs. masc., 'pride, arrogance, vain-glory, pomp,' perhaps also 'high spirit.'

Found only in its derivative adj. **uvarracch**, which see.

---

[1] In L the man's name *Meqqddrroiann* (genitive case) seems to = *Micdroghan*, i.e. 'line-fisher' or 'fishingline-maker.'

[Uvarracch] [Old Irish *úabrech*, Modern Irish *uabhrach*, *uaibhreach*, Highland *uabharach*, *uaibreach*]. Adj., ' proud,' ' spirited.'

Sing. gen. masc. **Uvvarrecch**, used as part of proper name, I (*edd M'qq Nu · Uvvarrecch*). The shortening of the *U* (indicated by doubling the *v*) is caused by the previous *u* in *Nu*.

The doubling of the *r* may or may not be due to the shortness of the *a* : see above under **Allhhallorr**.

The final *cch* represents the doubling of *ch* after a short vowel: thus in **O** aspirated initial *c*, when doubled after a short vowel in the previous word, becomes not *chch* but *hcc*.

The exact shade of meaning in the above case is uncertain. Windisch gives the Old Irish as ' übermüthig, prahlerisch '; O'Reilly the Modern Irish as ' proud, haughty, arrogant, vain-glorious '; the Highland Society's Dict. the Highland as ' proud, haughty, vain-glorious, spirited, full of spirit.' Its ambiguity is not lessened by the fact that ' Alexander the Great is always called " Uaibhreach " in Gaelic' (Nicolson, *Gaelic Proverbs*, p. 165, quoted by Kuno Meyer on the line ' feart Alaxandair uaibhrigh,' *Eine irische Version der Alexandersage*, p. 3).

Uvvarrecch. See **Uvarracch.**

THE COMPETITION AND THE CONTRIBUTORS

The following rules which I wrote will show what was in my own mind: in any similar competition the rules should be printed and a copy given to each competitor.

"I. Mention all the games played by children in Golspie. And describe any that have not got well-known names.

[For instance, if Golspie children play cricket, football, hop-scotch, or rounders, mention those games but do not describe them, because they are well-known all over the country. But describe the game in which children dance in a ring and then turn and dance the other way, because that is not well-known all over the country.]

II. Write out all the [1] rhymes and sayings that Golspie children use, *and say when it is that they use each of them.* If any are in Gaelic, write the

---

[1] I wrote 'rhymes' here so as not to puzzle the boys and girls. But I may tell them that 'rime' is the only proper spelling of the word—which has nothing whatever to do with the word 'rhythm.'

Gaelic and then turn it into English. Be sure not to forget the rhymes you use in your games.

III. Write out all the songs you know, or can find out, that you think have never been printed, and, if the words are Gaelic, write the English underneath. If you know how to write the tunes, write the tunes as well.

IV. If any stories are told in Golspie about fairies or ghosts, or the like, or any other curious old stories, write them out in English. If they are really Gaelic, say so, but [1] do not write the Gaelic—only the English of it.

> [You must not write down stories that are printed in books. For instance, you must not write down Jack the Giant-Killer, or stories which are in the Arabian Nights, or in Andersen's Fairy-tales, or in the histories of Scotland.]

V. If anyone in Golspie believes in witchcraft, or charms, or in stones and plants and trees and water having magical power, or in lucky and unlucky times and animals and things, write down

---

[1] This direction may seem a very mistaken one. But Gaelic is spelt so very unphonetically that few Gaelic speakers can write it—and the Gaelic stories sent in might have turned out to be almost or quite the same as stories of which Campbell has already printed the Gaelic: if not, it would have been easy for me to ask for the Gaelic afterwards.

what it is that is believed, and say whether most or many people believe it or only a few.

VI. Write an account of all the curious customs used in Golspie at different times of the year, such as [1] 'gizing.'

You may get as much information as you like from anyone else. But please say who told you each thing, and how old that person is. *And nothing at all must come out of books.*

You must compose your essay yourself. *Please write everything just as you would tell it in Golspie*, and do not try to write it as if you were writing a book. And do not change any words that you use because you think they are not found in books : for instance, if you speak about ' fog on a stone ' do not alter it to ' moss on a stone.' "

I also said " I may perhaps print what I think worth printing, and then I should also print the names of the children from whom I had got it. I will give 10*s*. for the best essay, and if there is a good second essay I will give 5*s*.[2] for that. And, if many boys and girls try, then I will give more than two prizes. All the essays sent in will belong to me to do as I like with."

---

[1] I had only heard the word once or twice, and did not see that it was 'guising.'

[2] Raised on seeing it.

The competitors were

Order of age	Place gained	Name	Age	Father's occupation	Parents Gaelic-speaking
1	1	Annie Cumming	15	Blacksmith	Both
4	2	Bella Cumming	13	,,	,,
3	3	Jane Stuart	13	Railway-surfaceman	,,
2	4	Willie W. Munro	14	Labourer	{ Mother can speak Father can understand
5	5	Andrew Gunn	13	Shoemaker	Neither
6	6 {	Henri J. MacLean	12	Draper, &c.	Father
7	{	Minnie Sutherland	12	Reporter	Both

In Stories, the first three were Jane Stuart, Annie Cumming, and A. Gunn. In Superstitions, the sisters Cumming were equal, and next to them Jane Stuart and H. J. MacLean also equal. In Customs the sisters Cumming were again equal, and W. W. Munro third. In rimeless Games the first three were W. W. Munro, Annie Cumming, and Bella Cumming. In Rimes, Annie Cumming, Bella Cumming, and Jane Stuart. And in Sayings A. Gunn, W. W. Munro, and Bella Cumming.

The competitors came out very nearly in order of age. The only noticeable exception was that of W. W. M., whose natural advantage over B. C. and J. S. in rimeless Games was far more than counterbalanced by their natural advantage over him in rimed ones.

Each competitor received a money-prize and a book.

ADDITIONAL NOTES TO THE CONTRIBUTIONS

Derivation of ' kilpie,' 'kelpie ' (p. 24).

The dictionaries I have consulted about this are either ridiculous or helpless. It is obviously derived from *kilpe, kilp*, or *kelp*, a name of various kinds of seaweed. About *kilp* or *kelp* itself they are equally ignorant. That again is obviously the Middle English *kelp* or *kilp* ' scabbard,' preserved in the name of the ' kelp-pigeon ' or ' sheathbill.' One of the commonest of our seaweeds is the very image of a pointed mediaeval scabbard, and doubtless from this, when the meaning ' scabbard ' became extinct, the name spread to other varieties.

The Old Gaelic (Old Irish) for ' horse ' is *ech*. Th re was also an Irish *oiche* = ' water,' and as Irish *oi* was dialectally pronounced *ĕ*, while the final *ĕ* of substantives was often dropped, it is quite possible that this also was sometimes pronounced *ech*, and that the confusion of sound assisted the notion that boys who were drowned when bathing by *kilp* or water-weed were the victims of a sub-aqueous horse whose mane floated on the surface.

Dread of the hare (p. 55).

Hazlitt in his *Popular antiquities of Great Britain* (iii, p. 191) says ' An opinion was formerly entertained both in England and abroad, that a hare crofling the path of any one was a portent of misfortune, and a warning to return, or retrace

one's fteps.' He gives references, and quotes a
passage from Sir Thomas Browne in which the
latter says ' the ground of the conceit was probably
no greater than this, that a fearful Animal paffing
by us, portended unto us fomething to be feared.'

Monday unlucky (p. 67).

I find the following instances of the supposed
unluckiness of Monday on pp. 30-33 of vol. ii of
W. C. Hazlitt's *Popular antiquities of Great
Britain*.

In 1617 Moryson says that the king and queen
of Poland lost many fair winds at Dantzic in 1593,
because they were afraid to sail on Mondays
or Fridays. Lord Burghley in 1636 mentioned
3 Mondays as having an unlucky repute—the first
Monday in April (when Cain was born and Abel
killed!), the second Monday in August (when
Sodom and Gomorrah were destroyed!), and the
last Monday in December (when Judas was born!).
On the last Monday in December — and on
March 22 and Aug. 20 when they fell on a Monday
—it was considered improper to eat goose, to be
bled, or to take a draught of medicine. ' Among
the Finns whoever undertakes any business on a
Monday or Friday must expect very little success.'
Finally, all Caithness gentlemen of the name of
Sinclair hold Monday unlucky because they crossed
the Ord on a Monday when going to Flodden
Field. So Hazlitt—who gives references for these
statements.

Witches as hares (p. 76).

In 1808 the Countess of Sutherland (the ' Duchess-Countess ') writes :

' You know that the last witch burned in Scotland suffered in Dornoch, to our everlasting shame, in 1722. Her daughter, a fishwife in a village about eight miles from hence, happened to have burned her hands when a child, which contracted her fingers, and the common people ascribed that misfortune to her mother's witchcraft, and imagined that this creature [1] could turn herself into a poney, and that being shod by the devil occasioned this blemish. Lord Stafford to-day, in walking near their village, met a man (a beggar) with his hands in that form, the son of this fishwife and grandson of the witch ; and the descendants of that family are still feared in the neighbourhood from that old *liaison* ' (Sir W. Fraser, *The Sutherland book,* i, p. 485).

Dornoch is only 8 miles from Golspie, and is the county-town of Sutherland—hence ' to our everlasting shame.' And in Dunrobin woods, close to the Gallows-hill, is a pit where the sink-or-swim test is said to have been applied to supposed witches.

The date of the judicial murder at Dornoch was apparently even later than the Duchess-Countess thought: for in Burt's anonymous ' Letters from a gentleman in the North of Scotland ' we have the following (1754 ed., i, p. 281):

[1] Dr. Joass tells me that it was also supposed that her mother had turned her into a pony in order to ride upon her.

' In the Beginning of the Year 1727, two poor Highland Women (Mother and Daughter) in the Shire of *Sutherland*, were accused of *Witchcraft*, tried and condemned to be burnt. This Proceeding was in a Court held by the Deputy Sheriff. The young one made her Escape out of Prison, but the old Woman suffered that cruel Death, in a Pitch-Barrel, in *June* following, at *Dornoch*, the *Head Borough* of that County.'

Burt was General Wade's agent in Scotland in 1724-8 and writes from Inverness. Although his letters were not printed till 1754, the ' Dictionary of National Biography ' says that evidence in them shows they were written in 1725 6. The above passage must have been written at least as late as 1727, but we may at any rate take him as a contemporary authority.

As regards the origin of the belief that witches were particularly fond of turning themselves into *hares*, I have seen no explanation of it; and in Scot's famous ' Discoverie of witchcraft ' (1584) the hare is not mentioned among the animals into which witches were supposed to transform them- selves—their favourite shapes being those of the wolf and the cat.

But Mr. J. Hutt, of the Bodleian, searching for me for such an explanation, has come across the following very interesting passages in Pitcairn's ' Ancient criminal trials in Scotland,' iii. pt. 2, pp. 602-611 :

'Confessions *of Iſobell Gowdie, Spous to John Gilbert, in Lochloy.*

(1.) Issobell Gowdies first confession. At Aulderne, the threttein day of Aprill, 1662 yeiris ' (p. 602).

'*Elſpet Chiſsholme* and *Iſobell More,* in Aulderne, *Magie Brodie,* . . . . . . , and I, went in to *Allexander Cumings* litt-hows [16], in Aulderne. I went in, in the likenes of a kea [17], the ſaid *Elſpet Chiſolm* wes in the ſhape of a catt. *Iſobell Mor* wes a hair, and *Magie Brodie* a catt ' (p. 605).

Again, at p. 607, in ' (2.) Issobell Gowdies second confession':—

'Qwhen we goe in the ſhape of an haire, we ſay thryſe owr :

'I sall goe intill ane haire,
With ſorrow, and ſych, and meikle caire ;
And I ſall goe in THE DIVELLIS nam,
Ay whill I com hom [againe!]'

And inſtantlie we ſtart in an hair. And when we wold be owt of that ſhape, we will ſay :

'Haire, [haire, God ſend thé caire!]
I am in an hairis liknes juſt now,
Bot I ſalbe in a womanis liknes ewin [now.]' '

Again, at p. 611, in ' (3.) Issobell Gowdies third confession ':—

'He [the Divell] wold ſend me now and then to Aulderne ſom earandis to my neightbouris, in the ſhape of ane hair. I wes on morning, abowt

---

' [16] Dye-houſe.' ' [17] Jackdaw.'

the break of day, going to Aulderne in the fhap of
ane hair, and Patrik Papleyis Serwandis, in Kilhill,
being goeing to ther labouring, his houndis being
with them, ran efter me, being in the fhape of an
haire. I ran werie long, bot wes forcet, being
wearie, at laft to take my own hous. The dore
being left open, I ran in behind an chift, and the
houndis followed in ; bot they went to the vther
fyd of the chift ; and I was forcet to run furth
agane, and wan into an vther hows, and thair took
leafour to fay,

> ' Hair, hair, God fend thé cair !
> I am in a hearis liknes now,
> Bot I fall be an voman ewin now !
> Hair, hair, God fend thé cair !'

And fo I returned to my owin fhap, as I am at
this inftant, again. The dowgis will fom tymes
get fom byttis [1] of vs, quhan ve ar in hairis [2], bot
will not get ws killed. Quhan ve turn owt of a
hairis liknes to owr awin fhap, we will haw the
byttis, and rywis, and fcrattis [3] in owr bodies.'

The 'confessions' (four in number) of this unfortunate creature fill 13 closely printed quarto
pages. We don't know whether she was tortured
or frightened into making them ; whether she made
them in the hope of saving her life ; whether, feeling
that she had no chance of escape, she conceived
a delight in magnifying her own importance as a

---

[1] ' Bites.'   [2] ' In the shape of hares.'
          [3] ' Tears and scratches.'

witch and in gulling her persecutors; or whether, as Sir Walter Scott thinks, she was simply a lunatic. The freedom with which she implicates other persons by name would make it charitable to believe that this last solution is the true one. But, if any-one wants to see how confessions of witchcraft *were* sometimes obtained, let him read the 9th of Sir Walter's 'Letters on demonology and witchcraft,' and a similar confession, though less detailed and extraordinary, was made by Janet Breadheid, one of the same accused parties. It is, however, possible that there were women and men who actually tried to become witches and wizards[1], and that there were men who associated with the women in a disguise intended to represent the Devil. When such persons were accused, having no innocent conscience to give them hope of deliverance, they may have delighted in publishing tales of imaginary achievements.

Whether Issobell Gowdie's story about the hares was her own invention or a repetition of earlier superstitions, it is clear that the belief goes back as far as 1662 at Auldearn. Auldearn is in Nairnshire, which you can actually see from the high

---

[1] Nor was it very hard for them to acquire a belief in their own power. It was so easy to 'wish ill to one's neighbour,' and, if the wish was realized, to mistake a coincidence for a consequence; while in the contrary event it was equally easy to suppose that the wish had been defeated by counter-spells. Image-killing must have been exceptionally 'successful' in times when the plague and smallpox slew their thousands, and when mortality, and infant-mortality in particular, was so much higher than it is now.

ground about Golspie, and between which and the
Sutherland coast fishermen must have conveyed
frequent communication. It is even possible that
the superstition was carried as far down as Yorkshire by coasters from the Moray Firth.

How to discover a cow-witch (p. 82).

In Scot's ' Discoverie of witchcraft ' (1584) the
following is given as *A charme to find hir that
bewitched your kine :*—

' Put a paire of breeches upon the cowes head,
and beate hir out of the pasture with a good
cudgell upon a fridaie, and she will runne right
to the witches doore, and strike thereat with hir
hornes ' (p. 282, p. 230 in the 1886 reprint).

Stand but(t) (p. 123).

I here describe the Oxford game of ' Iddy-iddy-
all ' from Mr. E. Gass's kind information.

A *tennis-ball* is thrown high up against the side
of a building, and the thrower calls

> Iddy-iddy-all
> Catch my fine ball,

adding the name of another player. The player
called, if he fails to catch it, throws it at the rest,
who are running away ; and anyone who is hit has
to stand out. The last left in may have three shies at
the hand of each of the others, held against the wall.

I presume that ' Iddy-iddy-all ' is a corruption of
' Heed ye, heed ye, all.'

And I think I played some form of the game about 1859 in the Middle School of Liverpool College.

See the robbers passing by (p. 127).

A company of girls having been selected, two of them join hands, and under their hands, which are held aloft, the rest of the girls (or robbers) pass. As they march along, one after the other, each holding the dress of the girl in front, the following verse is sung by all the company:—

> See the robbers passing by,
> Passing by, passing by,
> See the robbers passing by,
> My fair maidens.

Before (or as the verse is being ended) the last of the train pass under, the so-called "bridge" falls, and the girl being caught is questioned thus:—

> What 's[1] the robbers done to you,
> Done to you, done to you?
> What 's the robbers done to you,
> My fair maiden?

The above is of course sung by the "bridge"; and in answer the prisoner sings:—

> Broke my locks and stole my gold,
> Stole my gold, stole my gold;
> Broke my locks and stole my gold,
> My fair maidens.

[1] I.e. has. See p. 169, note 1.

Then she is carried away to prison to bear witness against the robbers, and, as she is being led along, the "bridge" sings

> *Off to prison you must go,*
> *You must go, you must go ;*
> *Off to prison you must go,*
> *My fair lady.*

The prison is supposed to be reached as the last word of the verse is sung, and, after they have remained a moment at the prison, the prisoner is brought back again, the bridge singing :—

> *Back from prison you must come,*
> *You must come, you must come ;*
> *Back from prison you must come,*
> *My fair lady.*

The prisoner is now set free, and stands aside while the game proceeds. The robbers, who have all this time been marching round the bridge, again pass under, again the last is caught, and the song is sung, and the girl is questioned as before.

Generally, but not always, the girls whose hands form the bridge choose before the game begins one of two things—apples or oranges, milk or tea, etc. The prisoners are each asked, after they have been brought back from prison, which of the chosen articles they like best, and each becomes the property of the girl whose article she has chosen. In this way sides are formed, and, when the game is finished, a tug of war takes place between the two parties.

[B. C.]

This is Mrs. Gomme's 'Hark the robbers' (i, p. 192), of which she prints 7 versions. None have 'passing by,' 5 having 'coming through' and 1 'going through.' None have 'maidens' or 'maiden,' but 6 have 'lady.' None have 'Broke my locks and stole my gold': the varieties are 'You have stole my watch and chain,' 'Steal your watch and break your chain,' 'They have stolen my watch and chain,' 'They have stole my watch and chain,' 'Stole my gold watch and chain,' 'She stole my watch and lost my key.' And none have the 'Back from prison' stanza.

As at Tong in Shropshire, the verses are sung to the tune of Sheriffmuir (see p. 198). B. C. has written it out for me.

'The music,' she says, 'is almost the same as that of 'My delight's in tansies,' but the time is slower. In the last two verses, however, it is quickened; for the prisoner runs to and from prison, and the music must always suit the movements.'

See the rob-bers pass-ing by, pass-ing by, pass-ing by;
What's the rob-bers done to you, done to you, done to you?

See the rob-bers pass-ing by, my fair mai-dens.
What's the rob-bers done to you, my fair mai-dens?

Rosy apple, lemon, and pear (pp. 139-40, 144-5).

I give the original form as nearly as I can conjecture it—

1. Rosy, happy, $\begin{cases} \text{merry, and fair—} \\ \text{maiden fair—} \end{cases}$

2. A bunch of roses she shall wear,

3. (And) Loving-silver by its side :

4. She's the one shall be $\begin{array}{c} \text{the} \\ \text{a} \end{array}\Big\}$ bride.

5. Take her by her lily-white hand,

6. Lead her to the altar ;

7. Give her kisses one, two, three,

8. For she's a lady's daughter.

Notes to the foregoing :

1. *Rosy apple* arises from *Rosy, 'appy* (see p. 145) : *fair* is given in two versions on p. 144.

2. So the version on p. 140 : see also the two on p. 144.

3. For *Loving-silver* as an emendation of ' Gold and silver ' see note to p 156.

Her side is possible and is found on pp. 140, 144, but *his side* suggests *its side*. Of course *his* was once equal to ' of it ' as well as to ' of him '; but the verses are not old enough for that.

4. *She's*. In North Midland *she* is *shoo* : hence *she's* would become *shoo's*, whence apparently ' Choose the one shall be her bride ' on p. 140. I am quite aware that this is in a Dorset version ;

but one doesn't know where the rime originated or what channels the Dorset version had passed through.

One, pronounced *wŏŏn* in parts of the North Midland district, would be liable to develope *who* (pronounced *woo-a*) in that dialect. Compare 'I know *who*' on p. 144, l. 4, and with this again compare 'Crying *out*' in the next specimen, where the accented vowels are the same if we pronounce 'Crying *oot,*' as a Fraserburgh child undoubtedly would.

Shall be.   So on p. 140.

The bride.   So on p. 139.   Or perhaps *a bride,* as two versions give 'her bride' (pp. 140, 144) and one 'and bride' (p. 144).

5–7. As on p. 140.

8. As on p. 133 and in the first version on p. 144.

Mother, the nine o'clock bells are ringing (p. 155).

The Rev. John Cort, vicar of Sale, Cheshire, kindly communicates through Dr. Joass the following as 'sung in Cheshire': I print it with no alteration except a few trivial ones in punctuation and the insertion of 'buy' in l. 7.

> Eight o'clock is striking;
> Mother, may I go out?
> My young man is waiting,
> To take me round about.

He will buy me apples,
He will buy me pears,
He will [buy] me everything,
And kiss me on the stairs.

Ten o'clock is striking;
Mother, may I come in?
My young man has left me:
He's an awful [1]sting.

He won't buy me apples,
And he won't buy me pears,
He won't buy me anything,
Nor kiss me on the stairs.

Poor Tom (pp. 201-2).

Mr. Andrew Lang, not in the least knowing that I was acquainted with any version of this rime, has called my attention to the following one. It occurs in *The forty-sixth annual report of the Deputy Keeper of the Public Records*, 1886, Append. II, p. 72, note—part of a report on the Royal library at Copenhagen by my friend the Rev. W. D. Macray, of the Bodleian. And it is quoted by him from a MS. of travels through Europe (New Royal Collection, fol. 129) the writer [2] of which picked up the rime in London, at some time in 1679-83.

'Who is there? Poor maid full of sorre and care. Whad will poor maid have? I beseech to rep poor Tham in. Is poor Tham dead? Poor Tham is dead. When did poor Tham dey?

---

[1] I. e. 'stingy one.'   [2] Oliger Jacobæus.

Yesterday in the morning grey. Partit poor Tham, and deid, deid, deid. I heared a bort sing in the wood, poor Tham is dead, we will drink a half for poor Thame's sake, for he was a right añish [*honest?*] man. I will drink a half w' play for me self w' so schall every man. Sup, pru, nel, mel, dal, Yohn.'

Comparing the two versions and making allowance for the Dane's imperfect knowledge of English, I would restore his original as follows:—

N. Who is there?

M. Poor Meg, full of sorrow and care.

N. What will poor Meg have?

M. A big sheet to wrap poor Tom in.

N. Is poor Tom dead?

M. Poor Tom is dead.

N. When did poor Tom die?

M. Yesterday, in the morning grey, parted poor Tom and died—died—died.

N. I heard a bird sing in the wood. [Poor Tom was *like* to die.]

[Chorus.] Poor Tom is dead! We will drink a half for poor Tom's sake, for he was a right honest man. *I* will drink a half and pay for myself, and so shall every man.

Sue, Prue, Nell, Mall, Doll, John!

At first I wrote *Tam*, and *Tamus* was a recent Folkestone pronunciation (Ellis, *Early English*

pronunciation, v, p. 143); but, as the Dane wrote
Dal for Doll and *añish* for *honest*, I suspect he really
heard 'Tom.' The Scottish form *Tam* is, indeed,
supported by the Scottish termination of *partit*,
but the Dane is weak in his final consonants, since
he writes *bort* for 'bird' and *whad* for 'what.'
'Poor Tit' in the Richmond version supports
'partit,' but it might have arisen quite independ-
ently out of 'parted.' There is nothing else in
the least Scottish about the dialogue, and the
names of the servants at the end look as un-Scottish
a selection as it would be easy to meet with.

Notes to the foregoing:

2, 3. *Meg* = older form of 'Peg,' but misheard
by the Dane as 'maid.'

4. *A big sheet.* Misheard by the Dane as
'I beseech.'

Tom. Probably the Dane inserted an *h* simply
because there is one in Thomas.

8. *Parted.* 'Part' = 'depart' is frequently used
by Shakspere. In acting this funeral-game the
repetition 'died — died — died' may have been
interspersed with sobs.

9. This I take to be a reply by the first person
= 'Yes, I thought he was likely to die, for I heard
a bird sing,' the idea apparently being that a bird
singing at night was a death-omen. See '**Cock-
crowing at night**' (p. 61), and Hazlitt, *Popular
Antiquities of Great Britain*, iii, p. 199, respecting

the night-jar: he quotes from Mary, Countess of Pembroke, this line referring to it,

'The night Crowes fonge, that foundeth nought but death.'

In the chorus, what has been taken for *w* in the Dane's manuscript is doubtless some Danish equivalent of *&*.

The names at the end of it are those of the servants of the inn, called to bring the liquor.

NOTES ON THE ILLUSTRATIONS

1. Specially taken by Mr. Dixon, from a point in the Dairy Park not far from the entrance to the gardens of Dunrobin. The Dairy Park is the long meadow between the Burn and those gardens, and the Castle dairy stands on the ridge at the end of it. The collotype shows clearly the old grass-covered Caithness road. The mountain on the right is Beinn a' Bhraghaidh, and the roundheaded one is the Silver Rock, which Dr. Joass believes to have been a place at which rents were received which were payable in silver instead of in kind.

3. Reduced from part of the 1-inch Ordnance-map of 1878, which the Controller of Her Majesty's Stationery Office gave me permission to reproduce. I have made the following changes and additions. The boundary of the parish has been rendered more visible. The position of the Battery (recently moved much nearer the Burn) has been altered. The names of the Sutherland Arms, Fishertown, the newly built Pier there, and Iron Hill, have been added. 'Highland Railway' has been inserted in one place and substituted for 'Sutherland Railway' in another. The former Sutherland Railway

Hotel at the W. end of the village having recently become a private house, the word ' Hotel ' has been taken out. The spelling ' Ben a Vraggie' has been altered to ' Beinn a' Bhraghaidh.' The outer border and some wave-lines have been taken out, a few names have been printed larger, and the scale has been transferred from the foot of the map to the right side in order to allow the collotyper more depth.

The School at Backies is not used as such at present: the Backies children come down to Golspie School.

11, 12. From a scarce work acquired by me for the Bodleian, ' Views · in · Orkney · and · on · the · north-eastern · coast · of · Scotland · taken · in MDCCCV · and · etched · MDCCCVII ·', by the Duchess-Countess of Sutherland. Whether it be the fault of the drawing, the etching, or the printing, the distance between the Castle and Loch Fleet (the nearest part of which is almost 4 miles off) has been greatly under-represented in 12.

William 'de Moravia,' the 1st Earl, was afterwards called ' de Suthyrland[1],' and Sutherland became the surname of his line. It ended in Countess Elizabeth, who succeeded in 1514, and had married in 1500 Adam Gordon of Aboyne in the Dee valley, 2nd son of George, 2nd earl of Huntly. In 1527 she and he resigned the earldom to their son Alexander. Dr. Joass tells me that in 1718

---

[1] *Registrum Moraviense*, p. 133, in a deed of 1237.

the Gordon name and arms were dropped by royal grant, and the Earl reverted to those of Sutherland. This second line ended in another Countess Elizabeth, who in 1785 married George Granville Leveson Gower, eldest son of Earl Gower. In 1803 he became Marquis of Stafford, in succession to his father, and in 1833 he was made Duke of Sutherland, whence his wife is known as the Duchess-Countess.

14, 15. Specially taken by Mr. Dixon, to whom my warmest thanks are due not merely for allowing me to collotype his various photographs, but for his generosity in making me a gift of all his own work towards the production of my book.

The seaward face of Dunrobin in 14 is merely modernized, as is the front nearest Golspie. The other old fronts have been hidden from outside view by new work.

The photograph was taken from a little knoll, on the edge of the beach, just 20 paces in front of the rifle-butt nearest the sea. The effect of it would have been better if the tide had been higher, but it is still the prettiest landscape-view of the Castle which I have seen.

The front cover shows
> Holl monie an' auld mone,
> At dip, at dip, o' day (p. 185).

www.ingramcontent.com/pod-product-compliance
Lightning Source LLC
Chambersburg PA
CBHW030903270326
41929CB00008B/554